COMPLETE
DREAM
HEALER

About the Author

Known only as ADAM, the author is a young and incredibly gifted distant-energy healer.

COMPLETE
DREAM HEALER

The incredible true story of
an energy healer – and how you can
discover and develop your own
healing abilities

ADAM

PIATKUS

This omnibus edition first published in Great Britain by Piatkus in 2009
DreamHealer Omnibus copyright © DreamHealer Inc. 2009

Previously published separately:

DreamHealer first published by DreamHealer Inc. in 2003
Published by Penguin Group (Canada), a division of Pearson Penguin Canada Inc., in 2006
First published in Great Britain by Time Warner Books in 2006
Copyright © DreamHealer Inc. 2003, 2006

DreamHealer 2 first published by DreamHealer Inc. in 2003
Published by Penguin Group (Canada) in 2006
First published in Great Britain by Sphere in 2006
Reprinted 2007
Copyright © DreamHealer Inc. 2003, 2006

DreamHealer 3 first published by DreamHealer Inc. in 2003
Published by Penguin Group (Canada) in 2006
First published in Great Britain by Sphere in 2007
Copyright © DreamHealer Inc. 2003, 2006

DreamHealer ™ is a Trademark of DreamHealer Inc.
Visit Adam's website at www.dreamhealer.com for information on workshops and ordering *DreamHealer* DVDs.

The moral right of the author has been asserted

All rights reserved
No part of this publication may be reproduced, stored in a retrieval system, or transmitted in any form or by any means, without the prior permission in writing of the publisher, nor be otherwise circulated in any form of binding or cover other than that in which it is published and without a similar condition including this condition being imposed on the subsequent purchaser

This publication contains the opinions and ideas of its author and is designed to provide useful advice in regard to the subject matter covered. This publication is not intended to provide a basis for action in particular circumstances without consideration by a competent professional. Your doctor should be consulted for any medical conditions noted in this book. The visualizations are NOT meant to replace advice from your health care professional. The author and publisher expressly disclaim any responsibility for any liability, loss of risk, personal or otherwise that is incurred as a consequence, directly or indirectly, of the use and application of any of the contents of this book.

A CIP catalogue record for this book is available from the British Library

ISBN 978-0-7499-2965-7

Typeset in Minion by M Rules
Printed and bound in Great Britain by Clays Ltd, St Ives plc

Papers used by Piatkus are natural, renewable and recyclable products sourced from well-managed forests and certified in accordance with the rules of the Forest Stewardship Council.

Piatkus
An imprint of
Little, Brown Book Group
100 Victoria Embankment
London EC4Y 0DY

An Hachette UK Company
www.hachette.co.uk

www.piatkus.co.uk

Contents

DREAMHEALER
A True Story of Miracle Healings
1

DREAMHEALER 2
A Guide to Healing and Self-Empowerment
125

DREAMHEALER 3
The Quantum World of Energy Healing
291

DREAMHEALER

A True Story
of Miracle Healings

Acknowledgments

I would like to express my gratitude to everyone who contributed to the making of this book by having the courage and open-mindedness to try something different. It has been an inspirational process every step of the way. Thanks to Dr. Effie Chow and Dr. Edgar Mitchell for their encouraging words of wisdom. Thanks to my sister for being herself and, most of all, thanks to my mom and dad for believing in me.

Contents

THE DREAM		5
CHAPTER 1:	DISCOVERY	7
CHAPTER 2:	THE JOURNEY BEGINS	15
	Healing Discovery	19
CHAPTER 3:	FINDING MY WAY	25
CHAPTER 4:	THE SCIENCE BEHIND IT ALL	35
	How I Heal	44
CHAPTER 5:	HOLOGRAMS AND COLORS	49
	Using Holograms	51
	Using Colors	57
CHAPTER 6:	HEALING HISTORIES	61
	My Most Difficult Healing	64
	Chronic Illness	66
	Injuries	70
	Cancer	70
	Healing Ronnie Hawkins	72
CHAPTER 7:	THE LEARNING CONTINUES	79

CHAPTER 8:	THE RETURN TO HEALTH IS A PROCESS	89
	Attitude Is Important	91
	Worry Is a Waste	92
	Visualization	93
	Intuitiveness	94
	Insights	97
	Reincarnation	99
	Open-Mindedness	101
CHAPTER 9:	LIVING WELL WITH THE SEVEN STEPS FOR LIFE	105
	Seven Steps for Life	111
CHAPTER 10:	YOUR DREAM	119

The Dream

The Dream is a mystical connection with universal energy, which expands life's perspective to a non-ordinary state of consciousness.

We interpret our reality through our five senses: sight, sound, smell, taste and touch. Our awareness is therefore based on very little input if we evaluate it only through those five sensory input areas. With our eyes, we see only a very small part of the electromagnetic spectrum. We hear only a fraction of the known frequency range. And we have no way of quantifying the amount or range perceived from our sense of smell, taste and touch senses.

But we are still bombarded with input, whether it is measurable or not. It is fair to assume that we have some awareness of it, and react to it. Therefore it is subjective sensitivity that interprets all of our sensory data. This leaves the door open for the extended human capacity to process information such as intuition, feelings, visions and dreams.

The dream is our vision of perfect health.
The healer is our guide along this path.

—Adam

Chapter I

Discovery

To perceive beyond ourselves is to truly see.

—ADAM

God must have a sense of humor. I don't know how else to explain the irony of my placement on this planet.

I was born into a regular middle-class family in a large cosmopolitan city. About 30 percent of the area's population is of Chinese descent, and had I been born into a home within this community, the cultural channels of Qigong or Taoism would embrace my uniqueness. It would be accepted as a rarity, not an oddity. The main thing is that it would be accepted.

The next largest visible minority in my city is East Indian, and if I had been born into this culture, I might have been spirited away to an ashram for mentoring. Again, the culture recognizes uncommon talents such as mine as gifts to be honed and developed. They are not only accepted; they are respected.

In contrast, the beliefs and customs of the Western culture to which I was assigned do not seem to welcome that which is not common. It purports to celebrate individualism, though in reality what is accepted is sameness. It is a culture that likes everyone to do the same thing, to be similar. Different is viewed as strange. At best, it is tolerated. What is valued is what we can process with the five senses and not anything beyond them. In Western culture, reality must be measurable.

I was born with a red birthmark shaped like a V on the center of my forehead. I have been told this is the "mark of a healer" because it is located on what is called the third eye. The third eye is where a healer channels his energy to connect with others for healing purposes. The V mark has faded considerably: It can barely be seen now, but I know it is still vascular because when I become emotional it shows up.

My great-grandmother on my mother's side saw auras. Auras are the energy fields that surround every living organism. She assumed that everyone else saw them too. It wasn't until she was about eighteen years old that she discovered no one else she knew did, and so she decided to turn off this ability. She still saw the auras, but she did not process the incoming information that her gift provided. She chose to ignore her ability rather than develop it. Many people who have such abilities decide to conform to the norm rather than explore the unknown within themselves. I have often wondered how my great-grandmother's life would have been different had she accepted and developed this gift.

My dad has North American Indian blood on his mother's side. Her family belongs to the Penobscot Indian Nation, which is based in Maine. I have always enjoyed the idea of my Native heritage and its connection with nature and the universal energy. After doing some research, I discovered that I am related to the last-known Penobscot shaman healer, Sockalexis.

Although some shamans used their power to do harm to their enemies, Sockalexis was known to do only healings, and because of this he was highly respected and not feared by his fellow tribesmen. Shamans need to be humble and aware of their own strengths and weaknesses in order to help others. They must be able to use their skills and powers to adapt to any situation. This requires a balance of mind, body, heart and spirit. Healing must be an intuitive quest of learning about others and ourselves.

The meeting of these two spiritual worlds from my mother's side and my father's side formed my unconscious awareness and unknowingly led me along my path.

Many things that I see are not visible to most people. For example, I see auras. An aura appears to me as a luminous glow, which I see in various colors and patterns. People, animals and even plants have auras, which show that the living organism is functioning. Because of this ability to see auras, I had no trouble distinguishing reality from the fantasy world of television. I remember watching TV as a little kid and telling my mom and dad that there were "real" people and TV people. Auric fields of people and all life are lost during the transmission of television signals; hence, I saw people on TV as totally different from other people. That was helpful in determining the difference between real and make-believe.

My abilities to see auras also created some problems for me, as you can imagine. As a kid, I didn't enjoy playing hide-and-seek. It wasn't that I was antisocial or too shy. I just couldn't figure out the point of the game. Someone might be hiding behind a tree, but he was still visible to me: His aura showed beyond the tree's outline. It seemed as ludicrous as a large man trying to hide behind a broomstick. I didn't know that others weren't able to see the way I did. That was something I had to learn. Before I did, the point of such games mystified me.

Every time I went with my family into the wilderness, I spotted wildlife long before the others. For me, the animals' auras were visible through the brush or forest. Many times as our car traveled along a highway, my family couldn't see what I did. But often enough, the others eventually spotted it too, and my sightings were believed. It is human nature to believe only what we can see. I once read that "vision is the ability to see what isn't there." I see and feel the universal connectedness of all living things—human, animal and plant. I always have.

By the time I was in high school, I had learned to tone down the auras I saw. They were glaringly bright and had become obtrusive. Toning them down had an interesting result: My intuitiveness, or psychic ability, increased. Instead of "seeing" auras and interpreting them, I was able to pick up the information directly through intuition. I just "knew" things, as a sense of knowing. In high school, accepting and understanding this phenomenon was never encouraged nor even acknowledged.

Many people can see auras or were able to see them at one time in their lives. When I look at babies, I can tell that most are very aware of a person's aura. If I change mine (for instance, by projecting, through my thoughts and intention, it higher above my head), the baby's eyes will follow. The seeing of auras is not nurtured in children mainly because most parents don't know their children have this ability. Some children are forced to suppress it, as the parents are fearful their child will be labeled mentally unstable. A family's religious belief might also pose a problem in accepting something like this. Doctors may want to prescribe drugs to "stop the hallucinations." Society has us thinking and believing that it is something that needs fixing.

Back in the 1600s, when people used their special abilities to heal, they were often called witches and burned at the stake. The leaders and scholars of the day would do their best to keep the public ignorant of what was really happening. They couldn't have been more wrong. Special abilities like mine need to be nurtured and understood in order to benefit all humankind.

But our thinking has a long way to go. For now, I know that what I experience is not understood and accepted. Rather, it is generally misunderstood and feared. I learned early in life that a regular kid in tennis shoes and a T-shirt had to keep quiet about being different.

Fortunately, my parents are rare and special spirits in that they came to accept my uniqueness. Even more, they came to realize my need for special guidance, or mentoring as it is sometimes called. They had the courage and the wisdom to allow me to be me. Within the context of a loving home environment and their open-mindedness, my gift has been allowed to grow and thrive. For this I will always be grateful. Because of my parents, I have a better chance of reaching my potential.

It couldn't have been easy for them. As I entered my teenage years and began to have telekinetic experiences, I was puzzled. I'm sure my parents were a little more than puzzled as well. Initially, they didn't believe me. Understandably, it was hard for them to accept it. It was especially difficult for my father, who looks for a scientific explanation for everything. It was easier for me because what was happening to me was my normal. I didn't know anything else.

Strange things seemed to always be happening to me. Objects often flew about the room when I went to touch them or pick them up. Sometimes the pencil I was writing with suddenly had a mind of its own and would take off across the room. This happened in school, and everyone figured I was throwing these objects. I let them think that. It was easier than telling them that they were trajected all on their own. I didn't know why or how this was happening, but I learned to live with it.

But the first time my bicycle did a 360-degree flip while I was riding it, I knew something was really different about me. My mom was with me when it happened, and she could hardly believe her eyes. I was glad she saw it. It is hard to keep overlooking happenings that you know are unusual. It's even harder when others discount them.

I tried to hide what was happening from the outside world, and was pretty successful at doing so. But it became impossible to hide it from my parents. We did a lot of activities together as a family, and they witnessed enough strange events that even my scientifically minded father could no longer deny it. He saw objects hit the ceiling with great force after I reached out to touch them.

The turning point for him, though, came one day while we were at the gym working out. A forty-five-pound barbell fell off its rack near where I was standing and missed my dad's head by just inches. We thought the rack was faulty so we spent a great deal of time trying to duplicate the event, to no avail. There was nothing wrong with the equipment. It was then that my dad finally understood that unexplainable events were truly happening.

After that, his attitude changed and he became insatiably curious about my abilities. Both my parents became focused on how they could help me develop my gifts. Together, we began a journey.

Chapter 2

The Journey Begins

*In the future, being able to heal
by thought will be the norm.*

—ADAM

My dad is the type of guy you want to have around in an emergency. He's calm, level-headed and unflappable. He's the one who will take charge in a crisis and step right into action. But Dad became worried and concerned at the onset of accepting what was happening to me. Was this dangerous for me? Was it dangerous for others? There must be answers out there somewhere, but where?

In a panic, my mom phoned Grandma with an SOS. In normal circumstances, Grandma's advice was usually acted upon. It soon became apparent that this was not a typical childhood situation, or one she had any experience with. Her advice at first was to call a pediatrician. It didn't take long for all involved to realize that this was not the route to take. Then Mom remembered a woman she had met years ago. This woman had the ability to see auras and what she called external energy flow. Mom phoned with an urgent request for an appointment. Fresh from my episodes of pencil-flying and bike-flipping, we went to see her. We had no idea what to expect.

It was great. For the first time I totally connected to someone who could discuss what I had thought everyone could see and feel: energy flow. She showed me various pathways and patterns to redirect my energy in order to achieve different effects and emotions. What I was feeling was visible to her as well as to me.

She explained that the bike-flippings were outbursts of energy, like unintentional static electricity, that occurred when I was not focused on my energy flow. I have lots of energy that must be patterned properly. It was a great relief to hear that I could do no harm to others or myself. I think that she was correct, as the bike-flipping has not occurred since I began to direct my energy in other ways.

She told me to stretch my arms out to the side as far as I could. I was to send energy out of one hand and encircle the earth with it, receiving it in the other hand. It was wonderful to see this energy, which she called an aura. That was the first time that I had heard this word. It was so reassuring to know that others can see this energy. We were both totally immersed in changing the patterns of my aura.

Mom sat speechless throughout the session; it was all new territory for her. But it was definitely not new for me. I understood with total clarity what was happening. I was finally able to control my energy. This came as a great relief to me, as well as to my parents. Having a sane adult describe what was happening helped us all understand that this was the normal state for me. Her parting words to my mom and me were that we should look into Qigong (pronounced "chee gong"). "Qi," sometimes spelled chi, means energy or life force. "Gong" means discipline or work.

"With the amount of energy he has, he could be a Grandmaster in a week," the woman told my parents. I've since learned that it often takes decades of dedicated study to reach that level.

As suggested, I made an appointment with a Qigong Master in town. It was interesting to watch as he demonstrated emitting chi, which was streaming out of his body through his fingertips. What an experience it was to be able to see this! He had a large, golden aura that seemed to flow harmoniously. I was curious and wanted to learn more about energy systems.

This encounter was a turning point for me. I had discovered that I could control and focus my energy. I wasn't flirting with madness but, rather, exploring a gift that others shared. From here, I embarked on the self-discovery part of my journey.

HEALING DISCOVERY

Two days after my meeting with the Qigong Master, my mom was in severe pain from trigeminal neuralgia, a stabbing pain in the face and ear that is caused, in my mom's case, by her multiple sclerosis (MS), a neurological disease. She had been diagnosed with MS when I was very young, and so this was not a new experience for any of us in the family.

That particular night, my dad, my sister and I were watching television and Mom was upstairs in her bedroom smothering her screams in her pillow. At times like this, we felt helpless to relieve her of her pain, and Mom preferred to be by herself. The pain was, as it was on many nights, unbearable. Finally, I went up to her room.

"Close your eyes, Mom," I said to her as I put my hands on her head. Why I did this I really don't know. It's as though I knew what to do. She complied, and I felt the pain leave her body and enter mine. It was a horrible pain.

I went to my bed and collapsed on it with a throbbing headache. My mom drifted off to sleep, pain-free. She has improved a great deal since that night and we are now able to do more things together as a family.

This was yet another turning point for me in understanding my gifts. It sealed my journey toward healing. Everything seems to evolve for a reason, and my mom's illness was no exception. This was no coincidence but a signpost. It allowed me to start my healing journey from a point of no fear, with the intention only of helping my mom.

If it weren't for my mom's illness, I likely wouldn't have dived headfirst into healing; rather, it would probably have been something I gradually came to years later. Seeing someone whom I love suffer was the inspiration I needed to react without thoughts of whether I could or couldn't help, of whether this was even possible. As if on autopilot, I did what I could do and made another self-discovery—I could heal.

But another challenge emerged for us. I had absorbed her pain and taken it on as my own. Once again, my parents were concerned. They certainly didn't want me healing if I was going to be ill as a result. Nevertheless, I was instinctively drawn to healing. While driving with my parents, I often noted injuries and medical conditions of the people we passed.

I recall sitting in a doctor's waiting room with my dad. Four other kids—one just a baby—were sitting across from us with their parents. This ability of mine to see auras is always on, so my attention was instinctively drawn to reading the kids' auras. Of course, they were unaware of what I was doing. I could clearly see that the aura surrounding the baby's lungs was alight with a problem. I felt upset that I couldn't say anything to the doctor about this, as the baby was unable to explain her symptoms.

Healing and health became a predominant theme in my life. Initially, I did some treatments on people from my dad's workplace. These people were socially separate from any of my high school friends or neighbors, so I didn't feel threatened by their knowing of my unusual abilities. Most were about my dad's age and typically dealing with old sports injuries and pain issues. One fellow had hurt his neck fifteen years earlier in a skiing accident. Even turning his head while driving was challenging for him. After one treatment, his range of neck mobility returned to near normal and his chronic pain disappeared. Word gradually got around the office, and I was kept quite busy. During this time, I learned a lot through practice.

But my parents were still not confident enough to be relaxed about my healing experiences. They wondered about the possibilities of my picking up some serious disease as I learned and practiced new techniques. After many sleepless nights, they called Dr. Effie Chow, a Qigong Grandmaster.

Mom met Dr. Chow years earlier at a Qigong demonstration. Dr. Chow is founder and president of the East West Academy of Healing Arts, in San Francisco. In July 2000, U.S. president Bill Clinton appointed Dr. Chow to the original fifteen-member White House Commission on Complementary and Alternative Medicine Policy. Dr. Chow has a Ph.D. in higher education and a master's degree in behavioral sciences and communications. She is a registered public health and psychiatric nurse, an acupuncturist and a Qigong Grandmaster with thirty-five years of experience.

Even with her qualifications and busy schedule, she managed to find time to come to our city and mentor me for three days. My time with her was valuable and played a major role in pointing me in the right direction. She told me about important things such as grounding and how energy moves. Most of all, she helped my parents stop worrying about my unusual abilities. She taught us to accept them for what they are and to understand that they are a gift. She also related little gems that we will always remember.

One that stands out is that "we all need at least three bellyaching laughs a day." I may have the ability to heal someone, but it is up to that person to stay well. He or she must be able to enjoy life and maintain a sense of humor. Laughter has been proven to help people heal and stay well. Whether it causes a certain chemical to be secreted in the body or it's simply the idea of having fun, laughter works.

Dr. Chow has given me guidance in so many other ways in the healing arts and I am grateful to her. It was great to talk with someone who was experienced in energy healing. She carried out amazing energy demonstrations at one of her workshops my dad and I attended.

To me, the energy demonstrations showed even further how interconnected we really are, as I was able to see by way of our connecting auras the energy that others could feel. Changing the energy field of one person affected all persons in or near that energy field. If someone is in a negative mood, all people around him will have a tendency to feel negative. If you are around someone who is positive, you will tend to be in a positive mood.

One of the most important techniques I learned from Dr. Chow was visualization. When I first met Dr. Chow, I had limited experience in removing people's energy blockages. She taught me how to visualize different tools for removing energy blocks, and I was able to be more effective with my healings. For example, when I first looked at someone with multiple sclerosis, the disease looked like grains of green sand. My usual approach was to envision picking up each grain and throwing it away. I found this technique extremely inefficient, as the blockages returned as fast as I could remove them. When I described to Dr. Chow what I was doing, she told me a more efficient visualization method for this. I found that it was more efficient to visualize the vacuuming up of these grains of sand and then the disposing of these energy blockages.

I learned that imagination is the most powerful tool in healing. This realization allowed me to actively participate in my own healing evolution. I became self-confident enough to learn by experience rather than depending on acquired skills from others. I began to experiment and learn what worked the most effectively for me. Some day, being able to heal by thought and imagination will be the norm. There are no limits in this new healing reality.

Chapter 3

Finding My Way

Every person is born with gifts.
Life itself is the most precious of them.

—ADAM

$\mathcal{A}$ journey is a sequence of events. It begins with the first step, which in my case was the recognition that I was different. I believe it is the responsibility of all of us to use the gifts with which we are born. I choose to use mine for the benefit of others. It would be a shame to ignore them and deprive others of this knowledge and benefit.

Life is one of the most precious gifts. Life gives one the connection to what I call the universal energy field. The science of quantum physics refers to this as the field of quantum information. Awareness of this connection is in itself a gift.

People's gifts and talents vary. My younger sister has the gift of a musical ear. Wherever she goes, she hears music. Whether she is in a shopping mall or in the wilderness, she is tuned in to it. She can't ignore her musical ear or turn it off. It is one of her gifts.

Similarly, visual artists must see a potential painting everywhere they look. Everyone can appreciate the incredible beauty of a rock-faced canyon with a river roaring through it toward the open ocean. Evergreens line the bluffs and their scent permeates our thoughts. Strong gusts of wind energize us as we feel our connectedness to the universal energy field, which engulfs us, connects us and is us. We can feel the oneness with all, but it takes an artist to see the emerging work of art; it is the artists who try to capture that feeling on canvas with their gifts.

Others are gifted with athleticism and are able to move with incredible agility or remarkable speed. They excel in mind–body coordination. All gifts are important. We are interdependent on each other's contributions, and no gift is any more or any less important than any other gift.

One of my gifts is being sensitive to our connectedness with the universal energy and each other. This connection goes by many names, but whatever it is called, it is a connection we all share. Calling it the universal energy field is perhaps most straightforward. Some people might refer to it by saying, "May the force be with you," but this is not really accurate, as the force is always with you. Some people are aware of it, and others are not, but it is there nonetheless.

So many things happen in life that one passes off as just coincidence. From some of my experiences, I have begun to think differently on this topic. Have you ever heard yourself say, "I knew that was going to happen"? Many of us have experienced this. We receive information from the universal information field constantly. It is just a matter of screening out what you don't need and making sense of what is useful. We must be aware of these coincidences and cultivate their messages and meaning. Most coincidences are messages that are sent for a reason. That reason may have to do with you. Or it might be intended for someone with whom you will be in contact—perhaps you are being used as a conduit for another person in need.

All information past and present is out there and available to us. The universal energy field is exactly that: universal. All inventions, medical cures and knowledge come from the universal energy field. Sometimes we access great ideas and surprise ourselves. The human ego being what it is, you might be tempted to assume you are very smart to have come up with the idea. There is nothing wrong with thinking highly of yourself. But you did not come upon this great idea solely through your own thought. You were assisted by many people who have their ideas filed in the universal energy field. We all share our thoughts and ideas in this way. And sometimes, it is accessed simultaneously. The refrigerator, for example, was invented at the same time by two different men in two different countries. They were never in touch with each other, but each accessed the necessary information at the same time.

A friend of my mom's is a talented graphic designer, and many of her clients and associates are in awe of her work. They frequently ask her how she comes up with her amazing designs, and some are disappointed with her answer. "I honestly don't know how I am able to create these results," she says. "But I don't feel as though they come *from* me. I feel as though they come *through* me."

I know what she means, and I appreciate her awareness. But it is often hard for those around her to accept it. They think that perhaps she has a self-esteem issue. I think she is simply aware of her connection to the universal energy field and routinely taps into it during her creative process, just as I tap into the universal energy field to do my healing.

Healing is something I can't ignore. This ability is not coincidental. It was given to me for a reason, and I plan to use it. I am still in high school and involved in regular social and sport activities. However, being able to remove illness from people is very rewarding. I just wish that I had more time to treat everyone who needs it, as well as play basketball, tennis, snowboard, chat with my girlfriend and just generally hang out with my friends. I am a regular sixteen-year-old . . . sort of.

Because of my gift of sensitivity to universal connectedness, I am able to heal. I think I always knew I could heal, but thought I needed to hide the ability from others. I would be alienated or rejected if I exposed this gift to those around me. Many other people who have unusual abilities feel they must choose between a social life and living with their uniqueness. I choose both, although integrating them is still very challenging for me. My social life is important to me. But so is the ability to share my healing gifts, so I must constantly balance the two.

I have had the privilege of working with other healers in many disciplines, such as Qigong and Reiki. Although what I do is based on what I experience, I found there was always something new to learn that I could incorporate into what I do. For instance, when I first began healing, I found it very draining, as I took the energy blockage out of the person I was healing by drawing it into me. So one of the things I had to learn was to heal in a way that didn't harm me. As I said earlier, that was important to my ever vigilant parents. My mom is especially watchful that I do not overextend myself and that I get enough rest. This meant I had to find a way to heal without taking on the other person's pain. So with some coaching from experts in the healing arts, and over time, I fine-tuned my own techniques.

My first step to understanding energy was to know that seeing auras or human energy fields is rare but certainly not unique to me. I soon realized that this ability is a gift, and I learned that I can control it. It can also be redirected and connected with any other life energy fields, including that of all humans, animals and plant life. This energy field connection could be used for healing. Many times I felt I was in uncharted territory as I explored this new gift. I have developed my own methods and style of healing through self-teaching. But that is not to say that I have not had input along the way.

The energy healing I do is not Reiki (Japanese healing art), Qigong, touch therapy or faith healing. It falls under no particular discipline. My ability to heal is what comes naturally to me.

I wanted to learn what other healers do so I met with many of them. With my ability to see auras, it is obvious to me what is happening as I can see the energy flow from healer to patient. What is invisible to most people, including many healers, is clearly visible to me.

One of the first healers I met showed me how to ground my energy, something Dr. Chow had told me about. Grounding is connecting one's life energy to the earth's energy. He explained that with exhaling, I should imagine the flow of my energy traveling down my body, through the soles of my feet, all the way to the center of the earth. This knowledge of grounding energy is essential to everyone. We connect to the universal energy field with each inhale—by breathing in and absorbing it. This completes the energy circuit, and we ground. I was thrilled with this knowledge and now my energy flows smoothly.

Another mentor I met with is a Reiki psychic healer, and I learned something of this type of healing. I engaged in telepathic communication or mind talk with this healer. To be able to do this was a first for me. We sat in the same room and had conversations without exchanging any words. Instead, we communicated by exchanging mental images. I enjoyed this form of communication, as it is so efficient compared with verbal communication.

Much of the information received from hearing someone speak is based on the receiver's interpretation of what was intended. Interpretations may vary widely from the speaker's original meaning. Communication through the use of mental imaging conveys a more direct meaning: A picture really is worth a thousand words.

Later I met another healer who also communicated to me with images. He had healed himself of terminal cancer and uses the knowledge he gained from this experience to help others. He works by increasing the vibrational level of the body. From him I learned about the vibrational levels of various colors and how this affects healing. Our bodies are tuned in to so many more aspects of the universe than we might think.

I also had the pleasure of meeting a local healer who discovered his healing ability by accident. Many years ago, he was first on the scene after someone was injured. He instinctively held his hands over the injury. Heat radiated from them and the person immediately noticed that his pain disappeared. Both the healer and the injured man were shocked by what happened. For fear of being ostracized, the healer tried to forget this event. He spent most of his life working in a high-tech field, trying to avoid his connection to healing. Of course, he found that he had to use his gift. It would wait until he was ready to use it, but it would not go away.

I found that each healer's strengths are different, and I have incorporated into my healings a technique or idea from most I have met. From all, I learned something valuable: We are all in this together, working toward the greater good.

Initially, I met people engaged in the healing arts who focus on the outer energy area of a person's body, or the aura. Healers use their hands and minds to smooth and repair the energy blockages negatively affecting the body. Many healers have found this to be an effective technique for dealing with health problems. Auras are an easy place to first notice illness or injury, as they are extensions and reflections of the body. Illness or injury prominently shows in one's energy field, leading the healer to the location of the problem. Various colors given off by this energy within the auric field provide lots of information.

The color is not the only visible indicator of trouble. I find that the entire aura of the injured or diseased part of the body is disturbed. In healthy areas of the body, the aura moves and swirls in a pattern and appears organized and in harmony. There is a flow. In an afflicted area, this flow is broken. The appearance is definitely that of disharmony.

Finding My Way

My vision goes much deeper than the aura of energy, which surrounds all living things. I have the ability to see energy fields, at many different frequencies, which enables me to do a type of body scan on a person. Dr. Effie Chow, in her book *Miracle Healing from China,* mentions this as a rare ability of a few Qigong Masters. It is sometimes referred to as X-ray vision.

It is possible for me to see these blockages or disruptions even before the person feels it, if it is a new blockage being created. When it is new, the area may not have been disturbed long enough to cause pain or become a noticeable problem. It can be an early warning of a developing problem. This may warrant a type of preemptive treatment. The earlier the problem is detected, the easier it is to fix.

Chapter 4

The Science Behind It All

*It will take the devotion of many
to awaken mankind to our connectivity.*

—ADAM

My dad has always said that there is a scientific explanation for everything. In our society, anything that we can't explain with our scientific knowledge is called a mystery. If something very good occurs and we can't explain how it happened, we call it a miracle. Doctors sometimes have patients whom they predict will live only a few months and to their surprise go on to live for years. The doctors refer to this as a miracle simply because the understanding of what took place is beyond their medical knowledge.

Many of the pioneers of science have been ridiculed for delving into that which was not in line with the scientific views of the day. I have had the honor of meeting a modern-day scientist who has no fear of exploring what he strongly believes. His name is Dr. Edgar Mitchell. His name will no doubt be familiar to many readers. On January 31, 1971, *Apollo 14* lifted off from Cape Kennedy (now Cape Canaveral) and three days later, Edgar Mitchell and Alan Shepard walked on the lunar surface. As could be expected from such a dramatic and meaningful experience, Dr. Mitchell's perspective on life and human consciousness was never the same again. A graduate of Cambridge's Massachusetts Institute of Technology, with a doctorate in aeronautics and astronautics, Dr. Mitchell has since constructed a theory that could explain not only the mystery of human consciousness but the psychic event as well. It is my opinion that Dr. Mitchell is one of the great thinkers of our time.

On Dr. Mitchell's return journey to earth, he became aware of a deep sense of universal connectedness. This overwhelming awareness set the course for him in years to come. For the next thirty-plus years, he studied the mysteries of consciousness and being. For years, Dr. Edgar Mitchell has studied the quantum hologram, which puts an important scientific description to human phenomena, including consciousness itself. The scientific papers he has written are complex and go beyond what I would like to cover in this book. Nevertheless, his ability to explain things to me in scientific terms has helped me understand my gift and progress with it.

"Magic," "miracles" and "natural phenomena" are labels we give to things we can't understand with our existing knowledge. When people refer to any healing I do as a miracle, I correct them. Everything I do has a scientific basis; we just have to discover it. Dr. Edgar Mitchell's paper entitled *Nature's Mind—The Quantum Hologram* comes closest to explaining what is happening when I connect to someone's energy field. It is always encouraging to come back to Dr. Mitchell for an explanation of any changes in what I am doing. He has been gracious and patient while helping me with my journey through this unusual time in my life. His mentoring has been invaluable to my understanding of the scientific meaning behind my ability.

I believe also that there is no such thing as random coincidences. Things happen for a reason, and I feel that my meeting Dr. Mitchell was an essential part of my development. The chain of coincidences started with my uncle, whose hobby is manned space travel. His house is full of model rockets and spacecraft. He also has most books ever written by astronauts, including Dr. Edgar Mitchell's *The Way of the Explorer*.

My uncle came to our house one day with a pamphlet advertising a conference entitled *Quickening Global Consciousness*. This was the first time I heard about the Institute of Noetic Sciences or IONS, the organization Dr. Mitchell founded thirty years ago. Among many other issues, it explores distant healing. This information came to me at the exact moment I needed it. Had this happened even a month before, I don't think I would have been ready for it.

My parents and I arrived for the conference early and found seats near the front. There were two extra chairs at our table and several empty tables at the back. There were about two hundred people in the audience. Just before the guest speaker was introduced, a friend of Dr. Mitchell's joined us, though we didn't realize her connection with him until we began chatting during the intermission. I was still uncomfortable with people knowing about my healing gift and had decided before arriving at the conference that I wouldn't reveal why I had come. Nevertheless, when she asked why I was there—I was the youngest attendee by twenty-five years or so—I decided to tell her that I have healing abilities. Dr. Mitchell's friend had recently been in an accident and was interested in me seeing the injuries.

When I looked at her, I could see that her neck and back were painful to her. I also noted a sharp foreign object in a spot on her neck. When I told her this, she was astounded. The previous week, her doctor had injected a painkiller into her neck in an attempt to lessen her pain. Unbeknownst to the doctor, the tip of the needle had broken off. An X-ray revealed that it was located where I saw what looked like a sharp object. She was so taken by what I told her that she immediately decided to introduce us to Dr. Mitchell.

Since then, I have appreciated the knowledge, guidance and insight Dr. Mitchell and IONS has offered me. It is reassuring to meet intelligent people who want to explore and understand the unknown. The world would not have advanced to where it is today if it weren't for people like Dr. Edgar Mitchell.

And people such as physicist Max Planck. Just over a hundred years ago, Mr. Planck wrote a mathematical formula that introduced the world to the concept of tiny bundles of energy that behave both as waves and as particles. They came to be known as quanta. His formula became the basis of quantum physics and gave birth to a branch of science in which reality does not follow the cause-and-effect rules of empirical science. This changed our most basic concept of our physical world.

Humans do not welcome change. There is great resistance to it in many aspects of life. Many people were shocked when it was first proposed that the world is round, not flat. Most people were determined to reject the concept.

Indeed, the Flat Earth Society of the time was adamant that anyone who believed the world was round had lost his mind. Within the scholarly community, it didn't matter how many people you asked—you got the same response. They all shared the same thought, theory and answers. Hundreds of years later, we readily accept that the earth is round and think that those who fought so hard to hold on to the belief and doctrine that the world was flat were out of *their* minds.

It is not uncommon for new concepts to be viewed initially with suspicion. There is a reluctance to accept change. This is true of any science of the day, including medical science. At any particular place or time in history, whether you ask one or ten doctors a particular question, the answer is based on the same body of knowledge—though the answer itself is, of course, not always the same. For instance, several hundred years ago it was common practice for doctors to bleed their patients, which was often considered a necessary procedure. Anyone who suggested anything different at that time was viewed with distrust. Today, doctors use surgery, radiation and toxic drugs to treat cancer and other diseases. Over time, many of these treatments and procedures will become obsolete. I am fortunate in that I am not restricted by the dogma of the day as to what is possible or impossible. Nevertheless, the scientific explanations of how I perceive life energies, or auras, became important in my understanding of what I saw and did. Validating these experiences was important to me.

Soon after I realized that I could see and influence these subtle energies, I discovered that all I needed was a photograph of someone to be able to see that person's body scan remotely. This is the technique I use when doing distant healings. It enables me to treat anyone anywhere in the world. The distance between us does not matter. A connection is made using this universal stream of information so I don't need to be physically near someone to heal her. We are all connected.

I have found that understanding some of the basic principles of quantum theory is necessary in understanding how distant healing is possible. The nature of reality in the quantum world is a giant leap from that of our everyday material world. For example, a quantum object (such as an electron) can be at more than one place at a time. It does not exist in ordinary space-time reality until we observe it as a particle. A quantum particle ceases to exist in one place, only to simultaneously appear in another, and yet we cannot say that it traveled through the intervening space. This is referred to as a quantum leap. The most important concept that relates distant healing to quantum physics is nonlocality, or quantum action-at-a-distance. A quantum object simultaneously influences its correlated twin object, no matter how far apart they are. This explains how energy can influence other energy elsewhere.

All particles are fundamentally connected to each other. All information and knowledge is available in the field of quantum information. Every physical object emits its own quantum hologram, or image, whether it is on this planet or on a planet located on the other side of the universe. My visual perception of the field of quantum information looks amazingly similar to what I see in a person's brain. When I see the inside of the brain at an energetic level, I see synapses clicking on and off at an astonishing rate through a network of pathways that connect every neuron in the brain. Each node in the field of quantum information I am viewing is a bright, dense light that looks a bit like a spider cocoon. Each cocoon has zillions of pathways that stretch out, each attaching to another cocoon. This pattern seems to continue infinitely.

The following words from the Vedas, collections of sacred writings of ancient India, are over seven thousand years old. It is interesting to me how they match my visualization of the universal energy field, or field of quantum information. The jeweled net of Indra—Indra was the supreme ruler of the gods in Vedic times—is a perfect example of how every point reflects to every other point. Interconnectedness and interdependency of everyone and everything in the universe is similar to the holographic view. Both the materialistic world of the jewels themselves and the nonmaterial world of energy as reflections of light exist as inseparable parts of the whole.

Indra's Net
There is an endless net of threads
  throughout the universe.
The horizontal threads are in space.
The vertical threads in time. At every crossing of threads
  there is an individual.
And every individual is a crystal bead.
The great light of absolute being illuminates and penetrates
  every crystal being,

And every crystal being reflects not only the light from every other crystal in the net,
But also every reflection of every reflection throughout the universe.

A person who is intuitive and energetically powerful can access this field and query it to find any information whatsoever. When an intuitive individual connects to another person, the information is received instantaneously because of this interconnectedness. The description of Indra's Net puts this complex concept into simple words.

The most important part of the quantum hologram that relates to my healing gift is that quantum attribute of nature called nonlocality. At the quantum level, action on two particles, which are part of a single system, occur instantaneously at a distance. It doesn't matter how far apart they are. This gives me a better understanding of how I am able to heal someone from a distance. I connect to a person's quantum hologram, which is a nonlocal information mechanism. I am then able to give information to the person's body through intentionality—my intention to heal—which causes the energy blockages to clear and allows energy to flow harmoniously and, thus, the body to change. The person's new state of wellness will then be emitted in the quantum hologram. With my intent to heal and the person's desire to get better, this can turn into real, positive results. I discuss this in more detail below, in "How I Heal."

In the last century, the early adapters of quantum principles have produced advanced technologies such as lasers, transistors and CT scanners. But in many areas, including our everyday lives, it is difficult for most people to think in terms of the quantum phenomenon. When we go to work each day, we like to know that our office is exactly where it was when we left it yesterday. It would be difficult for architects and engineers who are busy designing and building skyscrapers and bridges to think in terms of something existing in two places at once. It is not an easy reach, to say the least. But I believe that, over time, we will unravel the mysteries of this most interesting form of science and learn to apply the principles and concepts in many areas, to enormous benefit.

HOW I HEAL

I have been asked many times what I see, experience and know when I do a healing. When I first started healing, the person would be seated next to me while my arm and hand was outstretched toward her. This enabled my energy system to interact with hers. Now distance is not a barrier. It makes no difference if the person is sitting next to me or on the other side of the world. When I see a photograph of the person, I can instantly connect to her energy system.

Every physical object emits its own quantum hologram, which contains all information about it. From this field of quantum information, I can zoom in on specific information or views, which I project as holographic images in front of me when I am viewing someone for treatment. These holograms are the visual guidance, or three-dimensional maps. All the body's information is available in this manner. I discuss my use of holograms in more detail in the next chapter.

Once a hologram appears, I can manipulate the energy so that the person can find her way back to a healthy state. People who have observed me doing this tell me that it looks as though I am conducting an orchestra. My arms and hands wave through the air, and my fingers nimbly create patterns as I make energy adjustments. To the observer, I appear to be making mesmerizing yet patterned flowing gestures, like the dancing of flames in a raging fire. Through my intentions of healing, I provide information to the person I am treating. I do this by being in resonance with the person's body. This means that the frequency that we are tuned to is similar. In this way, the body of the person is interacting and exchanging information with me. This then stimulates the person to energetically alter her state of wellness, which is in turn reflected in the hologram. I can usually see this change starting to take place immediately.

Everyone's body knows its own way back to wellness—it just needs some guidance. These adjustments to the person's energy system help the body achieve this. I have done energy adjustments hundreds of times, yet my parents want to watch each time. Mom says that she can feel a tingly sensation every time I do an energy treatment.

As I developed and practiced my techniques, I found a way to dispose of the pain of the person I was treating, rather than taking it on. Now I send it to a black hole of sorts. I don't destroy it; it just seems to die on its own without the host organism (the person's body).

I had to learn to use the universal energy that flows through a person rather than using the energy that flows through me. This is more efficient because all healing is really done by the person herself, when she energetically alters her state of wellness. I have discovered that using the universal energy field is a far more efficient and powerful method of healing. This seemingly endless source of energy is much more efficient to use than using a person's own energy to heal. Every person knows where this universal energy is needed in the body in order to heal herself.

The following poem explains the relationship between healing and learning. The only true connection to knowledge and healing is that which we learn for ourselves.

Learning *can only be done by oneself.*
Nobody else *can learn anything for us.*

> Healing *can only be accomplished by oneself.*
> Nobody else *can heal for us.*
> Teachers *can mentor us, direct us to information,*
> *Encourage and assist us in the process.*
> Healers *can help us connect to our own energy sources, give us hope and guidance.*
> *When we are ready we will* learn *the knowledge ourselves.*
> *When we are ready we will* heal *our bodies ourselves.*
> *Our minds will* learn, *and*
> *Our bodies will* heal
> *Only when we are ready*
> —Adam

How did you know when you were able to start doing distant healings?
I always trust that when I am ready for more information, it will come. At that time I had a need to refine and develop my techniques as my outstretched arm that I used for healing became incredibly strained. My dad asked me to move farther away from the person and see if I could still connect effectively to the information that I "see." I soon found that if I was in the next room, the connection was just the same. Shortly after this, I was shown photographs of people and I was amazed that all of the data I received were just as clear to me as if that person were right beside me. We experimented with photographs of people in town and of people around the world. The information was just as precise, and so we discovered that distance is not a factor.

How are you able to prevent taking on the pain of the person you are healing?
Energy moves by intention. Through the intention of disposing of energy blockages, it is done. I have a clear image in my mind as to how I will do this; for example, launching it into black holes, or vacuuming it up and then throwing it in the garbage.

The ancient poem of "Indra's Net" seems very mystical. How is it related to modern-day life?

In spite of our technological advances, we still live within our connection to everything else in our universe. We affect and are affected by the entire net, as described in the poem. In this way, each and every one of us *is* the entire web of existence. Regardless of any scientific advances, our interconnectivity is the most fundamental law of the universe.

Chapter 5

Holograms and Colors

Through my intentions to heal, I can send new information to the person, allowing him or her to change to a new state of health.

—ADAM

I first started healing by using the overall energy holographic projections, or holograms, which shows energy blockages. I am constantly evolving new techniques and holographic layers for the new challenges I meet in healing.

USING HOLOGRAMS

When I first started healing, I saw and worked with one hologram to see, identify and clear energy blockages. I could do a virtual tour of the inside of someone's body with what appeared to me to be a still photo of all the organs and inner structure of the body. Energy blockages appeared prominently in the foreground, so I was able to easily see and remove them. I often found this work tiring and sometimes had a headache afterward. When I am working with a hologram, I lose all sense of time. I also had to be careful to remember to breathe rather than hold my breath. The breathing now comes naturally to me, but it was certainly part of the learning process. I definitely had much to discover about my techniques.

One day I was looking at a young man with a heart problem. All of a sudden, I found myself inside his body in real time. I was surrounded by the beating heart, pulsating blood, contracting arteries and moving valves. I couldn't escape this overwhelming realistic view. Graphic images surrounded me. I stepped back in awe and total shock of what I was experiencing. Believe me, it wasn't a pretty sight. I released myself during my step backwards and, once out, I felt ill, dizzy and exhausted. I had to go to bed immediately to sleep it off.

Since that experience, I have learned how to go in and out of this holographic view of one's body and remain in control, rather than letting it control me. I have a total sense of being there, and I can watch the entire body in action from the inside. I take a visual tour of the body of the person I am treating, *from the inside*. I can see every organ as it is functioning, or struggling to function. I see and hear the heart pumping. I watch cancer grow. I watch the traffic of synapses in the brain. Every cell and every activity can be visible to me as I go through the treatment. I call it "going in." I don't do this all the time. Usually I go into the energetic hologram, doing this physical real-time hologram only if it is needed for a specific problem.

When I go into someone, I can tune in to various subsets of information. It's kind of like changing channels on the TV. My mind acts as the remote control, which can adjust to different sets of frequencies, thus giving me different holographic views: I project a subset of information as a holographic image in front of me, and I am able to zoom in and out as required, as if I were using a microscope. I choose the hologram most useful for the ailment I am treating. The following are the seven holographic views I use most frequently, but I am sure I'll be using more as soon as I develop them.

Energetic Hologram

This is the first hologram I learned to use. It is at the most basic level and for many simple ailments it is the most effective. With it, I can see an overall view of the energetic body. The body's energy system grid shows the flow of energy, as well as any blockages, old or new. Energy changes provide a grid-type guide for a person's body to model for the path to healing: Reminding the body of its healthy state is often all that is needed. Through my intentions to heal, I can give new information to that person's body, which allows it to change to its new state of health.

If something is removed on the energetic level, it will soon disappear on the physical level. A woman I treated had been bleeding vaginally. Her gynecologist had ordered an ultrasound of her uterus, which showed a fibroid mass, or polyp. Surgery to remove it was scheduled.

I went in and had no trouble locating the bleeding area. It was a very small polyp that was causing the problem. I removed it energetically and saw that the woman's body was adjusting to the change. In her hologram, it looked as though her body would continue to heal itself. Six weeks later, when the surgery was performed, the gynecologist was amazed to find that there was no polyp. He later told the woman that he didn't understand how this could be but that "the case is closed," and if she had bleeding again, it was unrelated.

The energetic view is also the one I use to treat sports-related injuries. These types of injuries are often readily visible as a blockage and it is usually uncomplicated to manipulate the energy flow.

Brain Signals Hologram

In this hologram I can see the flow of electrical impulses along neurons and intuitively know their function. I can see damaged connections that are specific to certain brain functions. All the switches in the brain allow or prevent the passage of electrical impulses. The flow and blockages of these electrical pathways form a specialized holographic view of the brain. Any brain disease or injury shows up in the hologram as an area that brain signals do not readily and efficiently travel through. This area is the energy blockage, causing all signaling to reroute itself. The brain signals hologram is a useful tool for healing headaches, migraines and neurological disorders. For certain recurring problems, the brain needs to be reset.

Viewing the brain signals hologram in real time is like being in the middle of a three-dimensional superhighway. There are electrical impulses flying along pathways everywhere, and I do mean flying. The speed at which they travel is incredible. It took some practice until I felt comfortable viewing this hologram.

A woman I know was misdiagnosed many years ago as having MS. This was before the current diagnostic tests were available. Recently, she had an MRI and was told she does not have MS. Rather, her cerebellum has simply stopped functioning. She has great difficulty with mobility (she had to use a walker), which contributed to the MS misdiagnosis. Her neurologist could not establish what caused her condition but said that it did not appear to be progressive.

When I first went in, I could see right away that part of her brain had no functioning neurons. I used her brain signals hologram to get the flow of energy going in this area. After a few sessions, I could see an energetic difference as new pathways began to develop. The woman, however, felt no change but thanked me for my efforts.

Several months after our sessions, I heard from her. She had noticed a gradual but marked improvement in her mobility and coordination. The physical improvement *did* follow the energetic strides I saw. Her body just took some time to react.

Real-Time Physical Hologram

The real-time physical hologram involves the nervous, musculoskeletal and energetic systems, as well as the organs. I can see any of these at a cellular level, if need be, and adjust it to its best healing potential. I like to use this hologram to observe the functioning of different body systems. From here, I can determine the next course of action.

This hologram is particularly useful when the person I am treating has a musculoskeletal disorder such as fibromyalgia or rheumatoid arthritis.

Smart Energy Packets

Through intentionality, I send these Pacman-like units into the body's information to reduce the unwanted blockages and replace them with good energy. I call them smart energy packets (SEPs).

SEPs are an extremely useful healing tool for me. It is a tool that I use to eliminate things on an energetic level that would require ongoing work, as SEPs can continue to heal long after my treatment is finished. I use SEPs on infections, cancer and other such problems that have a great potential to reoccur.

SEPs are more than a "seek and destroy" device. They have a sack on them that spreads good healing energy along their path. They can also reproduce themselves and communicate with each other, sending signals to each other to shock or jump-start the system. I am constantly developing more efficient and effective SEPs.

Pattern Energy Grid

The pattern energy grid can reveal if there is a dysfunction or disease occurring because the source of the problem stubbornly remains. When I look at three-dimensional contour maps, I can quickly tell if there is an imperfection in the graph. In a similar way, I detect dysfunction or disease in the pattern energy grid. There is harmony and flow in the hologram of a healthy system, and a disruption around the dysfunction is clearly visible as energy reroutes itself around blockages. Old, stubborn injuries appear prominently in the pattern energy grid hologram. New injuries are not as pronounced. This view is not of the external aura but of much deeper energy patterns in the body.

If the body recognizes its healthy state, the deviation will also be recognized and dealt with by the body's immune system. The pattern energy grid is also useful after a treatment to hold the new energy pattern in place.

Heat Hologram

I have found this hologram useful in my treatment of cancer. Every visualization has variations, including different ways of applying heat. The only limitation on the number of applications is imagination. To me, cancer cells appear as green. After red heat is energetically applied, these cells gradually turn white and disintegrate like dust. Then I energetically vacuum up the dead bits. A variation is energetic red heat, or high-frequency energy, which can be used to pop cancer cells from the inside out. They explode on the energetic level and die. If something is dead on the energetic level, it usually dies on the physical level shortly after.

Overall-View Hologram

I compare how this hologram looks before and after each treatment to see if the person has accepted the new pattern of health. If energy blockages have been removed, that should appear obvious to me. Some people and some conditions appear to shift toward health in one treatment. Others take more treatments and time—the effectiveness of a treatment varies with each person. This overall view is how I know what impact the treatments have had and whether more treatments are needed.

Genetic Hologram

This is my eighth and newest holographic image. Genetic diseases are complicated, as the body sees the defect as part of its rightful and healthy state. I'm not yet ready to use this view. But I know there are many applications within the information contained in this hologram, and I will continue researching it so I can fully understand its potential.

USING COLORS

Each color has its own energy frequency. Colors are applicable to any hologram for healing. I know that there have been many suggestions as to what each color means and how it can be used for manipulating moods and even healing. I have simply observed colors, their vibrations and their effects. Over time, I have figured out how they work by watching auras and studying energy fields. I watch how auras look and move when people are sick and when they are healthy. That is how I have come to know which color to use, and when.

I have been asked if the average person can help himself or someone else by visualizing the appropriate color around him or around the afflicted area. My answer is that it depends on the person. Most people who are willing to discipline themselves and learn to focus can use colors to help themselves and others. Everyone has the ability to heal to some degree. The "Seven Steps for Life" section of this book outlines how everyone can maximize this capability.

If you break anything in the universe down to its basics, you have energy. Light is the visible frequency range of the electromagnetic energy spectrum. There are many other frequency ranges that we cannot perceive with our five senses, yet we know they exist. If we are exposed to large doses of electromagnetic waves in the upper frequencies, such as ultraviolet, X-rays, gamma rays or cosmic rays, we will eventually die from this exposure. It is no surprise that cancer will also die from exposure to high-frequency electromagnetic waves. This technique is used in a number of medical technologies to kill cancer. The problem is that this often kills the normal cells surrounding the cancer, causing serious side effects.

One of the methods I use to treat diseases is applying high energy directly to the diseased area, without damaging normal cells. The only side effect is from the body adjusting to a new, and therefore unfamiliar, healthy state. I see the energy that I apply in the form of colors inside the body. During this process I am able to access colors outside the standard spectrum, colors I can see only in my mind. These are of a much higher frequency and are extremely useful in healing. These colors are impossible to describe. It's like asking someone who can see only the color green to describe the color red.

The concentration of a certain color of light is made denser when it is focused like a laser beam. This makes it more effective for healing small areas. There are so many combinations of colors and densities that it is impossible for me to summarize all the different results at this stage in my discovery. Some combinations of colors are synergistic. White and purple, for example, work well together. Here are brief descriptions of the colors within the standard spectrum that I use most frequently.

Yellow: Yellow is used when an organ or localized area requires treatment. It is used to increase energy when someone suffers from a lack of it. Yellow encourages the growth of good energy and will rejuvenate a person's energy system.

White: White, although not technically a color, is used in similar situations as yellow to give energy. It boosts one's energy system by joining forces with the immune system to eliminate energy blockages.

Purple: Purple works somewhat the same as SEPs. It floats around until it finds blocked energy, then attaches to it like glue, penetrating the blockage and eliminating it from the inside out. Purple is one of if not *the* most difficult color to work with.

Using purple takes tremendous focus and concentration, and if not properly applied, it will simply dissipate.

Red: Red is used as a healing color in the heat hologram. It is useful in the energetic treatment of cancer. Red can be used as a glue, which holds the areas to be healed in place. This enables me to then use the other healing colors to treat the area.

Blue: Blue is most effective in the form of positive thought. It is positive thought in liquid energy form. Blue prepares the body to be receptive to the healing intentionalities, thereby overshadowing any negative mind–body connections that may exist.

If each physical object emits its own hologram, how do you see multiple holograms for the same person?

When I connect to a person's hologram, all the holographic information contained within it becomes available to me. Each person emits just one hologram, but I am able to make better use of this information if I tune in to a specific view of it. Each holographic view, whether it's energetic, brain signals, real-time physical, or so on, constitutes a subset of all information contained within a person's hologram.

Think of this process as similar to your being an architect viewing blueprints of a proposed renovation. The existing building is physically in front of you, but the vision of the future or your goal or plan is what you must visualize in your mind's eye. Each future view can be seen on the blueprint. During a treatment, I redirect the energy flow of the hologram in accordance with the optimum state. At each stage between this perfect vision and the present health situation, adjustment and time are required. The problem must be removed, just as in a renovation. Most importantly, the person being treated and the healer must keep the vision of the desired end result in his mind's eyes. Some of the holographic images I see are more useful than others in viewing certain problems, just as some blueprints reveal certain details more clearly than others. The electrical blueprint is needed for accessing certain information, while the floor plan is more useful for other aspects. All are needed in order to complete the renovation.

Which colors do you use most often for healing?
I used to use purple most often, as it grabs hold of a problem most readily. This made removing energy blockages efficient. More often now I use pure white energy, as this encompasses a much wider range of frequencies. Working with the full spectrum of light frequencies allows more healing energy to be absorbed by the person being treated. Everyone subconsciously knows where they need this healing energy, and white light is more diversified for people to use.

You often describe seeing problems in the body as green. Does this mean that the color green always indicates a problem?
Although I generally see problems in what I would describe as a fluorescent green, every person sees energy blockages and thus problems differently. It is all a matter of the healer's interpretation of the information he receives. Often the colors are beyond the physical spectrum, which makes what you are seeing difficult to describe in terms of color.

Chapter 6

Healing Histories

*I don't need to be physically near someone to heal them.
Distance is not a factor.*

—ADAM

The energy healing that I do is a manipulation of internal energy, which in turn is reflected in the aura of a person. This is a deep and permanent healing.

I go into the person's quantum hologram to view the inside of the body. At this point I use my energy, the other person's energy and the surrounding energy to focus on removing the energy blockages causing the disease or affecting the injured area. An injury or diseased area stands out as a bright green. Older injuries are seen as a darker green. When I am viewing inside people, I also have intuitive knowledge of what and where the problem is. Basically, I travel through the person's body and observe. This process I refer to as "seeing."

When I first started to heal, I was looking at only the most basic energy level. Now I am able to view many levels at once. I view several holograms of the person for energy diagnosis and healing. I am also able to bring up another person's hologram alongside to compare the different functions of the body. This is useful when I am not sure what a normal functioning body should look like. Now my healings are much more effective because I can approach the illness or injury from several fronts. I know there are many more levels for me to develop as I become more experienced.

Another important development of my gift is the ability to go down to the cellular level and actually see whether cells are in a precancerous or abnormal state that may lead to trouble. This is extremely important in energetically diagnosing illnesses before a dangerous situation develops.

I have enjoyed working with many people and find healing comes naturally for me. At first, it was important for me to work within a confidential and isolated group in order to develop and understand my gift. My school life and personal friends had to be kept separate from my healing work. For this reason, I saw people whom my parents knew weren't associated with my friends. Most came as nonbelievers and skeptics and left in awe.

As my skills developed and people began hearing about me by word of mouth, I started to be contacted by others in the healing profession. I worked with a group of naturopathic doctors who consulted me when the patient was interested in my ability. One such patient was an elderly lady with an extremely sore leg. I immediately pointed to an area on her hip as the source of the pain. It was nowhere near where she felt the pain. When the doctor touched the spot on her hip, an area where two muscle groups met, the woman's leg flew up, nearly kicking him. "That's it!" she exclaimed. "That's where the problem is!"

Working with these doctors was a great experience for me. I was given no background information about the patients beforehand, yet every diagnosis I gave was accurate.

MY MOST DIFFICULT HEALING

Last year, my parents decided to take the family to Mexico for a break from the healings and all the emails we were constantly receiving. I felt that I needed a brain break, and I knew that a rest would make me more powerful. We also thought that it would be exciting to spend Christmas in a different country.

The vacation got off to a great start. We stayed in a resort, part of an all-inclusive package, where my sister and I could order drinks all day. My dad made sure the bartender knew how old we were. As soon as we arrived, he took my sister and me to meet the bartender. He introduced us as his son and daughter and informed him that "they don't drink alcohol." We were able to order endless virgin strawberry daiquiris, though.

Two days into our vacation, my dad was playing with my sister and me in the resort's swimming pool. Dad had just thrown my sister into the air and over his head. At the same time, I was surfacing out of the water just behind him. The timing couldn't have been worse. My sister landed on my head, fracturing one of my neck vertebrae. Numbness spread down my body. It was a cold feeling. I somehow managed to get out of the water before I lost feeling in my legs.

My parents called an ambulance. The pain in my neck was unlike anything I had ever experienced. I felt like I should pass out, but I knew I was the only one who could fix my neck. Despite my pain, I was able to go in and see it. It was bad.

It was very difficult to heal myself because I was in excruciating pain. When I try to view an injury in my own body, it always looks foggy. I had to try my hardest to use all the power at my disposal. I worked on the fracture and the swelling for about half an hour. In that time, I could see that I had managed to heal the fracture and bring the swelling down. It is important to reduce the swelling as quickly as possible, because the swelling itself can create problems. By the time the ambulance arrived, I was walking, but the attendants insisted I put on a neck brace and go to the hospital.

X-rays were done on my neck as soon as I arrived at the hospital. The neurologist arrived with his little reflex hammer. He checked to see that all my reflexes were working. I passed with flying colors. When the doctors looked at the X-rays, they pointed out that I had a congenital defect on my C2 vertebra. Otherwise, everything was fine.

I knew that the defect was not congenital. It was the area that I had just damaged and subsequently healed. My parents brought the X-rays home so that we could compare them with ones taken a few years ago when I injured my shoulder playing tennis. As I expected, there was no sign of a defect on the earlier X-rays.

I felt that I had passed a major test of willpower and healing ability. I surprised even myself with what one can do if confronted with the need. It had been more difficult than any other healing I had done.

CHRONIC ILLNESS

Living with chronic illness is a reality for millions of people—children as well as adults. Out of necessity, people get used to tolerating constant pain, so this to them becomes the normal state of health. Many have forgotten the pain-free time of their lives. In order to heal, they must first remember this. They must have a contrast in their mind and set their goals accordingly.

A number of people with chronic illness have come to me. Because the illness has been with them for so many years, many think that it might take a lot of work to fix. Sometimes it does, but not always.

Under the Western medical system, there are no cures for many illnesses—just ways to manage and live with them. Sadly, this has caused some people to give up hope of ever getting better. However, I have treated a number of these people, and their pain is sometimes eliminated within two or three treatments. Often one treatment produces amazing results. These results have been long lasting and in many cases the chronic problem has been eliminated.

One man came to me with a sore neck that had been bothering him for four years. I quickly found the problem and spent about five minutes treating him. He reported that he felt immediate relief. He was amazed that for the first time in four years his neck was not sore or stiff. I guess he felt so good that he decided to go skiing. Unfortunately, he re-injured his neck and I had to do another treatment. The second treatment was also successful, but this time I made sure he understood that muscles and ligaments take a bit of time to adjust to the new state of wellness. I asked him to refrain from any physical strain for a while.

The return to health is a process, meaning a sequence of changes must occur. The mind is already there or the healing wouldn't have occurred. The mind and the body are connected, but the mind can get there quicker than the physical body can. People I have treated must gradually let their bodies catch up. It takes time. Those who have suffered with chronic pain for years frequently overexert themselves at first, since they feel so good and are so glad to be pain-free. In their enthusiasm, they sometimes return to activities they have been unable to do for a long time, before the body has had a chance to finish the healing process. It is important to give the body sufficient time to complete the process.

Another fellow came to me with a sore back that had been bothering him for years. When I went in, I could see that the third and fifth disks in his lower back were damaged. He confirmed that these areas had been diagnosed as the problem but didn't think anything could be done about it. I treated him, and his back pain has improved considerably. He returns from time to time for maintenance treatments. It is very rewarding for me to be able to help people who have suffered for years.

I had the pleasure of meeting a woman who was planning her wedding yet was in too much pain to try on shoes for her big day. She was motivated to improve her health, so we began treatments. As a preteen, she was athletically inclined. Competitive sports kept her schedule full. With a mix of summer and winter activities, she was always on the go. Then she started feeling extreme pain in her arms and legs. A diagnosis of fibromyalgia soon followed. As many people with chronic pain experience, the sleepless nights became a major problem in and of themselves. Fatigue rules the day and night. Next, depression set in, as she was unable to continue with her activities. She had to change her active pastimes to sedentary ones in an attempt to adapt to her limitations.

This act of redefining self is difficult. One grieves for one's old self and past abilities. We all redefine ourselves gradually throughout our lifetimes. Illness or injury often forces this upon one without any adjustment period. Feeling like an eighty-year-old is expected if you are eighty. However, if you are a teenager, or even twenty or thirty for that matter, the physical pain is accompanied with feelings of resentment. How could this happen? Why did this happen to me? This is so unfair!

I started doing energy treatments with the bride-to-be and felt positive about it. She felt tingling throughout her body and got goose pimples. They were powerful experiences for her; she could feel a storm of energy moving inside her. Sometimes she became dizzy and pale right after the treatment. The day following a treatment, she always reported that she slept well right through the night, which was unusual for her. Upon waking, she felt refreshed. After four treatments, she felt reenergized. It certainly helped that she was sleeping right through the night. She had a wonderful time on her wedding day, too!

I treated a man who had chronic pain after being involved in a bad car accident many years ago. He had little success with conventional medicine and requested my help. Immediately after the first treatment he noticed that his constant headache had vanished. He also had digestive problems, particularly stomach aches, caused by injuries he had sustained in the accident. These too disappeared. As is often the case, physical recovery led to significant improvement in his ability to focus and concentrate on mental tasks.

A woman contacted me who had had severe chronic asthma for many years. When I looked at her photograph I could see a haze over her lungs and the airways leading to them. With most lung conditions, I apply heat to the hologram, as I find that this is the most efficient way to correct it. During the treatment she felt the heat that I applied, followed by a tingling sensation. Instantly she felt that her lungs were lighter and more elastic. Breathing was easier for her and she became so relaxed that she fell asleep. As a result of unlabored breathing, her mind was clearer.

I was also contacted by a woman in her fifties who had peripheral neuropathy, which caused painful nerve sensations. Shortly after the treatment began, she noticed that the constant sensations of numbness, pins and needles, and burning in her extremities had left her. She felt that her quality of life had returned.

A woman who had chronic stomach problems called me. She told me that she ate poorly and felt tired most of the time. In addition, she said she rarely slept and suffered from occasional depression. The morning following her first distant treatment, she woke up pain-free. Her stomach did not ache with every breath she took as it had before. Her new painless state brought with it a feeling of peace.

A man who had been in a bad accident many years ago contacted me requesting a treatment. He is quadriplegic and since he was diagnosed with a complete spinal sever, I cautioned him to have no expectations going into the treatment but to keep an open mind. During the treatment he noticed that his triceps and biceps were tingling, whereas he had had no feeling in them for the last twenty years. He also had experienced chronic pain and stiffness in his neck and shoulders, which reduced in intensity after the treatment. He was most excited about the tingling that he felt in his lower body.

I met a woman who had been diagnosed with syringomyelia, a degenerative spinal condition. After one treatment her pain was significantly reduced, allowing her to stand erect and to roll over comfortably while sleeping. Now she was able to sleep through the night, making all the difference to her outlook.

INJURIES

I have had the opportunity to work with several athletes who had sports-related injuries. One baseball player had thrown out his shoulder by pitching. He hadn't been able to play any sports after that and was in constant pain. The movement of his shoulder was restricted. After one treatment, he was pain-free and he regained his full range of motion in his shoulder. Many sports injuries are fairly quickly resolved with treatments.

CANCER

One of the things that I find interesting is how the inside of a person's body looks when she is undergoing or has undergone chemotherapy. It looks like a war zone. Cells are fighting each other in an exhaustive battle of survival, and it doesn't look like there are any real victors.

I am often amazed by how fast the cancer or a tumor can grow. If I go in to a person whose cancer has advanced throughout her entire system, it is almost impossible for me to stay ahead of the growth. I am much more optimistic about influencing cancer when it has not spread. It is more straightforward to focus on an isolated area, such as an organ.

Standard Western therapies to destroy tumor cells include radiation and chemical treatments. The genetic code tells cells to grow and divide, thus spreading the cancer. Radiation is energy and it is used in cancer therapy to destroy the cancer cells or alter cell activity and slow growth. But radiation also affects normal cells, which in turn causes side effects, such as nausea. Many radiation treatments will prolong a person's life. Chemotherapy may also be recommended, causing even more side effects in a body that is already ravaged. In making decisions about cancer treatment, the quality of life should be an issue. It is a delicate balance. Of course, sometimes chemotherapy and radiation is successful.

On an energetic level, I see the cells within a living organism communicate with one another. Cancer cells are no exception. I also see on the energetic level that cancer cells absorb energy and modify according to intention. When cancer cells communicate, they pass on information about any changes within their immediate environment. When I am energetically treating cancer, the death of the cancer has a domino effect. One cancer cell appears to receive the energy, modifies itself according to intention and passes the message along to the next cell. The surrounding healthy cells are not damaged because they are not modified. The only side effects are slight, and are from the body adjusting to being healthy again.

This technique is applicable only to cancer that is localized, such as a single tumor, not to a malignant spread. Imagine a sealed-in city occupied by cancer cells with no communication with the outside world. The only communication is with one another. When I make energetic changes to the cancer cells, they spread the news around to each other, and in this way cause their own destruction.

If the cancer is spread out, as it is with advanced lung cancers, there are cancer cells outside the "city" that could warn the rest of the cancer and prevent the changes required to kill them off. In effect, I "see" that the cancer cells at the first cancer site send distress signals to the other cancer locations. In this situation, I resort to a combination of reasonably high intensity yellow, purple and white light energy. I would not use light that is focused like a laser because the cancer is spread out too much for that to be effective.

Sometimes during treatment the person can feel the activity or process. Some people describe it as a tingling sensation in the area I am treating. Others feel as though ping-pong balls are ricocheting inside them. Occasionally, people feel sleepy (some have even fallen fast asleep during the treatment) or dizzy or nauseous. And some people feel nothing. Everyone is different. How they feel it, or even if they feel it, doesn't seem to affect the outcome of my treatment.

HEALING RONNIE HAWKINS

On September 21, 2002, I read an article in our local paper on rock legend Ronnie Hawkins. It reported that he had been diagnosed with inoperable pancreatic cancer. I had never heard of Ronnie Hawkins before, but my dad told me he enjoys his music.

Ronnie Hawkins has lived in Ontario since the late 1950s, when he immigrated to Canada from his native Arkansas. Many consider Ronnie to have been the performer who brought rock and roll to Canada. Ronnie is perhaps best known outside of Canada for his backing band—some major stars played in it at one time or another. The original name of The Band, legendary in the 1960s for backing Bob Dylan, was The Hawks. Ronnie has been in the business for decades. When John Lennon and Yoko Ono were in town during their 1969 peace crusade, they stayed at Ronnie's place.

I had not healed anyone of pancreatic cancer before but I

wanted to try to help Ronnie. According to the newspaper article, on August 13, 2002, Ronnie had surgery to remove the tumor. However, when the doctor cut him open, he saw that the tumor was much larger than the anticipated three centimeters. It was wrapped around an artery and couldn't be removed. Chemotherapy was apparently not an option for Ronnie. His cancer was diagnosed as terminal, and I thought he might be interested in my healing ability.

I contacted Ronnie's daughter-in-law, who is his manager. Mary was open-minded and felt that they had nothing to lose by seeing me. Talking to Mary, I realized that Ronnie wasn't just a rock legend but a loving husband, father of three and grandfather. There were a lot of worried relatives.

When I had looked at Ronnie's photo, my first impression was that he was an honest man. When I told Mary this, she said that comment shook her. Ronnie is as honest as they come, she said, and one of the funniest people you will ever meet. Ronnie was quite willing to try my healing approach, since the doctors had not held out much hope for him. Distant healing was certainly a new idea to Ronnie and his family, but they were keen. "If Adam can pull this off, tell him we'll send him an autographed Hawk T-shirt," Ronnie said with his trademark good humor. "Five of the best doctors in the world have told me that this is it. They said three to six months, tops—I'm gone."

In September 2002, well-known Canadian producer and composer David Foster, also an alumnus of Ronnie's backing band, hosted an intimate gathering in Ronnie's honor in Toronto. Many major celebrities attended, including former U.S. president Bill Clinton, comedian Whoopi Goldberg, singer and composer Paul Anka, Ronnie's tycoon friend Don Tyson from Arkansas and Canadian industrialist Peter Pocklington. Paul Anka had written another version of his song "My Way" and dedicated it to Ronnie. Bill Clinton, David Foster and Paul

Anka sang their parts of the song. Ronnie, with his wife, Wanda, at his side, had his guests laughing through their tears throughout the evening.

A few weeks later, the City of Toronto declared October 4 Ronnie Hawkins Day. That day started off with Ronnie being inducted into Canada's Walk of Fame. Many people feel that it was an induction long overdue. Usually, this recognition is formally made in May of each year. However, because of the dire state of Ronnie's health, it was done a few months early, in October.

That evening a tribute concert was held at Massey Hall to honor Ronnie. Ronnie got up on stage and joined his band with the song "Hey Bo Diddley." Kris Kristofferson and the Tragically Hip highlighted a special four-hour concert of stars. "If there is a God of rock 'n' roll, I know he looks just like this guy," Kris Kristofferson said in his tribute.

When I first went into Ronnie's hologram on September 21, 2002, I could see a tumor the size of a tennis ball—approximately ten centimeters in diameter. I spent the next few weeks treating Ronnie's tumor on the energetic level, helping his body fight off the cancer and reduce the tumor. From the beginning of my treatment, Ronnie felt a quivering in his abdomen. His jaundice improved and his overall health seemed to be getting better. He no longer felt or looked like a dying man. On September 23, 2002, I got news that he was looking wonderful. Everyone was encouraged, especially Ronnie. He told me to "Keep on rockin."

I continued treating Ronnie intensely every day. We all felt positive about the treatments. On September 27, 2002, I energetically compared Ronnie's pancreatic functioning to that of my dad's. I did this by visually bringing in front of me the quantum hologram screens of both. I noticed that Ronnie's pancreas was blocked and my dad's had a constant drip. I manipulated the energy and got Ronnie's pancreatic juices flowing. From what I saw energetically, it started with a gushing flow; there was probably a lot of buildup. My parents spent a sleepless night worrying about this, but I assured them that his body knew how to regulate it. I later learned that the pancreas secretes insulin and many enzymes which would have been blocked by the tumor.

Ronnie continued to feel and look great, and his blood sugar levels improved. He was walking better and his eyes looked clearer. Ronnie *wanted* to get better. He has such a love for life. This is his greatest strength.

By the time November arrived, rather than planning a funeral, Ronnie was planning a CD release and a TV show. Ronnie continued to feel better and the fluttering feeling in his abdomen persisted. I could see energetically that the cancer was gone and that the remaining tumor tissue, no longer growing, was being removed by Ronnie's own system. This takes time, which explains why the quivering in his abdomen continued. But he was now thinking more about living than dying.

A CT scan done on November 14, 2002, determined that Ronnie's tumor was approximately four and a half centimeters. From its original ten centimeter mass I had seen on the energetic level, the tumor had shrunk in half. But the doctors still believed that Ronnie had cancer and was going to die.

On November 27, 2002, Ronnie had a biopsy to check on the cancer. The biopsy was negative. There was no cancer.

All the treatments I did on Ronnie were from three thousand miles away. I started working on Ronnie's energy system September 21, 2002, a month and a half after the surgeon sewed him back up and told him there wasn't anything he could do for him. The doctor expected that Ronnie would not live to see Christmas. I treated his energy system on a daily basis for a few weeks and fairly regularly after that. All my indications on the energy level were that his body had managed to kill the cancer and that the tumor was shrinking rapidly.

On February 27, 2003, Ronnie's CT scan showed no evidence of any tumor. He now performs onstage with his band and sings all night. This is an amazing change because it was only months before that he was a dying man. An MRI done April 11, 2003, confirmed that Ronnie is cancer-free.

Shortly afterward, my autographed T-shirt arrived safely in the mail. I have since met Ronnie and his family on several occasions and we enjoy keeping in touch.

Why was healing yourself the most difficult healing?
Generally, when I am treating myself it is similar to treating anyone else, so it is quite straightforward for me to do. However, when my spine was fractured I was in excruciating pain, which made it difficult to concentrate. It took a great deal of concentration just to stay conscious. This is why healing myself in this instance was so challenging.

Why is it that it can take months from the time you start treatments until you get positive confirmation through scans and tests?
Many variables are involved in any treatment. People's thoughts, emotions, beliefs and attitudes differ, as well as their lifestyle habits. The illness may be categorized similarly, but how it develops and manifests itself may vary considerably.

Generally, a person with a more positive outlook notices beneficial effects sooner than someone with a less positive attitude. An illness that has just recently developed reacts more quickly to treatments than does a chronic condition that has existed for many years.

The first treatment I did on Ronnie Hawkins for his terminal pancreatic cancer was on September 21, 2002, and seven months later his MRI scan showed no evidence of a tumor.

During this time I did about sixty treatments from a distance of about three thousand miles. I sometimes worked intensely for forty minutes in one session. Energy treatments are not a magic wand, and their efficacy has as much to do with the person being treated as with the healer.

Chapter 7

The Learning Continues

What is in the mind is always reflected in the body.

—ADAM

What have I learned from helping people heal? Many things. For one, I have learned that disease starts in a person's energy field and shows as a blockage of the energy flow in the body. And as I mentioned in the previous chapter, often I can see this before the person feels any symptoms. The word "disease" can be broken into two syllables: "dis," meaning opposite, and "ease," referring to the flow of healthy, harmonious energy. "Dis-ease" is the unpatterned flow resulting from an energy blockage. Most diseases or illnesses have their own signature—that is, each has a similar appearance in the hologram I view. This similarity became clear to me after treating many people with similar problems. However, I've discovered that people react differently to each type of treatment, whether it's one of conventional medicine or energy healing.

Each person's journey to wellness is an individual process. Healing the *person* rather than just eliminating the ailment is vital. Sometimes the cause of disease is a poor lifestyle choice, such as improper diet, lack of exercise, smoking, drinking or taking excessive drugs (be they street drugs or prescription drugs). I've had to set some tough boundaries for those people who continue to make choices that will negatively affect their health. For example, when a person with a smoking-related disease continues to smoke, treating him or her would not result in recovery, as the root of the problem has not been addressed. In one man I was treating, I could see abnormal cells continue to develop. I knew that if he continued to smoke cigarettes, there would be no point in giving him healing energy, as the cancer would generate faster than I could kill it. I informed him that he *had* to quit smoking, and he did when I told him that I would not attempt further treatments until he did. Often lifestyle changes *must* be made in order for the person to be healed.

It is also difficult for me to see clearly inside bodies of people who are on medication. Ideally, I do the treatment just before it is time for a person to take the medication. This usually allows me to see clearly enough to carry out a treatment. I saw a forty-year-old woman who had been in a debilitating car accident and was on painkillers and anti-inflammatory drugs. The medications made the energy blockages jelly-like and I was unable to move them during treatments. I suggested that she reschedule another treatment that would be just *before* she took her medication. When she did, I found her energy blockages much easier to move, and she reported that she noticed the positive effects more intensely.

Muscular and structural maladies are fairly straightforward. They are easy for me to spot on the body, as I see breaks in the person's aura. I can go in and show the body its natural energy grid. Sometimes the injury or whatever is causing the malady is so old that the body has forgotten what the natural healthy state is like. It is very helpful if I can show it the map of health. The body is an amazing thing and will strive to return to a healthy state if given the chance. Reminding the body of this ideal state and providing a push in the right direction is sometimes all that is needed.

Another thing I have learned is that some people have underlying psychological and emotional issues that affect the energy body and so must be addressed before healing can take place. A person's negativity, guilt or fear will work against the path to wellness. Be prepared for some personal work and perhaps some lifestyle changes if you want to achieve a lasting state of wellness.

I remember going in to help one woman and thinking that I couldn't do anything for her. The antidepressants she had just taken prevented me from doing my healing. So we rescheduled the healing to a time of day when she hadn't just taken her medication. During that treatment, I was able to remove some energy blockages, but I intuitively noted a strong psychological basis to the illness. This became obvious, as the problems immediately rebounded after treatment, which is common for emotionally based illnesses unless the root cause is dealt with. She mentioned that, before I treated her, there were about five other unrelated problems bothering her. My feeling was that she needed to address the underlying origin of these concerns before I could improve her state of wellness.

One man I treated had a stomach condition with symptoms similar to those experienced by people with irritable bowel syndrome. Those symptoms include abdominal pains, severe diarrhea and reactions to certain foods. He claimed to be allergic to milk or dairy products and took great pains to avoid these foods. I went in and took a look. I could see that his stomach was irritated, but I could see no physical cause. I am not saying that it was all in his head. I know that the symptoms he experienced were real to him—and painful. It seemed to me that he processed his emotions and his anxieties through his stomach. I suspect that if he hadn't created the stomach condition, he might have had to create another physical malady. I could treat this man every day, but his condition would return unless he formed a new strategy to deal with and process his emotions. The body is amazingly complicated in that our health involves a mind–body connection. What is in the mind is always reflected in the body.

I have also learned that some people have difficulty accepting their newfound wellness. Perhaps the illness or injury serves another purpose, and so the person wants to subconsciously hold on to the disease. If they become well, the purpose served by the illness is not achieved. There are many possible psychological reasons for illness. Sometimes the real reason a person becomes ill is because she has been seriously disappointed and has become disenchanted with life. Illness is a form of retaliation. That person may feel that life has injured her, and she retaliates by not fully participating in it. Or if someone feels deprived of attention and recognition, illness (particularly if it is chronic) can bring the person the attention and recognition he wants. His condition may range from requiring a special diet to being bedridden. The disorder becomes reality in the body because of what was first perceived by the mind. For the body to return to a state of total health, these issues of attention and recognition must be addressed. One can't just heal the body and expect lasting effects if the mind is not in alignment with this objective.

Avoidance behavior is another root cause of disease. For instance, a person may be suffering from a work-related injury because that person is desiring a new career. But switching careers can be a scary thing, even if the person wants it: A major life change is not an easy thing for many people to make. Creating the chronic condition replaces the desired change.

Family members can also be a factor in our health, by affecting the decisions we make about our health and treatment. One day, I received an email from a woman who was clearly panicked. She had terminal cancer. She did not want to pursue chemotherapy or radiation, but wanted to explore energy healing. Her family wanted her to have chemotherapy and radiation.

Even after X-rays showed that the tumors had significantly shrunk after several of my treatments, she continued to waffle about chemotherapy because of the pressure from relatives. Eventually she decided to go the route of chemotherapy.

For the most part, however, people are ready, willing and accepting of my energy treatments. With that receptivity and a positive attitude, I have had the honor and pleasure of helping many people return to health. For some, however, it is their time. A man whose elderly father was in an extended-care hospital after suffering a stroke contacted me. He was concerned that his father was dying. I went to the hospital to do an in-person treatment on the father. He was lying in bed and was nonresponsive when I first saw him. During the treatment, I saw a strong spirit in the man, and I could tell that it was not his time yet to die, but that it was near. The next day, after only one treatment, he was able to sit up in bed, talk and even complain about the food. A couple of months later, his entire family came from out of the country to visit him. By this time, he was well enough to leave the hospital on a day pass and go with all of them to his favorite restaurant, and he even purchased a lottery ticket. He died later during their visit, but he died peacefully, having been able to say his goodbyes to those he loved.

Another thing I have learned from my healings is that many people are interested in energy healing only as a last resort, rather than as a first choice. This doesn't make sense to me, as I personally would be most interested in trying the least invasive treatment first. I have been contacted by several people with cancer who have been through surgery, chemotherapy and radiation. Now that they are terminal, they ask for my help. The majority of cells in their bodies are either cancerous or negatively affected by the disease or the medical treatments they have undergone. Energy healing is often considered only as a last resort, after every other avenue has been exhausted.

I had a father email me a week before Christmas with an urgent plea. His son had leukemia, and had a fever of 105 degrees Fahrenheit and blood in his urine. He and his wife were staying in a motel near the hospital where his son had been a patient for many months. He had no idea how he was going to pay the $100,000 hospital bill, a bill that was climbing each day. All he and his wife knew was that they desperately wanted their son to get better.

When I looked at the boy, I knew right away that his body had decided to shut down. All I could do was give him positive encouragement and some energy. I managed to get his temperature down below a hundred degrees for a couple of days. He was actually able to get out of bed and play with his toys—something he had not done for weeks. However, the illness was too far along to halt and he died on Christmas Eve.

I never realized how many sick people there are in the world until I was able to do something about it. Most of the people I see are in need of some positive thoughts as part of their healing. By the time they have turned to something they view as radical, such as energy healing, they have usually already been turned away by the mainstream Western medical system. Being told that there is nothing more that can be done and that you will die in six months' time is not easy to hear.

But sometimes it is a self-fulfilling prophecy to be told that you will die in six months. (Of course, often patients themselves demand to know.) Keep in mind that the brain is like a supercomputer that interprets incoming information. Any thoughts are greatly influenced by what we experience. In addition to our own thoughts, our brain is constantly being fed information by those around us and will respond to positive or negative thoughts accordingly. We must take control of this computer rather than allowing it to control us. What I am suggesting is that no one rush quickly to a conclusion when there might indeed be something that can still be done. Exhaust *all* possibilities.

We must always keep in mind that everything in the human body is interconnected, and one change, whether a dysfunction or improvement, affects everything else. This is very important for people to realize, both in a personal and a global context. According to this perspective of interconnectedness, we are at one with the whole existence of all time and space, all interwoven into a unified state of being.

What do you "see" as an illness signature; for example, how would you describe the multiple sclerosis signature that you see?
The first time I looked at someone with MS was when I helped my mom with her trigeminal neuralgia. I saw this painful symptom as a throbbing fluorescent green ball of light in her head and instinctively pulled it out of her. At the time, I didn't reflect much on the signature of the illness, as I had no reference point. Since then, I recognize MS as fluorescent green flecks of sand that appear to be bubbling up through the spinal cord and into the brain. I tried removing them from my mom's hologram, but it was like trying to separate different colors of sand with my fingers. It wasn't effective at all. Then I used my imagination and decided to visualize vacuuming up the sand particles. This was far more useful. While using visualizations, if one way presents a difficulty, I find another approach. I need to be creative and flexible.

Does the medication a person is taking cloud your vision when you go in? What do you actually see?
What I see depends on the person involved and the particular drug they are taking. Even off-the-shelf and over-the-counter medications can affect how clearly I see. Of course, the more

toxic the drug, the more obscured everything appears. When someone is on strong medications, it often seems as though I am viewing his reflection in a warped mirror. Other times the reflection appears cloudy, misty or foggy.

Sometimes the medication gives a blockage a jelly-like texture that is difficult to grip on to when I attempt to remove it. However, bombarding the blockage with energy helps a great deal because the body knows what the problem is and will direct the energy appropriately. The person receiving the energy bursts intuitively knows where to focus his attention. If I'm unable to move the energy block, I suggest rescheduling the treatment to a time when the medication is not so intensely present in the person's body—usually shortly before he is due to take the medication.

Does a person have to believe in energy treatments for them to work?
It certainly helps. We all have many filters through which we sift incoming information. These filters are our beliefs. We can have so many of them that virtually nothing gets past them. When this happens, we are our own worst enemies, as we have effectively blinded ourselves to all possibilities.

When one is blind to the potential of energy treatments, nothing can get through. An open mind will allow change as long as one can be flexible to incoming information. Of course, if you truly believe that energy is the invisible power of you and the universe, your possibilities are limitless. As with everything else in life, you are responsible for your own limitations.

Chapter 8

The Return to Health Is a Process

*You must step out of the box of conventional thinking.
You need courage to take that step.*

—ADAM

𝒟isease is the absence of health. It is an energy system out of balance. It is a body that is not recognizing its natural grid, or code, for proper functioning. Disease can take many forms. Sometimes it shows itself as chronic pain. Sometimes the body will grow a tumor. Sometimes it will grow cancer. There are many ways that disease can manifest itself, and there are just as many causes for it.

Ideal health is a state of no energy blockages, where energy flows freely throughout the body. Everything works together in harmony. There is no physical, energetic or emotional conflict in the body. Perfect balance exists.

Perfect health should be everybody's goal. Old scars and injuries make achieving it impossible, but we can work toward achieving the best balance possible within these limitations.

ATTITUDE IS IMPORTANT

From beginning to end, attitude is important. Whatever a person's religious or spiritual beliefs are, they should be maintained during treatment, as they are important to that person and therefore to the healing process. No matter what one's belief system is, the most important factor of all is a positive attitude. *Believe* that good things are going to happen.

Attitude is a powerful tool in the healing process and is the foundation for returning one's body to good health. A person must be able to show thanks to others and be thankful for the good things in her life. By dwelling on the bad things in our lives, we are unable to appreciate all the good.

You must step out of the box of conventional thinking. You need courage to take that step. There is no authority other than you as to whether healing (or anything else, for that matter) is going to work. People delegate authority to others who are deemed as experts. Perhaps they feel that it relieves them of the responsibility, but it doesn't. The choice and authority is still ultimately yours. Courage and a positive attitude will lead you along your path to wellness.

Each of us can achieve our own personal best with a positive attitude. Having an open mind will help you achieve any goal. And I believe that all people have a certain degree of power to heal themselves and others. It is merely that some people are more sensitive to the universal energy connection, just as some of us have a natural gift for playing the piano or playing sports. The point is that we may not all be Mozart or Tiger Woods, but we can all learn to play the piano or golf if we dedicate the time and our focus. I think it's the same for what I do. We can all do it if we try hard enough.

WORRY IS A WASTE

Worry is a waste of time. Worry is fear of the future, which has yet to be determined. It is harmful. It is harmful to the worrier and to everyone close to that person. Nothing good comes of worry.

Worry leads to guilt. Guilt leads to negativity and loss of self-empowerment, and then it affects our health. And then it affects everyone around us through our interconnectedness. Some people are so disconnected from themselves and their own energy systems that relating to others and the connectedness is challenging.

Worry can cause disease. I can make the body aware that things can be different, but unless the person I'm doing the treatment on can see through his own negativity, nothing will change. This will affect the efficacy of the treatments. It is far easier for me to treat someone with terminal cancer and a positive attitude than someone who has a minor ailment but a negative attitude.

Some people cannot get out of their negative thought loop. If you say, "Hey, isn't it a wonderful sunny day?" they reply with something like, "Yeah, but it's probably going to rain tomorrow." They are insulated by negativity. From past experiences, they paste various negative labels on life. The excuses range from parents to guilt issues. They tend to blame others, especially their parents, but that is useless. Whatever your excuse is, you've got to deal with these issues and move on.

VISUALIZATION

Never underestimate the power of visualization. When you are imagining, you are visualizing. When you are visualizing, you are accessing the universal knowledge base, scientifically known as the field of quantum information. Intuition is the ability to tap into this field that surrounds all of us and emanates throughout the universe.

See yourself in the state of wellness you want to achieve. Do this in as much detail as you can. *See* yourself doing what you will do in this state of wellness. *Feel* how it will feel in this state. *Hear* the sounds you will hear around you. *Smell* the air. Do this every day. Make time for it, and look forward to spending this time with yourself each day. This state of wellness is your personal goal, your dream. Your dream of your path to wellness will help you achieve your goal.

Therapists have helped people by suggestion. They ask their patients to visualize the illness in their body and then have them visualize its removal by various means. When doing this, the mind is telling the body to heal itself. This might be successful with a few people who have a vivid imagination and are able to hold the healing thoughts for long periods. What I do is similar except that I influence the mind–body controls and bypass the person's need to successfully carry out the task of visualization. If someone was able to do this visualization while I do my healing, that would make my job easier.

INTUITIVENESS

As with any modality of healing, the beliefs and goals of the healer are as important as those of the person being healed. In this and the following sections, I elaborate on my own beliefs based on what I have experienced so far. Whether you agree with the specific details is not what is important, but understanding the beliefs I bring to energy healing will help increase your comfort level, and this in turn will help in your healing process and, thus, your return to health.

My ability to tap into the knowledge base that surrounds us is always improving. When I first started healing, I had to see a picture of someone in order to receive any information on them. Now, when someone simply mentions a name, I sometimes make the connection to that person. When I tap into information on a person this way, it goes through the person mentioning the name, so if someone else has the same name, I still connect to the right person. The path of linking to another person happens very fast, and I have not been able to map it out or even fully understand it yet.

Intuitiveness can be a strange thing. My parents were going to a friend's house for dinner one night and they told me who was going to be there. The name of one person brought an image into my mind of his ex-wife. They had been separated for ten years. I mentioned that she had some kind of neurological problem that was affecting her reasoning. I also said that this happened about ten years ago and that she was doing much better now. At the dinner, my parents were able to confirm that all of this had taken place.

I usually know or sense what is wrong with a person before she says anything or before I go in and see. Of course, I get much more detail when I actually go in and look at the person's energy system. When I am healing someone, I receive intuitive information as well as visual holograms. I feel that this is because of the interconnectedness of everyone. Again, the television provides a good analogy of the way I can receive the information. With the remote control, you can change the channels and connect to different movies. When I go into a person, I don't have to manually change the channels; they are changed instantaneously by thought. I believe that the information I access is coming from the field of quantum information.

To continue the television analogy, suppose that you want to watch a particular movie. Now imagine that your remote control can read your thoughts. The device picks up your thought and switches the television channel to the station showing the movie. This is similar to what happens when I scan a person for injury or disease.

The controls that I use are extremely sophisticated. I might tune in to the person's doctor's information, or in to the person's mother because of their close association or in to someone who might be aware of this person's injury. All the information I obtain is pertinent to the injury and becomes part of my analysis. In this way I am connecting to the field of quantum information for my healing.

This intuitive ability to receive images goes hand in hand with the healing. I see what and where the problem is, and I collect the intuitive information to complete my healing treatment. The information I receive is not in words but in images. They must be interpreted into something I can explain. Much of the time I use my own nonmedical terms to describe what I can see in a person.

I looked at a woman who had a total hysterectomy. She had endometriosis—the endometrial tissue, which lines the uterus, had attached to other organs in the pelvic cavity. She had the hysterectomy ten years ago, and although her uterus was removed, some of the endometrial tissue still remained on the other organs. The doctors said they could do nothing about it. The tissue I saw had connected to the kidneys. It looked like a plant growing on the outside of the kidneys, which at the time seemed strange to me. But after she described her health history, it all made sense.

Another woman had a problem with fluid in her lungs. She said that she could feel the fluid but was unable to cough it up. I went in and looked at her lungs. I told her that the inside of her lungs looked like they were sealed with some kind of coating. The liquid that she felt in her lungs was behind this coating. She then informed me that she had an operation for breast cancer and the doctors had to apply a sealant on the inside of her lungs after that operation. This explained what I saw in her lungs.

The image information I receive is not always exactly as it appears physically, which can be a challenge for me. One man I looked at had damaged disks in his lower back. What I saw was his lower spine being held in place by two thin perpendicular strings. My interpretation of this was instability in the lower back. He confirmed that his doctor had told him exactly that only a few days before my seeing him.

Intuitive abilities are becoming a major part of my energetic healing and diagnosis. Now, at the mere mention of someone's name, I am sometimes able to pick up information that lets me know what the problem is and whether I am able to help. And sometimes I receive information that isn't directly relevant to the injury. For example, I gave a woman one treatment and then didn't hear from her again. I knew it had helped her, but I also knew that her husband was against this type of treatment and was trying to talk her out of it. She eventually did contact me, and when I mentioned this issue to her, she wanted to know how I knew. Her husband had indeed tried to talk her out of it, but she had decided to proceed because her arthritis had improved so much after just one treatment with me. Since then, her arthritis has improved considerably.

When I look at a person, I can often tell whether or not he will be receptive to energy healing. I can also frequently see if it is a person's time to die. There isn't much that I can do if this is the case. When the body decides that it can't hang on anymore, it shows signs of shutting down. This is evident to me, and I feel that it would be futile to try to reverse it. I can give that person energy and in some cases help him become more accepting of the inevitable.

I feel that I am constantly in touch with the field of quantum information. It doesn't take much thinking for me to quickly connect to a certain area of the hologram. I also believe that this will get stronger as I grow older and more experienced.

INSIGHTS

Being able to tap into the field of quantum information opens my consciousness up to receive information about many things. The information available is vast. Sometimes I receive knowledge about events that will occur in the near or distant future. I believe the mind does some sort of instantaneous statistical analysis of all the information available and comes up with a probable event. This is similar to the ability that Edgar Cayce had to make some incredible predictions.

Edgar Cayce (1877–1945) was one of the most amazing psychics ever. He was able to diagnose illness in people he had never met, and then prescribe the medical treatment to heal them. He was also a devout Christian who wrote volumes of studies on how clairvoyance and reincarnation are not in contradiction to the teachings of the Bible. I recommend the reading of his material to anyone with an interest in this. Edgar Cayce became renowned for his ability to make predictions about future events. Many (but not all) of his predictions turned out to be correct.

If everything were to happen exactly as he foresaw from that moment, the prediction would come true. If a prediction did not come true it was probably because what he predicted was in a snapshot of time, but an unforeseen event came into the picture. Let's take a horse race as an analogy. A person reads the statistics on a horse and it seems there is no way it can lose the race. All the other horses are real duds and the horse you want to bet on once won the Kentucky Derby. The track is dry and this is when your horse does its best. For an instant in time, everything points to your horse easily winning the race. As the race gets under way, your horse gets bumped by another horse, causing it to break an ankle. So much for that prediction. Unforeseen events altered what seemed like a predictable outcome.

It is the same with psychic predictions except more information is involved. The closer the prediction is to the event, the more likely it is to happen. I was driving home one night with my dad. It was around ten o'clock. All of a sudden I told my dad, "I feel death coming." I said it was a horrible feeling and that hundreds of people were going to die soon. He told me not to worry and that we could check the newspapers in the morning. But my dad's driving became more cautious, as though he was beginning to wonder if we were about to be involved in an accident.

The next morning when we read the newspaper, we learned that an airplane had left Taipei, Taiwan, at 3 P.M. and went off the radar screen about twenty minutes after takeoff. Over two hundred people died in the crash. We checked the time difference and the time that it went off the radar was exactly when I had the feeling of death coming. Why did I get this feeling? Perhaps I got an energy connection from one of the people on board the plane. Or perhaps it was because so many people were heading for death at once, and because they knew it, I was able to pick up on their emotional distress.

REINCARNATION

Whether reincarnation is part of your belief system or not will not affect your healing process. This is just another level of spirituality that I personally accept. In the cycle of life, death is an inevitable and often very emotional part. I believe that we have all died many times and will continue to live and die. Our path is defined by our accumulated intentions. Death is a fact of life in a material sense, although I believe that our energy transforms itself, or reincarnates.

At first, reincarnation was difficult for me to accept, and I probably risk losing some readers by discussing it. It is hard enough to accept that it is possible to heal people without touching them or even meeting them. I am not a Buddhist and I haven't read much on Buddhism. My views on reincarnation come solely from my insights and ability to see the past lives of others and myself.

I believe that we have each had many lives in the past. Sometimes, our illnesses have something to do with our past lives. I also believe that some of the scars we obtain throughout our lifetime are related to something that happened to us when we were in a previous life.

Many people have experienced déjà vu, the feeling that you've experienced that same experience before. Many people when visiting another country for the first time feel a deep connection, as though they'd been there before. Or upon meeting someone for the first time you may have a sense of familiarity, as if you have known that person for a long time. Sometimes it is an uneasiness you feel when meeting someone, almost like a fear of being around them that you cannot explain. Then there are the times you find yourself coming up with information you never realized you knew. I believe that these are indications that this life is not our first.

I am actually able to see many of the past lives that people have experienced. When I go in to someone, I usually see present injuries as well as old injuries. I have yet to find someone who doesn't have something wrong with them. However, every person has a bright white light inside which I can go into. Inside this white light, I see what looks like a pure body with no scars or injuries. Maybe this represents what we refer to as the soul. From this bright light I am able to access a person's past lives. There are so many past lives that I seem to access a different one each time I go in. When I see these past lives, I receive vivid details. I looked at my dad and saw him at war with troops that carried a British flag with a battalion number. I have also seen him as a fisherman who lost his life at sea. My dad has always been terrified of swimming in deep water, and I don't think that this fear is coincidental.

Sometimes our past lives are not what we might want them to be. I went into the past life of a friend and saw that he had been a sheep farmer. There is nothing wrong with being a sheep farmer, but most people expect something more glamorous. They want to have been a king or queen in a past life. Whatever your past consists of, it makes up the person you are now. You are like a quilt fabricated from many different patterns to make something that is beautiful.

OPEN-MINDEDNESS

As with any form of healing, if you are not open to the idea of it being successful, it very likely won't be. We all have the ability to close our minds and therefore narrow the outcome possibilities of any experience. Conversely we can be open-minded enough to accept the possibility of positive change.

A person can be both open-minded and skeptical at the same time. You have to be careful that you don't become so committed to skepticism that your ability to be open-minded is lost. Good researchers have open and inquiring minds. There is no shortage of published formal scientific studies to support the validity of distant healing. Yet, the mere mention of distant healing to most people is considered almost taboo. Even people who profess to be open-minded have no interest in learning about it.

It is difficult for me to face this rejection from people, since I experience my special gift every day. It has fueled my ambition to educate and inform the world about the existence of these abilities. Many scientific inventors were ridiculed by their contemporaries. It was only later in their lives that they became great men and women in the eyes of the world.

Take Alexander Graham Bell, for instance. In 1876, he invented the telephone but had difficulty finding anyone interested in it. Chief engineer Sir William Preece at *British Post* said, "England has plenty of small boys to run messages." Sir William Preece was a Fellow of the Royal Society who had studied under the great chemist and physicist Michael Faraday. Sir Preece outdid this judgment when Thomas Edison announced that he had invented an electric light. Preece said it was "a completely idiotic idea."

But the best example of all has to be the Wright brothers. Although they had photographs of them flying their plane and held many public demonstrations which local dignitaries attended, their invention was dismissed as a hoax by most American scientists and top science magazines.

There are several memorable quotes from skeptics. Prominent British mathematician and physicist Lord Kelvin stated in 1895 that "heavier-than-air flying machines are impossible." A couple of years later he said, "Radio has no future." An editorial in the *Boston Post* in 1865 proclaimed, "Well informed people know it is impossible to transmit the voice over wires and that were it possible to do so, the thing would be of no practical value." In 1899, Charles H. Duell, U.S. Commissioner of Patents, made this statement: "Everything that can be invented has been invented." And finally, Thomas Watson, chairman of IBM, said, "I think there is a world market for maybe five computers."

Thankfully, my search has led to a number of well-educated people who are very knowledgeable and willing to help me understand my healing ability. They are courageous people. It takes a strong individual to go against mainstream thinking and pursue answers to the many unexplained events around us. I truly respect these people and hope they will be vindicated someday from all the attacks by their critics.

It is interesting how people whom I have known all my life are so doubtful when I explain distant healing. But it is reassuring that most people can eventually understand and accept this concept. I have changed the thinking of many people simply by demonstrating what I do. When people actually feel sensations in their body from a distant healing and notice a definite change in their health, they find it difficult to deny that it works. Of course, there are people who are skeptics just for the sake of being skeptical. I almost feel an obligation to change their thinking, because it seems like such a shame for someone to go through life and miss out on something so simple yet so profound. There is joy in the healing of a person, and there is also joy from changing a person's views on distant healing. I am unable to heal everyone, but I can make people aware of the existence of this connection, which we all potentially have access to. The "Seven Steps for Life" outlined in the next chapter will help you unlock your own self-healing ability.

How do you see the relationship of healing to spirituality or the soul?
Healing is far more than a physical experience. Emotions and spirit can and should be part of the healing experience. It is arbitrary to separate emotional, physical and spiritual realms of yourself. They are all interconnected and intertwined as one experience. Creating a positive frame of mind will propel you in your healing journey.

Are emotional issues related to physical ailments?
Which came first: the chicken or the egg? Emotional issues can create energy blockages that may eventually physically manifest as a problem. Physical ailments can cause a plethora of psychological issues. It is important to address them together as being integral parts of you. Your emotional and physical being is one. Improving your health and well-being is only complete if you can reflect on your total self.

Does one have to believe in order for energy healing to work?
Energy healing works through the intentions of the healer and the person being healed. If that person doubts it will make a difference, this may affect the outcome. It is important to keep an open mind in order for any form of healing to take place.

Chapter 9

Living Well with the Seven Steps for Life

*Everything is interconnected,
so one change affects everything else.*

—ADAM

*I*t is essential that we find happiness in our everyday lives. A positive approach to life and all that it brings will ensure that good things happen. And this in turn equates with better health. Research has shown that not only are levels of stress hormones reduced in people with a positive attitude, but their wounds heal significantly faster than those of people who feel negative. Positive feelings make the immune system stronger and give it direction. Negative feelings and emotions have been shown to weaken the immune system.

Difficulties and challenges are daily occurrences, and severe problems occur from time to time. What makes a difference to the outcome is not so much the details of the problem but how you perceive and handle the problem. *How* you react to something is more important than *what* is happening. And that's where people have much more power and control than they realize. You always have a choice as to how you are going to react. And your choice can often, if not always, strongly influence the outcome.

You can always choose your attitude. Your attitude determines how you react to something. It also determines how much stress is attached to a situation. People bring much more stress into their lives than they need to, simply by reacting inappropriately to situations. By choosing a positive attitude—a positive reaction—you can immediately diminish your stress levels. Few situations in life merit an over-the-top reaction. It is better to learn to relax, go with the flow, and enjoy the simple pleasures of life.

It is also helpful if you can approach life with a sense of humor. Kids are naturals at this. The average kid laughs or chuckles about 145 times a day. The average adult does this only about four or five times a day. A big difference!

Children also know how to enjoy the simple pleasures of life, such as splashing in puddles. This is because they have a different concept of time and its passing. It wouldn't occur to young children to concern themselves that they might get wet or dirty from puddle-splashing. They live in the moment of the fun, appreciating the present, the now. Future concerns, consequences and worries don't even enter their psyche. Children live in the present. Somehow over time we lose this perspective, yet it is essential for maintaining health.

I believe it is lost when our lives become controlled by time. We start school at a certain age during a certain time of year, on a predetermined day, at a prescheduled time. Time is all of a sudden of extreme importance to us, even though our understanding of it is still vague.

In school, some days pass quickly. For me, it's sports days. On other days, time slows down, as when we are being taught something in which we are not the least bit interested. Time varies a great deal on the same day, depending on our interest level in the activity. The academic part of school usually passes slowly, but then lunchtime passes so quickly that sometimes we hardly have time to eat, let alone get a good game of ball going, before the bell rings and it's back to class.

For me and many of my classmates, the afternoon in school has to be the slowest that time could possibly move without standing still. By this time, most kids have had enough of sitting. Finally the bell rings, and happy yelps of freedom echo through the hallways. The next couple of hours skip by in seconds before we have to be home for dinner.

Gradually, we learn how to tell time, and most kids eventually get a watch, and consider it an essential item to have with them at all times. We are no longer told what time it is by the sound of the school bell ringing or the turning on of the streetlights. Time is now a precise measurement. No longer does our mother gently wake us from our dream state. We have now grown up enough to have our own alarm clock scream in our ears at a designated time. Each day starts with an incredible and unnatural adrenaline shock to our system.

As we become adults, we are conditioned to equate time with money. We are expected to get jobs that have specific hours of work. The normal workday starts at 9 A.M., lunch is noon to 1 P.M., and the day ends at 5 P.M. So the workday schedules our time and events for five days out of every week. Here's the schedule of a typical, albeit simplified, weekday:

7:00 A.M.	Alarm clock rings, wake up, shower
7:30 A.M.	Breakfast
8:00 A.M.	Catch the bus or drive to work
8:45 A.M.	Get to work early, looking sharp!
9:00 A.M.	Workday begins
12:00 P.M.	Hungry or not, it's lunchtime
1:00 P.M.	Back to work
5:00 P.M.	Workday ends, commute home begins
5:30 P.M.	Get home, start making dinner
6:00 P.M.	Eat, whether hungry or not
6:30 P.M.	Chores and evening activities
10:00 P.M.	Wind down so we can wake up at
7:00 A.M.	And start the whole thing again

In short, we wake at a specific time, rather than when our bodies tell us that we feel adequately rested. Many people keep functioning without enough sleep, relentlessly keeping in stride with the clock. Functioning this way is a major contributor to stress. Fatigue is epidemic in our society and leads to errors in judgment, accidents, strained relationships, frayed nerves and deteriorating health.

We eat at the designated time, not necessarily when we are hungry. If you ask some people if they are hungry, they will look at their watch before they answer. Eating becomes an activity within our off time. This may lead to overeating as a habit or social pastime. It is seen as beyond something that our bodies require. This may result in addictive behavior, which can lead to obesity, a growing health problem in our society. Eating can easily become a comfort-zone activity during scheduled timeout. Then it becomes an activity we treasure because it is beyond the bounds of our stressful time-constrained day.

Many notions of measuring time create stress for us. In school, exams must be written at specific times, which may not be the time of day at which we function most effectively. But we do it to avoid failing; we must keep up with our grades.

People who have been told by their doctors that they are terminally ill are given a death sentence. Many people who are told they have only six to twelve months to live will take that as an indisputable fact and die within this prescribed time. We tend to forget that nobody knows this as fact and of all people on earth, *you* have the most to say and do about this. Indeed, it is well known in the medical field that some patients will hang on to life until they are able to see someone important or significant to them. Earlier I mentioned a man who recovered sufficiently from a stroke until all his significant family members were able to come see him. This often happens. We have more control over our conscious and subconscious thoughts than we are often led to believe.

The point is, if we don't want to hear something, we can always choose not to listen. If something is doing us psychological harm, such as being told that we are going to die in six months, we can deflect it. Always take the opportunity to empower yourself. You have the power until or unless you choose to give it to someone else.

We can learn a great deal from little children about the importance of time. Almost all preschoolers could give us the following valuable advice, through their actions: Let time be. This is particularly hard for type-A personalities, or high-strung individuals, but the best thing they could do is leave their watches at home. Our societal obsession with creating structured time is the ultimate source of many illnesses. Time is structured only through the eye of the beholder: You!

The Seven Steps for Life that follow will help you unlock your self-healing ability. At first glance they may appear simplistic. Sometimes the most important observations are the most obvious, and often the most overlooked. Read this information carefully and objectively examine what changes you can make to your life for your maximum benefit.

SEVEN STEPS FOR LIFE
Step 1: Feel Your Own Energy and Be Aware of It
To feel your own energy, rub your palms together in a circle. Be sure to rub the spot right in the center of your palms. Feel the generation of heat. It is your energy. Then hold your palms an inch or two apart and feel the magnetic push and pull. Move your palms farther apart, until you can no longer feel your energy field. Play with your energy and have fun with it. Our energy system is what this is all about, so become aware of it.

This flow of energy is our life force. It is more important than any other single body system because it involves all of them. Yet, our digestive, respiratory, circulatory, metabolic and nervous systems are better known in Western medicine. We have created lots of tests to measure the efficiency and health level of each of these. We have yet to develop a measurable level for our energy system, and so it is ignored. Yet, it directly affects all aspects of our health. Learn to feel it, work with it and, most of all, enjoy it.

Step 2: Breathe Abdominally and Be Aware of It
Breathe deeply. Many people usually breathe shallow breaths, from their chests, and are actually somewhat oxygen deprived. Breathing using your diaphragm and abdominal muscles promotes relaxation and reduces tension. Athletes and singers require lots of oxygen intake and this is the method of breathing that they use. The body gets enough to function, but would function even better with deep, full breaths. Singers and athletes are very aware of how proper breathing enhances their performance. We all need air in order to reach our maximum potential.

Breathe in through your nose and imagine filling your abdomen with air. Once full, exhale through your mouth and pull in your belly. Your shoulders should not go up and down with breathing. It may take a bit of time for you to develop good breathing habits, but stick with it. I know some people who make a point of deep breathing on their daily walk. They count to four as they inhale, hold for another four counts and then breathe out over four counts. This is a good exercise to practice proper breathing. Increase the number of counts as your lung capacity expands over time.

Step 3: Ground Your Energy and Be Aware of Its Flow

It is important to ground your energy often. Think of your energy as circulating through and around you, connecting you to the universal energy above and below the earth. With each breath, breathe in air and energy from above and around you. When exhaling, imagine forcing that energy down the front of your body, through the soles of your feet to the center of the earth. Feel your soles connecting to the earth's core. The exhale connects you to everything on the planet. The inhale connects you with all in the universe. This is grounding, which is all about being aware of our connection to energy systems. Grounding will increase your physical energy and strength by unifying your aura with other energy systems. It will cleanse your aura and generally improve your health.

Step 4: Drink Water

Drink water. Lots of it! Our bodies are nearly 80 percent water—it composes that much of our body weight. We are water-based creatures, and we must respect this. Every day, drink the eight glasses your body needs. Drink filtered water, if possible. If you want a more exciting taste, add a twist of fresh lime or lemon.

Our bodies need water to operate optimally. If we face an additional health challenge because of an injury or illness, water is a vital part of our recovery. Our bodies remove unwanted and unnecessary materials by excreting them along with the water. This is our natural purification process. Without water, toxins that could easily be removed on a regular basis accumulate in our bodies. Dehydration can be deadly.

Consuming water is the easiest habit to change, and the most overlooked. Water is readily available to most of us and sometimes can alone achieve remarkable results. You would never think of trying to run your car without adding oil and gas. Why would you treat your car with more respect and care than you would your own body? We have been given this fabulously effective body, and it shouldn't be taken for granted.

Step 5: Develop Emotional Bonds with Others
Many of us, but not all, are fortunate enough to have loving family members. And, at any moment in time, each and every one of us has the opportunity to bond with others as friends. We all need these emotional connections. It requires a give-and-take of trust to make relationships work, but it is well worth the effort. Welcome it, and your world becomes a wonderful, loving place to live, a place filled with good, harmonious energy.

Stable and loving relationships have been shown to have a strong and positive influence on health. Those who have made the effort and commitment to develop close relationships with family members and friends are healthier than those who lack these relationships. If they do get sick or injured, they recover much faster than people who do not have a network of supportive family or friends.

Step 6: Think Positively in the Present Tense and Feel Its Effects
The power of your own positive thoughts helps balance your mental, physical, emotional and spiritual aspects. This balance empowers us, making us able to achieve our dreams and keep us healthy. Stay in the now, as the past is over and, although it is good to have dreams, fears about the future are futile.

Dream of what you truly love to do and do it. Only *you* can make a lasting change in yourself. By looking inward, it is possible to re-create yourself. Be aware of your feelings and your power to adjust and control them.

Put yourself into a quiet meditative state. Picture a three-dimensional holographic image of yourself. This takes lots of concentration and practice. Make it an exact image of yourself. If your eyes are blue, imagine the image of yourself having blue eyes. Visualize it. Concentrate on seeing your eyes exactly as they are. Work on perfecting this image until it is an exact image of you, exact in every detail. Even someone who lacks imagination can do this.

Once you have this clear image in your mind, repeat to yourself that you are all better and problem-free. Concentrate this beam of positive thoughts on the injured area. For example, if you have an elbow problem, project these positive thoughts like a laser beam toward your elbow.

Do not think of the problems. You do not have any problems in the image you have put in front of you. Think of the perfect hologram, one with no injuries. I know this can work for you because of what I do. I heal people with my ability to connect to their energy holograms. Once I connect to a person, I use my thoughts to perform the healing work that I do.

I understand that this ability to connect to a person's hologram is a gift. I also know that we all have the ability to make the connection to our own holograms and use the power of thought to heal. This does not come easily, but with the desire to learn and with some practice, you will succeed. By continuing to practice, you will find that it gets easier and easier, and that your ability to do this increases. Once you master it, you will find this an effective method of improving and maintaining your state of wellness.

Step 7: Understand and Appreciate the Connectedness of Everyone and Everything

Everything affects everything else in the entire universe in a weblike manner. Positive thoughts and actions taken by one of us affect everyone else. While the people most affected are those closest to us in the web—family, friends, workmates and acquaintances—the entire web is indeed affected. It is this interconnectedness that enables distant healing to take place.

Feel grateful for your life—it is precious. Be thankful for all the wonderful people who have connected with you along your journey. Look forward to the adventures that each day brings. We all face challenges, but our attitude as we face them makes all the difference. The positive outlook of each of us is contagious.

The Seven Steps for Life will help guide you along your personal journey to wellness. Use them as a motivational guide to keep you on course with your healing journey. Keep them handy and get in the habit of referring to them often as a useful reminder of the essential steps for your health.

Seven Steps for Life
1. Feel your energy and be aware of it. Make it a habit to feel your life force energy daily.
2. Breathe abdominally and be aware of it. Practice this every chance you get until it becomes second nature.
3. Ground your energy and be aware of its flow. This can be done any time of the day and anywhere, such as when you are standing in line at a store.
4. Drink water. Make a mental note of every time you have treated yourself to a glass of water.
5. Develop emotional bonds with others. Be consciously aware of doing something positive to make another person's day a little better.
6. Think positively in the present tense and feel its effects. Make a point of relaxing peacefully at some point throughout your day, whether in a state of meditation or self-reflection.

7. Understand and appreciate the connectedness of everything and everyone. Express appreciation for one thing that you are grateful for each and every day. Feel gratitude, smile and be happy.

Chapter 10

Your Dream

*People have much more power
and control than they realize.*

—ADAM

I have helped many people, and the most enjoyable part is receiving their appreciation. It is such a pleasure to have them understand the connection that we have shared. I have received many letters and emails from people who understand and accept that their health has improved. This show of gratitude inspires me to help others. When I help a grandfather with cancer, I know I am helping not only him but also his wife, daughters, sons, grandchildren and friends. The wellness affects as many people as the sickness did.

I am living my dream.

I am always amazed and somewhat amused at the response I get from people when I tell them of my abilities. If someone asks me to explain my ability, I might say, "I do distant healing by connecting to the quantum hologram of another person." Some friends and relatives whom I have known almost all my life have reacted in a similar manner—either dismissing the subject or deflecting it with a response along the lines of, "Lovely weather we're having, isn't it?"

Those who are receptive and understand what I do often find themselves in the same predicament as me, trying to explain it to others. It's almost as if it is taboo to talk about something that doesn't fit mainstream thinking. We all have to change this mentality in order for humankind to advance at a conscious level—the level of knowing and understanding everything within us and around us.

Usually, people need to be alone with me before they will engage in a conversation on the topic. When there is more than one person present, a giggle factor often kicks in. It is a form of human self-defense when our brains can't stretch far enough to grasp an idea or concept.

Accepting change or a new way of thinking is referred to as a paradigm shift. There have been many examples of dramatic paradigm shifts throughout civilization, and there is no reason to believe that there won't be many more. I always thought that one characteristic of humankind that prevents us from moving forward is ego. A dramatic example of how ego can have a major impact on how we perceive things is the Ptolemaic system, which came about in the second century A.D. Scientists, accepting the view of Greek astronomer and geographer Ptolemy, claimed that the universe rotated around the earth. With billions and billions of stars and planets in the sky, how much bigger can one's ego be? But nonetheless, this scientific proclamation was widely accepted.

The Ptolemaic system was so entrenched in medieval society that many people were put to death for thinking differently. We might find that shocking, but what it really should do is remind us that we must continue to question today's science and not just accept it. We must always be able to subjectively analyze knowledge beyond our current scientific base of information. We should learn from our past and not blindly accept all current science as truth. We've been mistaken before.

If you tether an elephant to a small post with a rope that is simply placed over the top of the post, the elephant is unable to move away. Despite that it is not tied, and even though the elephant with its massive weight could easily pull the post from the ground, the elephant will not move. In its mind, it thinks that it is securely tethered and can't possibly pull away. Obviously, that couldn't be further from the truth, because all the elephant has to do is walk away. This analogy can easily be applied to our day-to-day thinking about what is possible and impossible. Our limitations are self-imposed.

There is a swell of change taking place in the world today. With freedom comes the ability to question the medical and scientific dogma that we confront on a daily basis. It wasn't long ago that you wouldn't dare tell your doctor that you would like a second opinion. Today, many doctors go out of their way to explain their medical diagnoses in detail in order to meet the demands of inquiring patients. This is, in a small way, a paradigm shift. People are finally coming to the realization that doctors really aren't gods (though their opinions should be respected). Ultimately, health choices are one's own responsibility.

More and more of us are becoming aware of people with special abilities. There are many things that we don't understand and science cannot yet explain. We are coming to the realization that if science can't explain something, that doesn't mean it's impossible. Another belief that is tough to change is that experts are all open-minded and willing to explore science. Even top scientists have paradigms they don't want to breach. Change is difficult and humans resist change. However, we must change in order to move forward, and this will happen naturally when the critical mass of consciousness is reached. This means that when enough people become aware of our connectedness, our conscious awareness will change with it.

One force joins us. One idea keeps us apart. Love is the unifying force. Fear is the underlying separation of beings. The future of humankind depends on how we apply this unifying force. Love and cooperation is needed.

Fear and material competition must be left in the past with

ego. They only intensify our perception of separateness, which leads to conflict. Human survival is the ultimate goal of every being and can be accomplished when our commonality, not our differences, is our focus.

My goal is to make people realize that many things exist that are beyond our five senses. We have to be able to open our mind's eye and see beyond the societal and scientific paradigms that exist in our world. Everyone must become fully aware of our interconnectedness. Only then will we be able to heal ourselves. Believe in yourself and everything becomes possible. There is more to this universe than we know.

Stay tuned!

DREAMHEALER 2

A Guide to Healing
and Self-Empowerment

You have the rest of your life to change your future.
—ADAM

Contents

Acknowledgments	131
THE JOURNEY CONTINUES	133
Healing Is a Choice	136
CHAPTER 1: ACCEPTING RESPONSIBILITY	139
The Role of Habits	142
The Role of Attitudes	143
The Role of Emotions	146
CHAPTER 2: THE LIVING AURA	149
The Aura of a Healthy Body	152
The Aura of Illness	155
Energy Exercises	157
CHAPTER 3: THE MIND–BODY CONNECTION	169
The Immune System	171
Awareness of Children	173
Reintegration of Self	174
CHAPTER 4: HEALING INFORMATION	179
Intuition	181
Energy Connections	182
Energy as Information	183
Seven Steps for Life	183
Analyze Your Lifestyle	188

	Telepathy, Intuition and Intention in Healing	190
	The Evolution of Self-Healing	193
CHAPTER 5:	GROUP HEALING	195
	The Master Hologram	198
	Lessons from Native Culture	199
	Group Healing Workshops	203
	Steps in Group Healing	204
CHAPTER 6:	THE PHYSICS OF ENERGY HEALING	215
	Matter as Energy	217
	The Universal Energy Field	219
	Our Energy Links	220
	Distant Healing	221
CHAPTER 7:	SKILLS FOR SELF-HEALING VISUALIZATIONS	223
	Fine-Tuning Your Ability to Visualize	225
	Projecting a Hologram	227
	Recalling Details	228
	Four Strategies for Enhancing Your Visualization Skills	231
CHAPTER 8:	GENERAL VISUALIZATIONS: RE-CREATING WELLNESS	237
	Fire and Ice	241
	Lightning Bolts	244
	Smart Energy Packets (SEPs)	245
	Explosion	247
	Waterfall	248
	Holding Your State of Wellness in Place: The Patterned Energy Grid	250
	When and Where to Do Visualizations	252
	Customizing the General Visualizations	252

CHAPTER 9:	VISUALIZATIONS FOR	
	SPECIFIC CONDITIONS	255
	Cancer	258
	Leukemia	263
	Neurological Conditions	263
	Respiratory Conditions	264
	Heart Conditions	266
	Infectious Diseases	272
	Gastrointestinal Conditions	274
	Pain Issues	274
	Joint Conditions, Chronic and Acute	277
	Back Injuries	279
	Muscle Injuries	281
	Broken Bones	282
	Fatigue and Emotional Problems	283
	Customizing Your Visualizations	286
	Conclusion	289

Acknowledgments

Thank you Ivan Rados, for all the effort and dedication you have put into the art for this book. When we first discussed the illustrations required, it didn't take long to come to the realization that some of them were too complex for me to explain to you in words. You suggested that I telepathically send images. I thought this might work because it is one of the techniques I use to help people in comas. I telepathically send them images of familiar people, places or things.

Your intuitive ability has enabled you to receive the information I sent you, and your extraordinary talent, creativity and true artistic vision have created images that closely resemble what I had envisioned.

Thanks Ivan, for giving this book illustrations that go far beyond my stick-man level of art.

Also many thanks to Dr. Doris Lora, who encouraged me throughout the writing of this book.

Most of all, thanks to everyone whom I have had the pleasure of meeting when our paths have crossed.

The Journey Continues

I have always been able to see and feel energy fields around humans and all living things. What I didn't realize for many years is that not everyone else can. One day I was drawn to help my mom, who was in agonizing pain from trigeminal neuralgia, an affliction caused by her multiple sclerosis. Without being aware of what I was doing, I took her pain away. Now years later, what was a frequent symptom for her has never returned. Thus, my healing journey began.

The view of the external aura provides useful information about a person's state of health, but I do not use this with what I do. When I perform a healing, I am able to project holographic images in front of me, which are three-dimensional charts of information emitted by the person. I call this "going into" the person because I am able to "go into" their energetic hologram, to directly access their holographic information. This can be accomplished when I am physically with a person, or through a connection made by looking at a photograph. From these holographic views, I can "see" where energy blockages exist and can manipulate energy in the form of information in order to facilitate healing. The person themselves does the healing based on the information they receive.

It doesn't matter how many miles separate us physically—distance is not a factor. I can do what I refer to as "distant healing." The ability to do this exists because of our inherent interconnectedness to each other and to everything else in our universe. This knowledge is essential for our own expanding consciousness.

Healing is something that we are all capable of doing and increasing our skills in. Our own wellness is the responsibility of each and every one of us. It is with this purpose in mind that I have written *DreamHealer 2: A Guide to Healing and Self-Empowerment*, which includes instructions for visualizations you can use to help balance your own energy system back to wellness.

The purpose of my first book, *DreamHealer*, was twofold: to tell the story of the discovery of my healing ability and, more importantly, to help people understand that we all have the capacity to heal and be healed. Soon after the publication of *DreamHealer*, I became aware that many people needed more information on the powerful influence that we all have on our own health and healing. Readers were enthusiastic but often puzzled. They expressed doubts about their own abilities to heal themselves. They peppered me with questions about how to heal.

This second book, *DreamHealer 2: A Guide to Healing and Self-Empowerment*, is an effort to answer that need. It also has a twofold purpose: to provide detailed information on how each of us can heal ourselves and others and, as a result, to address the enormous need for healing on our planet.

Since the release of *DreamHealer*, I have been contacted by many knowledgeable and enlightened people with messages of encouragement and support. I also received thousands of emails from individuals in need of healing. Some contacts were desperate pleas for help from people who lacked a basic understanding or knowledge of the connection we all share. In this book, I discuss at length our connections with each other and with universal energy.

Many requests for healing have been heart wrenching beyond words. I have been confronted by people who are at the end of their rope and "willing to try anything." I have been asked to quit high school, friends and hobbies to allow for more time to heal others. One fellow even suggested I sleep less. Even if I were healing 24–7, there would not be enough time to address all these needs. This book is a step in the direction of meeting that need.

As a healer, I must always be aware of how much energy I can give to others and how much to reserve for myself. Consider this parable: There was once a healer in New Zealand who became famous. He had been an alcoholic, but his life took a turn when he discovered his ability to heal. People came from far and wide seeking his help. There was always a lineup of people stretching from his front door far down the street. For several years, he gave to others all the help he possibly could, while sacrificing his own needs. Then one day he collapsed under the awesome responsibility that healing brings with it. He took up drinking again as an escape. He never healed again.

Every healer knows this to be true: Give of yourself, but *always* save lots for yourself. Maintain your own life, your own interests and the space you need. In doing so, you can remain devoted to helping others.

It is clear that with a world population of approximately six billion, we need millions of healers. My goal is to teach as many people as possible, since everything we need to heal ourselves is already within us. We just need the tools to effectively tap into the mind–immune system connection and use it to heal. Teaching effective healing tools is the focus of *DreamHealer 2: A Guide to Healing and Self-Empowerment*. With this book, I hope to assist in empowering millions of people to become self-healers.

HEALING IS A CHOICE

All healing is participatory, no matter what the method. Even Western medicine, which is allopathic— dealing with disease with treatments, including drugs, that have the opposite effect to the symptoms—accepts the idea that patients must be willing to improve their own health in order for their health to improve.

Many people have been encouraged to leave all the responsibility for their wellness in someone else's hands, usually a medical authority. Each of us must realize that we ultimately choose every aspect of our health care. We are in charge. In this way, we become our own masters; we claim our birthright of total self-empowerment. At every turning point in life, there are decisions which we make ourselves. We define and create our own futures. Our wellness—physical, emotional and spiritual—is part of this creation.

It is our choice whether we smoke, drink, take drugs, worry or place unnecessary stress or risk in our lives. Each lifestyle choice has consequences, but we ultimately make the decision. Generally, people want to remove themselves from the responsibility of their illnesses. They tend to pass that responsibility on to someone else, particularly to a healer such as myself. However, everyone must understand that healing themselves is ultimately their responsibility.

When people tell me that they will leave their healing in my hands, I have a serious discussion with them. I will not do a treatment on anyone who doesn't accept the participatory nature of healing. The healer does not do the healing directly. The healer simply creates an efficient connection in order to facilitate the healing.

We also have other choices that influence our health. We can choose to ignore our own energy systems or we can dedicate time to understanding them. A healthy energy flow pattern will help each of us. To achieve this, everyone should strive to maximize his or her potential. When you are being your best self, the positive energy will radiate out in waves of healing that will affect everyone and everything, well beyond your conscious awareness.

Chapter I
Accepting Responsibility

The most powerful tool to heal yourself is yourself.
—ADAM

What is the most extensive untapped resource in modern medicine? It is the power of every person to heal himself. Millions of people put the responsibility of their personal health care in the hands of others. In many cases, the underlying cause is rarely dealt with. I challenge you to take charge of your own health. Make sure that your lifestyle choices are healthy ones. Accept the primary responsibility for maintaining your health. After all, no one is more interested in your health than you are. Learn about your body and how to avoid illness.

Your best defense against illness is your immune system working at its optimum level. What you think directly affects the efficacy of your immune system. Do some research so you can make educated decisions about what is best for you. For instance, if you have a pancreatic problem, get an anatomy book and learn where the pancreas is located, what it looks like and how it works. Learn everything that you can about the pancreas. Then you can use this knowledge when you do the visualizations I outline in this book, making them much easier to do and more effective.

Set new intentions to counter old habits. Habits play a part in reinforcing behavior. They can strengthen our resolve through positive habits but can also intensify problems through negative thoughts and beliefs. Because of their routine nature, they are counterproductive to positive change within yourself. Only you can change yourself. All true and permanent change comes from within. Understand that in order to improve your well-being, you must first believe that this is possible. The following three statements illustrate the progression necessary to bring your belief system in line with the possibilities of self-healing.

1. I can be well again (possible)
2. I will be well again (probable)
3. I am well again (being well)

Wellness involves looking carefully at your lifestyle: at your habits, attitudes and emotions. Those seeking better health must have a true desire to reach the goal of being well.

THE ROLE OF HABITS

In many illnesses, the individual's habits are a contributing factor. The first step to healing yourself is examining your habits and practices from a nonbiased, or objective, point of view. Recall everything that you did today that may have had a negative impact on your health. If you are having difficulty doing this, ask a close friend or relative who knows you well. Ask that person to tell you honestly how she thinks you could improve your lifestyle.

It may be more difficult to recognize an underlying negative lifestyle factor, such as stress, than a more obvious poor choice, such as smoking. Changing your lifestyle for the better can have only a positive impact, so it is essential to have the willpower and discipline to make the necessary changes.

This approach to analyzing your lifestyle involves not only becoming aware of negative aspects that are causing problems but focusing on those that will create a positive impact in your life. Make all your choices healthy ones. Decide what habits and practices you must change and take the appropriate action to change them. Take control of this power that you have to change any unhealthy habits and, consequently, your life. This amounts to only a fraction of the incredible potential of self-empowerment at your disposal.

I have received many emails from people seeking help who have lung-related diseases, only to learn that they are still smoking. If they cannot throw away the cigarettes, do they sincerely have the desire to get better and heal themselves?

It would be unwise to spend my time and energy helping someone who refuses to make such changes and continues the behavior that may have caused or at least contributed to the problem in the first place. The desire to take positive steps for your health is the same desire that will empower you to get better. The healer points the body in the right direction for healing: It is *you* who must continue in that direction. It is your body, so take care of it. You are ultimately in charge.

THE ROLE OF ATTITUDES

The second step toward self-healing is creating a positive social environment that will enhance your healing ability. The attitudes of those around you have a huge effect on your well-being. Therefore, not only must you change your habits, diet and thought patterns, but you must influence people around you to change their attitudes and be more positive. When those around you observe your efforts to improve your own health, many will radiate positive thoughts. When you and all the people around you are thinking positively, you are creating a perfect healing environment and increasing the effectiveness of your healing process. Conversely, when people around you are always negative, their negative attitudes interfere with and counter your positive healing process.

Be aware of the impact that other people's thoughts and attitudes have on you and your well-being. Make mental notes about when you feel best and in whose company. The choice is ultimately yours as to what energy you expose yourself to. You are responsible not only for your own attitudes but also for those that you allow to influence your own. Surround yourself with positive, like-minded people.

Negativity is the most common attitude problem that people face today. Your positive outlook will guide you hand in hand with your physical recovery. Everyone must put his past difficulties behind him. The past is past; you cannot change it. You can only change your present, which impacts your future possibilities.

Imagine two people in the hospital with identical illnesses. One believes and so is thinking that he is getting better and will be home in a few days. The other believes his illness is going to be with him forever and is thinking that he will probably never leave the hospital alive. Which of the two will recover faster? The positive person, of course. We have all had the pleasure of meeting these people in life who accept any challenge with a positive expectation of outcome. And guess what? Good things *do* happen to them. The power of thought cannot be overestimated.

All thoughts and intentions radiate throughout the universe. Everything is connected to everything else because the universe is composed only of energy. Thought or intention is a form of energy; therefore, every intention you have radiates out forever, affecting everything in its path. It is like a ripple in a pond. Every molecule in the pond is affected to some degree by that ripple.

Start today by having a positive outlook from this day forth. See the glass as being half full, not half empty. In any situation there is always hope. Be the optimist. This positive attitude is essential to the success of your healing.

It helps enormously to have a regular companion with you while doing the visualization techniques that are explained in the upcoming chapters. If someone close to you has the same common intention and visualization, the effect of that intention will be greatly amplified.

Finally, cultivate an attitude of open-mindedness. Many people are skeptical of what they cannot perceive with their five senses. A popular children's book says in its wisdom that everything important can be seen with the heart, which is, of course, invisible to the eyes. In this way, we must look beyond our familiar paradigms and keep an open mind about that which we cannot see. Always remember that a closed mind can be locked only from the inside. It therefore follows that a closed mind can be unlocked only from the inside, too.

Wellness involves an open, positive, responsible and participatory attitude toward one's own well-being. The old parable about giving a man a fish versus teaching him to fish nicely explains the participation required in any healing: Give a man a fish, and you feed him for a day. Teach a man to fish, and he feeds himself for life. Teach him how to make a fishing rod, and he will teach his children how to make them.

Giving a man a fish is like the healer healing a person without any participation on the part of the healee. The expectation on the part of the healee is sometimes referred to as the magic wand syndrome: No participation is required. No change in lifestyle is expected, and there is no need to reflect on how the illness occurred. A totally passive relationship is created. The healer provides what is needed, and the healee gives away the responsibility for his own health.

On the other hand, teaching a man to fish requires two-way participation, just as with healing. The healer gives instructions on how to participate in one's own wellness. Both healer and healee understand that healing is a two-way process. The healer's responsibility is to examine the lifestyle, stress and emotional responses that led the person to this point and to suggest the necessary changes that will prevent health problems from reoccurring or continuing. It is understood that this is a lifetime challenge that requires constant attention in order to affect permanent change. A participatory relationship leads to lasting changes in health.

However, teaching a man how to make a fishing rod ensures he has a lifelong tool. Similarly, the healer teaches the healee the concept of self-healing and maintaining a state of wellness. Consequently, the healee achieves a state of complete self-empowerment. Total responsibility is with the healee, as he handcrafts his own fishing rod or state of health. A creative process has been achieved.

Ideally, people should understand the dynamics of the healing process completely so that they can improve the design for maximum efficiency for themselves. People should understand that the ability to re-create their reality lies within each and every one of us. Accessing this ability requires imagination and a sense of knowing this to be true, based on personal experience.

When the healee achieves a firm understanding of the healing modality, he is then able to teach others. This should be the ultimate goal of both the healer and healee.

THE ROLE OF EMOTIONS

Emotional problems are usually very complex and, in many situations, they develop into physical problems. Often we let emotions dictate our subconscious intentions and, therefore, our wellness. If you master the control of your emotions, you are in control of your immune system and thus your health.

To master our emotions, we should practice tuning in to ourselves in order to understand what makes us tick. What more worthwhile endeavor could there possibly be in this lifetime than to develop a deeper appreciation of ourselves? We can start by being aware of what pushes our buttons. What situations drive us to distraction? What characteristics in others drive us crazy? What triggers our positive and negative emotional responses, which in turn flood our systems with energy? Only when we understand what makes us tick can we set out to control these reactions.

It has long been established in all types of medicine that emotions play a major role in the efficacy of our immune systems. Listen to what you tell yourself; notice what replays in your mind. Is this working toward your own good, or is it providing negative reinforcement? The good must be given every opportunity to flourish. What you don't need must not be given the strength and resources it needs to exist. You don't need it, so get rid of it.

Visualize cleaning your room and throwing out all of the old, unused stuff—broken items, stray parts of things whose origins you have long since forgotten. Be thorough and selective. Keep only what you need to help you achieve the goal of re-creating your new positive reality.

This housecleaning of your past is necessary in order for you to understand what you have experienced, how you have interpreted those experiences and what emotional baggage needs to be addressed. It is like eliminating the junk emails from your computer. If you don't do this on a regular basis, your entire system slows down, becoming less efficient and eventually dysfunctional.

Habitual emotional responses are difficult to change. An established pattern creates a tape loop of sorts in the mind, going around and around on the same circuit. Break the pattern and move on, as it is detrimental to your health. Understand that your happiness is not dependent on what happens to you and around you, but how you process things within you. Your emotions depend on what you think, and you control your thoughts.

Life is for learning. What better goal could we have than to learn as much about ourselves as we can in this lifetime? Through learning about how we react to various situations, we also develop the ability to relate to others in a more meaningful and compassionate way. This new state of awareness sends out ripples of positive energy. Our concept of self, or "me," becomes more connected to everyone and everything around us. Improving the energy balance of one person ultimately affects us all.

Chapter 2
The Living Aura

*The harmonious flow of one's energy
defines one's health pattern.*

—ADAM

*E*very living organism emits an energy field, which is visible to many people in the form of light. This energy field is commonly referred to as an aura. The aura is a reflection of the organism's intentions and its physical and emotional structure. This aura surrounds every living thing. The physical structure of the organism appears to influence the manner in which the energy flows. The auras around plants appear to be colorless and look like heat waves shimmering and rising from a hot road in summer. In humans, an aura looks like a bubble of swirling colored waves.

I know many of us are born with the ability to see auras because when I change mine in front of a baby—by projecting it above my head, for instance—the baby's eyes tend to follow the change. But this ability gets suppressed as we grow up. It is not something that is accepted in Western society, so over time people lose this ability, whether deliberately or not. With a little practice, we can retrain ourselves to see auras.

A person's aura is like a fingerprint or genetic marker that uniquely identifies the individual. Twins can be genetically identical yet their auras look completely different. No two auras are alike. They differ in color, intensity, size and shape. Emotions seem to influence change in the aura's color. People are always interested in what colors their auras are. However, I don't see the value of categorizing aura colors into "red means this and blue means that." The important aspect is the dynamic, harmonious flow of energy.

THE AURA OF A HEALTHY BODY

In a state of good physical health, a person's aura looks like an ocean of colors flowing around the body; there is harmonious flow of color throughout the aura as the colors smoothly transition from one to another. The manner in which a person's energy flows outside and inside her body is a unique identifier of the individual. Some people have a translucent flowing energy near the surface of the body. Others have another brighter layer that contains colors of swirling energy. Some people have lots of colors in their auras and others have very little color. Some auras extend well beyond the body, and others barely extend beyond the physical body. The same person's aura can appear very different under different conditions, depending, for example, on the degree of emotional stress.

These observations have taught me that the most important aspect of a person's aura is how it flows. Harmonious flow of one's energy defines one's health pattern. A splatter painting may contain exactly the same paint and materials as the *Mona Lisa*; the difference is in the pattern in which the materials are applied. A symphony being practiced by an orchestra may contain all the same notes as the perfected performance; the difference is in which notes are played with others. Harmony or coherence, in these examples, is what distinguishes chaos from order.

As a problem begins to develop, the energy begins to lose this harmony. The energy in the aura near the problem becomes stagnant. All the cells in a person's body are working in unison and share an interconnectedness to each other; therefore, a change in one cell affects all the others.

None of us has a perfectly healthy body. We all have something that causes breaks to show up in our auras, whether it is an old injury, an existing ailment, or a developing issue. Re-establishing this harmonious flow gives each of us a goal to constantly work toward. Many people have the ability to see these auras with varying degrees of intensity and can easily determine where a problem exists in the body.

The external auric view of the physical body gives me a broad perspective and is a good indicator of general problems in the body. When the problem is deeper within the body, I have to be able to see the body's inner energies to cause lasting change. I do this by connecting to the person's quantum hologram.

In order to understand the quantum science, there are some basic quantum concepts you need to wrap your mind around. In the quantum world of subatomic particles, a quantum object such as an electron can exist at more than one place at a time. Until we actually observe it as a particle, it behaves unlike our perception of space-time reality. It seemingly moves from one site to another without moving between the two locations. Rather than being like motion as we know it, the process is more like disappearing from one place and reappearing elsewhere. This is referred to as the quantum leap.

Quantum physics also explains how someone's holographic information can be accessed and influenced from anywhere, making distance not a factor, and therefore distant healing possible. Information about everyone and everything is intertwined, or interconnected. On a subatomic level, one quantum object simultaneously influences a correlated twin object no matter how far apart they are. This is called quantum action-at-a-distance and is the basis of nonlocality phenomena, including distant healing. For decades, physicists have shown this—it is no longer just theoretical.

Every physical object emits its own quantum hologram, or

information, that contains all past, present and future data. All particles are fundamentally connected to all other particles. I see this field of quantum information as a web, or network, of pathways connecting everything to everything else. This is what I am able to access when I do an energy healing on someone.

During a treatment, I project holographic images, or holograms, in front of me. If the person is not physically with me, I use her photograph to make a connection to her. Holograms are the visual guidance, like three-dimensional maps, that appear before me when I am viewing someone for treatment. All the body's information is available in this manner. From this field of quantum information, I can focus or zoom in using specific information or views, which I project as a hologram.

When I go into someone and access her hologram, I can effectively tune in to various subsets of information. It's kind of like changing channels on the television. My mind acts as the remote control, which adjusts to a different set of frequencies, thus giving me different holographic views of the person's health data. These subsets or layers of information become visually accessible to me. For example, I am able to see the nervous, musculo-skeletal and energetic systems as well as the organs. Selecting a particular body system is similar to looking at a computer screen. My thought or intention is the cursor click on the screen that accesses the information I need.

Once this holographic information appears before me, I can manipulate the energy so that the person can find her way back to a healthy state. People who have observed me doing this tell me that it looks as though I am conducting an orchestra. My arms and hands wave through the air, and my fingers nimbly create patterns as I make energy adjustments. To the observer it appears to be mesmerizing yet patterned flowing gestures, like the dancing of flames in a raging fire. Through intentions of healing, I provide information to the person I am treating. I do this by being in resonance with the person's body. This means that the frequency that we are tuned to is similar.

In this way, the body of the person is interacting and exchanging information with me. This stimulates the healee to energetically alter her state of wellness, which is in turn reflected in her hologram, as intentions manipulate the shape of the aura. I can usually see this change starting to take place immediately. Everyone's body knows its own way back to wellness; it just needs some guidance. These specific adjustments to the energy system help the body achieve this.

Think of this process as similar to an architect viewing blueprints of a proposed renovation. The existing building is physically in front of you. The vision of the future or your goal or plan is what you must visualize in your mind's eye. Each future view can be seen on the blueprint.

During a treatment, I redirect the energy flow on the hologram in accordance with the body's optimum state. At each stage between this perfect vision and the present health situation, adjustment and time are required. The problem must be removed, just as in a renovation. Most importantly, both you and the healer must keep the vision of the desired end result in your mind's eye.

Some of the holographic images I see are more useful than others in viewing certain problems, just as some blueprints reveal certain details more clearly than others. The electrical blueprint is needed for accessing certain information, while the floor plan is more useful for other aspects. But all are needed in order to complete the renovation.

THE AURA OF ILLNESS
If someone has an illness or injury, I see the problem as varying shades of green energy inside the body. This sluggish energy has

lost its direction. I refer to these areas as energy blockages. With different visualization techniques, I can eliminate these energy blockages and return the body to a state of wellness. While I am doing this, my intuition usually allows me to pick up other related information that may help me to more efficiently redirect the person's energy so that it in turn is flowing more efficiently.

Many illnesses have specific appearances, or signatures, that define them. Fibromyalgia and chronic fatigue syndrome show up as a hypersensitivity of the nerve endings, so I use the nervous system hologram to view these. Multiple sclerosis looks like grains of green sand bubbling up from the base of the spine and collecting in the brain. Organs that have problems have a cloudy ring around them. Cancer has a unique, radiating green glow to it. With experience, I am learning how to more effectively and efficiently do this specific energy work. Each healing is part of an ongoing learning experience.

The auras that I saw in my high school's crowded hallways were overwhelming. I sometimes needed my girlfriend to guide me down the hall, as the auras were overpowering my vision. I found it challenging to see while navigating through the hallway. For this reason, I made the conscious decision to turn down the auras, as they were far too much information for me to process. Once again, trying something new was an amazing learning experience for me. After I consciously turned down the intensity of the auras I was seeing, I found that I received far more intuitive information than before. This basically saves me a step, as I don't need to interpret visual input, which I receive in the form of auras. I can bypass this step and access the information directly.

Our pattern of wellness is like a coiled spring. If you pull the spring out and let it go, it will return to its original shape. It is quite flexible and forgiving. However, if you pull it too often, the spring eventually will stay in its stretched shape. Our objective should be to stretch that spring as infrequently as possible. By maintaining our health, we won't risk stretching ourselves beyond our limitations to rebound back to our healthy state.

The following are five main points about the aura:

- An aura is flowing energy and changes color constantly.
- Every living thing has a unique aura.
- Auras vary in intensity in different people.
- An injury or illness shows up as a break in the aura.
- In perfect health, the colors of the aura are bright and the flow is unimpeded and harmonious.

ENERGY EXERCISES

The following exercises will help you develop your skills in feeling and seeing your own energy, and then bringing in universal energy to your body.

I. Feel Your Energy

1. Rub your palms together in a circular motion. Feel the generation of heat. This is your own energy.
2. Now hold your hands about two inches apart, palm to palm. Push your hands toward one another without actually moving them. That is, visualize your hands pushing toward one another. Feel the resistance, similar to two like magnets repelling each other.
3. Spread your hands varying distances apart and feel the same resistance.
4. Establish the threshold distance at which your palms can be separated and you still feel your energy. With practice, you will be able to increase this distance as you become more sensitive to energy.

Illustration 1 depicts both the energy around your hands and the resistance you should feel when doing this exercise.

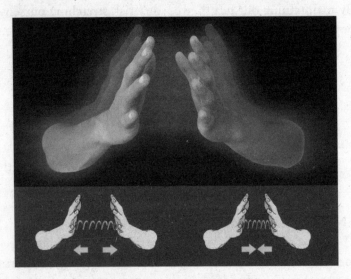

Illustration 1: Feel your energy

2. See Your Energy
1. Against a dark background, hold your hands in front of you with your fingertips pointing to the fingertips of the other hand, about two inches apart (see Illustration 2).
2. Move your fingers slowly up and down and in and out. Think about the energy flowing from one fingertip to the other. You will see a faint line of energy passing between them. At first this may appear as a hazy band.

Practice this exercise against backgrounds of various colors. With practice, the energy flow will look more defined.

3. Bring in Universal Energy
1. Imagine all the energy of the universe circling above your head, available for your use.

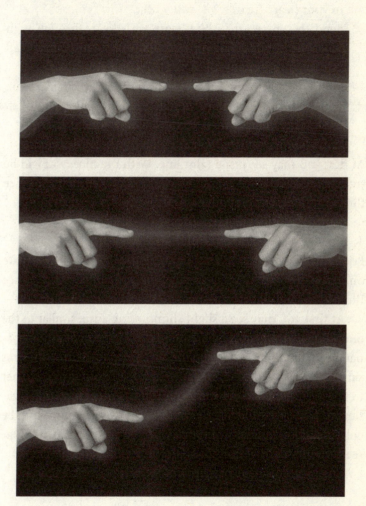

Illustration 2: See your energy

2. Bring in energy through the top of your head and collect it in your heart area.
3. Send the energy from the heart area down through your right arm, through your right fingertips, back into your left fingers and up through your left arm and to the heart.
4. Continue to imagine this flow as an energy circuit; from your heart to right arm, right hand, right fingertips, to left fingertips, left arm and then to the heart.

At first you may see just a faint line. With practice, you will be surprised at how quickly you will see defined energy flow. (See Illustration 3.)

4. How to See a Person's Aura

Look past the person whose aura you want to see. Concentrate on an area about two inches above his shoulders or head (see Illustration 4).

At first you may see a slight shimmering aura, similar to the one shown in Illustration 5. The aura may appear as a faint emanation surrounding material objects. Some people describe this as similar to heat waves, others as a misty fog. It will likely be far easier to see the aura after you've done a treatment using the visualizations discussed in this book. Few people will see the aura with the color intensity shown in Illustration 6, but with practice, you may see the defined flowing colors. Keep practicing!

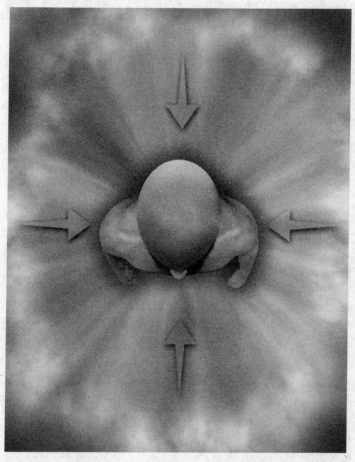

Illustration 3: Bird's-eye view of bringing in universal energy

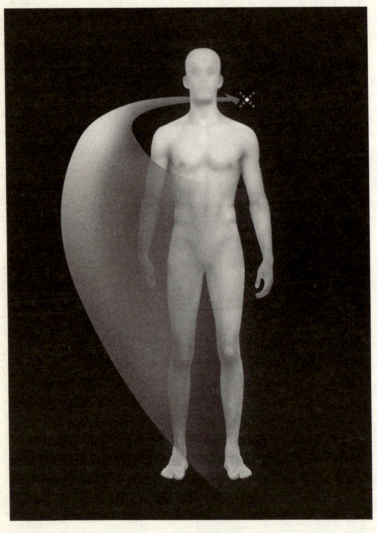

Illustration 4: *Seeing an aura:*
Focus on a spot behind the person

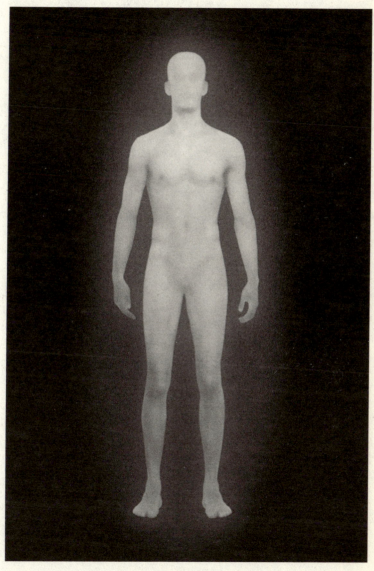

Illustration 5: A slight, shimmering aura

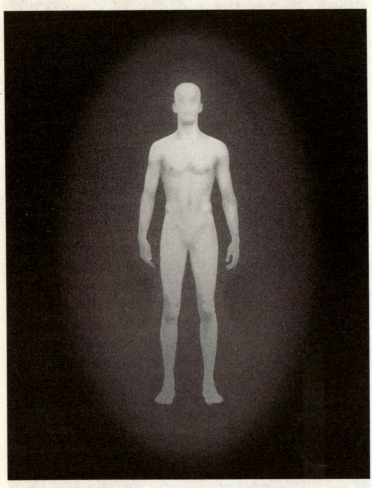

Illustration 6: An aura with defined flowing colors

5. Energy Flow Representation

A body without injury or illness would have harmonious energy flow. A body developing an injury or illness has energy that is beginning to lose its path or direction. A body with a fully developed injury or illness has a break in the energy flow, as depicted in Illustration 7, and can't find its way back to a harmonious energy flow, or wellness. Here is an advanced exercise to see energy flow; keep it in mind as a long-term goal.

1. Stand in front of a full-length mirror.
2. Relax your eyes.
3. Practice seeing and feeling your own energy flow.

Try doing this in both light and dark conditions. You can do this exercise with another person as well, practicing to see each other's energy flow. At first, you may be guided primarily by intuition—by feeling the energy. Soon you will be able to see it as well. As you develop this skill, you will find that your intuitive sense increases along with your healing ability. Trust that you can do this.

What do you experience when you connect to another person's hologram?
To connect to a person I look at a photograph of him and then rapidly connect to him through his eyes. Everything in the room I'm in goes dark and then I see three-dimensional images of the person in front of me, laid out before me like charts of information. While connected to someone, I pick up a great deal of intuitive information also. For instance, I am often keenly aware of a person's attitude stemming from his belief system. I feel whether a person is sincerely interested in pursuing this type of treatment. I just get a strong sense of knowing, but it is not necessarily from anything I saw. I also get a deep sense of interconnectedness.

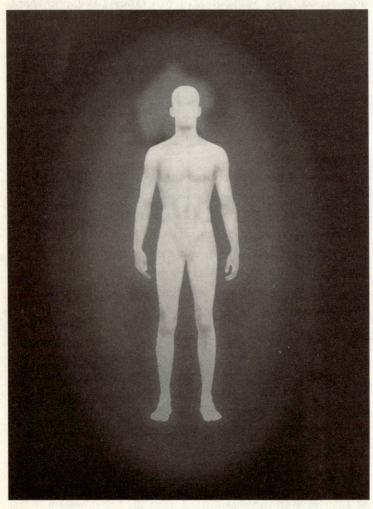

Illustration 7: A break in the aura, in the head area

How do you explain the idea in distant healing that distance is not a factor?

Many people have great difficulty accepting that a person's health can be influenced from a distance. Yet, my healing is done with intention, which is not restricted by distance at all. Science has many sound explanations for our interconnectedness to each other and how the intentions of one affect another instantly, regardless of the distance between us. This is explained in quantum physics mainly by the phenomenon of quantum nonlocality, where a change to one object instantly influences its correlated twin object, regardless of distance.

Many people can accept how someone can be healed when within arm's reach of a healer but cannot understand how this could work from farther away. There is no distance at which the healing will be ineffectual. The idea that distance is a factor is simply a paradigm that develops from living in our Newtonian physics–based everyday reality. When doing distant healing, we are operating beyond the material limitations on objects being either here *or* there in time and space. Information is present at all times and all places simultaneously.

Chapter 3

The Mind–Body Connection

The subconscious mind is molded by what we tell ourselves.

—ADAM

THE IMMUNE SYSTEM

People tend to think of the mind and the immune system as two unrelated entities. Yet, you were born with an integral connection between the mind and the immune system as a natural self-defense mechanism. The mind directly influences the immune system. The mind is the command center. Illustration 8 is a portrayal of how all things are interconnected. When the mind is sending helpful signals to enhance the proper functioning of the immune system, the immune system in turn allows for a healthier functioning mind. This is why it is important to always keep the relationship depicted in Illustration 8 in mind.

When you are injured, your mind is subconsciously directing the immune system to heal the injured area. Your immune system responds by initiating various chemical reactions where needed. For instance, you don't have to think about healing a cut on your finger. The healing occurs automatically.

Your goal in self-healing is to reach this level of control over your immune system on a conscious level. We all have that ability and can learn to direct it consciously for more serious problems. There is an increasing number of medical studies confirming the mind's ability to control the immune system.

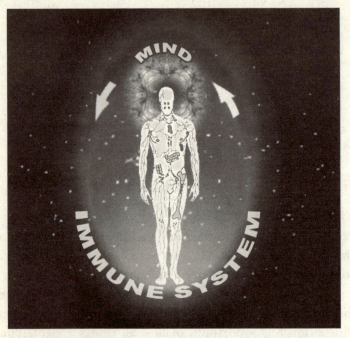

Illustration 8: Your mind directly affects your immune system

This is the key to the process of self-healing and to maximizing its benefits.

From conception until birth, each of us had a vital connection to another being, as we all shared every necessity of life with our mothers while in the womb. This bond was our first experience of totally being at one with another physical person, where every breath of air, every bite of food and every feeling is shared. When I look at expectant mothers, I can see their baby reacting to the mom's energy pattern. A happy mom sends harmonious healthy energy flowing to her baby. A happy mom is a happy baby.

AWARENESS OF CHILDREN

At birth, our own mind–body connection is complete. Every cell understands its connection to every other cell, and they all function as one.

It is common knowledge that salamanders have the capacity to regenerate a severed limb. A medical fact that most people don't know is that humans have a similar ability until around the age of twelve. If a child has a finger cut off up to the first knuckle, the missing portion will regenerate within ninety days. The energetic patterns of our DNA mobilize to rebuild the missing part. What is even more amazing is that there is no scientific explanation for this. Surely this phenomenon warrants more attention and investigation.

What we do know is that the genetic memory of the complete finger apparently still exists within one's energy field. Why is it that children are able to tap into this effectively until the age of around twelve, and then the ability disappears? One reason may be that children's boundaries of "possible" and "impossible" are not yet well defined. For them, psychic and mystical experiences, extrasensory perception (ESP) and seeing auras are everyday events. It's just that these phenomena have never been discussed.

I had the pleasure of doing workshops with kids at the International Healing Gathering in Saskatchewan, Canada. Most were Native, and had a cultural appreciation of our energetic connection. All were younger than eighteen. During my demonstrations to show energy, they all could clearly see the energy right away. One kid exclaimed, "Oh, that's what that is!" The others nodded in agreement. They had not yet been taught that seeing energy is impossible. They still experienced all events as being equally valid.

Over time, this open state of mind and unlimited expectation is taught out of us. The seeing of energy is beyond the boundaries of our acceptable reality and is dismissed and not discussed. We are told there is a time and place for such science fiction notions and nonreality-based possibilities, separate from everyday life.

Children expect nothing more in life than to experience everything to the fullest. They are excited about what each new day may bring and meet it with radiating self-confidence and a readiness to learn new things. As we get older, we adopt the cultural view of ourselves as separate from everyone and everything else in the physical world. Our "me" ideas develop. We are taught one set of expectations for our minds and another for our bodies. Our minds are supposed to achieve academic excellence at school. Our bodies are expected to grow strong independently of our minds.

Before I entered school, I thought that I was artistic. Then I met kids whose doodling looked like the drawings in professional comic strips. My opinion of my artistic abilities plummeted. Every one of us has experienced this shattering of our self-confidence at one time or another. It is vital that we get this back.

At school and in our leisure time, we compete with each other mentally (through academics) or physically (through sports). This is how we learn to view ourselves, and how others relate to us. We become known for our traits and become labeled: the runner, the nerd, the loner, the popular kid.

REINTEGRATION OF SELF
Society has placed perceived but artificial boundaries on each of us. The fragmented self can be reversed so that we function as integrated beings. In reality, we are one with ourselves and one with everything. Our consciousness and the universal consciousness is an interconnection of constant information exchange. Some day, a truth as obvious as this won't have to be seen as a self-revelation but instead will be readily accepted.

Subconscious and conscious thoughts should work together to achieve the same goal of wellness. The subconscious mind is molded by what we tell ourselves and what we physically do. It should be focused on the goal of maximizing wellness, and this focus must be constantly reinforced.

Our subconscious thoughts and background self-talk are equally powerful for wellness and should be synchronized with the conscious mind. The conscious mind influences the subconscious mind, and the subconscious mind is at one with the immune system. As a result, your conscious intentions have an effect on your immune system.

The most efficient way to direct the immune system through the mind is through visualizations at or near your sleep state. You are closest to your subconscious mind when you are sleeping or in a relaxed or meditative state.

When awake, make sure that you are constantly reinforcing positive thoughts toward others and yourself—and toward your future self—which you are now in the active state of reinventing. Think of this process as weeding the garden: Keep only what is helpful to you. If what you need flourishes, there is no room for that which you don't need.

When I connect to a person's energy system, I resonate at the frequency of that person in his subconscious healing state. This allows my treatments to usually have a very strong impact on that person's immune system. You can do the same within your own body by understanding the important link between your immune system and your mind, and how it functions as an integrated whole. You have complete control over your conscious and even your subconscious thoughts. Therefore, you also have complete control over your immune system and consequently your health.

For most of us, this thinking requires a paradigm shift. Not only does Western (allopathic) medicine view the body as separate from the mind and spirit, it also separates the body into its anatomical parts, with various medical specialties encompassing each of these parts. There is little or no awareness of the energy body. Every adult needs to relearn what they once knew as children but have since forgotten. Children view people as energetic beings, and as a *whole* being rather than a sum of their parts. This philosophy or vision is the key to our state of wellness. We hold this key. Go with it. Explore it. Enjoy it. Move forward with your new healing attitude.

Why do you think that many people in our society have such difficulty accepting energy treatments?
We are trained from an early age that seeing is believing. This reinforces that what falls beyond the limitations of our five senses should be dismissed and disregarded. Our energetic self and treatment of it challenges what we are taught.

Science has been granted some leeway in this, as most people accept that there are many observations that can be measured by technical equipment yet cannot be seen with the naked eye. The scientific pioneers who initially searched for these invisible effects were doubted—Louis Pasteur, Madame Curie and Nikola Tesla, to name just a few. These scientists not only risked their reputations but endangered their lives in the course of their experiments in order to advance science.

We must accept that many things exist beyond what our five senses can detect. Try seeing from your heart and feeling with your eyes. You may be surprised by what you can learn this way.

How can we assist ourselves in mind–body healing?
In order for mind–body healing to be effective, the healee should view the mind, body and spirit as one. It is impossible to energetically affect one area without influencing all. Every aspect of us and our being is affected by everything else that we think, say and

do. Through self-reflection and understanding ourselves we can directly assist ourselves in our healing journey. Be aware of your conscious and subconscious thoughts.

How do I influence my subconscious mind?
The subconscious and the conscious mind are constantly interacting, resulting in a back-and-forth influence. Your conscious thoughts are manifested from your subconscious self. Your conscious experiences are recorded in your subconscious mind, thus influencing your subconscious mind. Because of this interaction, you are able to affect your subconscious thinking. Your subconscious thinking can be changed.

For instance, an alcoholic may find it difficult to quit drinking if he continues to hang out with his old drinking buddies. If he is serious about breaking his addiction, he will find it easier to do so if he is not in a setting that triggers drinking associations for him. By changing his actions and conscious awareness, he is reprogramming his thought patterns, thereby influencing his subconscious.

Chapter 4

Healing Information

You are always the person in charge of your own wellness.

—ADAM

INTUITION

We all have the ability to heal, but not all of us have developed our healing skills. Learning these skills is like anything else we do: It takes practice. There is no doubt that Wayne Gretzky was born with a special ability to play hockey, but he still worked hard to be able to play hockey incredibly well. Many other athletes play great hockey; they just had to work a lot harder at it than Wayne did, and even then they didn't achieve his level of excellence. Nonetheless, their hard work brought results.

In any athletic endeavor, the top athletes depend on intuition or feel. Perhaps they feel the energy shifts but are unable to actually see them. This is called "anticipating" the opponent's move or "reading" the situation—or simply being "in the zone." It is this awareness of intuitive abilities and being able to use this gift strategically that separates the good athletes from the great ones in any sport.

The same is true in business. All the charts and graphs—the facts—of an economic issue must be interpreted in order to determine a move forward or shape an executive decision. The process of interpretation necessitates the involvement of intuition; that is, how one feels about how events will evolve.

Learning to trust your intuition and "go with it" takes practice. The same is true in every aspect of our lives. Trust yourself.

ENERGY CONNECTIONS

The universe is all energy, which is received and interpreted by us as information. This links all of us. Ripples in the energy system are like ripples in a pond: Everyone affects everyone else.

Can you imagine how powerful an influence it would be if all good news were given front-page status and all bad happenings were relegated to the back pages? Every morning we would awaken to an upbeat connection with each other. The positive intentions would ripple outward and reach everywhere. Don't you wonder why this seems like such a preposterous idea?

I have already, in Chapter 2, briefly covered some principles of quantum physics as they relate to distant healing. At the quantum level, there is no difference between "here" and "there." In quantum physics, this is referred to as nonlocality. The effect we have on each other extends far beyond merely the direct physical contact that we experience with our five senses.

The study of quantum physics has been around for only a hundred years. There are many published reports and studies investigating the major role that quantum physics plays in the energy field in which we live. However, the mere mention of the word "quantum" evokes a mental block of sorts in our minds—kind of like when you say the word "calculus" to high school students. We feel anxiety. It's true that quantum physics is complicated. But there are certain aspects of it—energy as information, for example—that can be explained so that everyone has some understanding of its role in our connectedness.

ENERGY AS INFORMATION

Every physical object emits information in the form of quantum data. We can pick up this information. The body's field of quantum information is accessed and then assessed by the healer. The healer looks at the quantum information of the body in its current state. The healer notices the areas of difficulty. He then sends new information to the person, which facilitates a change in the existing quantum hologram of that person's body. The body's new goal is to update the physical to match the newly accessed quantum information.

This is not as mysterious as it sounds. When we accurately perceive a common event—who is at the door or who is phoning, for instance—we are receiving nonlocal quantum data referred to as intuitive information. This ability can be developed further through practice. We often call this ability our sixth sense. Some people are predisposed to this sixth sense for tuning in to this nonlocal information system.

When I am doing a treatment, I project the three-dimensional image of the person in front of me and change the information through intention. This affects change at the information's source, which in this case is the person's physical body. It is this technique that I am teaching.

The following Seven Steps for Life serve as a great starting point for anyone embarking on a healing journey. These steps should be referred to often and followed as closely as possible. Focus on ways in which you can incorporate them into your everyday life. We are all healers.

SEVEN STEPS FOR LIFE
Step 1: Feel Your Own Energy and Be Aware of It
To feel your own energy, rub your palms together in a circle. Be sure to rub the spot right in the center of your palms. Feel the generation of heat. It is your energy. Then hold your palms an

inch or two apart and feel the magnetic push and pull. Move your palms farther apart, until you can no longer feel your energy field. Play with your energy and have fun with it. Our energy system is what this is all about, so become aware of it.

This flow of energy is our life force. It is more important than any other single body system because it involves all of them. Yet, our digestive, respiratory, circulatory, metabolic and nervous systems are better known in Western medicine. We have created lots of tests to measure the efficiency and health level of each of these. But we have yet to develop a measurable level for our energy system, and so it is ignored. Yet, it directly affects all aspects of our health. Learn to feel it, work with it and, most of all, enjoy it.

Step 2: Breathe Abdominally and Be Aware of It

Breathe deeply. Many people usually breathe shallow breaths from their chests and are actually somewhat oxygen deprived. The body gets enough to function, but would function even better with deep, full breaths. Singers and athletes are very aware of how proper breathing enhances their performance. We all need air in order for us to reach our maximum potential. Breathing using your diaphragm and abdominal muscles promotes relaxation and reduces tension.

Breathe in through your nose and imagine filling your abdomen with air. Once full, exhale through your mouth and pull in your belly. Your shoulders should not go up and down with breathing. It may take a bit of time for you to develop good breathing habits, but stick with it. I know some people who make a point of deep breathing on their daily walk. They count to four as they inhale, hold for another four and then breathe out over four counts. This is a good exercise to practice proper breathing. Increase the number of counts as your lung capacity expands over time.

Step 3: Ground Your Energy and Be Aware of Its Flow

It is important to ground your energy often. Think of your energy as circulating through and around you, connecting you to the universal energy above and below the earth. With each breath, breathe in air and energy from above and around you. When exhaling, imagine forcing that energy down the front of your body, through the soles of your feet to the center of the earth. Feel your soles connecting to the earth's core. The exhale connects you to everything on the planet. The inhale connects you with all in the universe. This is grounding, which is all about being aware of our connection to energy systems. Grounding will increase your physical energy and strength by unifying your aura with other energy systems. It will cleanse your aura and generally improve your health.

Step 4: Drink Water

Drink water. Lots of it. Our bodies are nearly 80 percent water—it composes that much of our body weight. We are water-based creatures, and we must respect this. Every day, drink the eight glasses your body needs. Drink filtered water, if possible. If you want a more exciting taste, add a twist of fresh lime or lemon.

Our bodies need water to operate optimally. If we face an additional health challenge because of an injury or illness, water is a vital part of our recovery. Our bodies remove unwanted and unnecessary materials by excreting them along with the water. This is our natural purification process. Without water, toxins that could easily be removed on a regular basis accumulate in our bodies. Dehydration can be deadly.

Consuming water is the easiest habit to change, and the most overlooked. Water is readily available to most of us and sometimes can alone achieve remarkable results. You would never think of trying to run your car without adding oil and gas. Why would you treat your car with more respect and care than you would your own body? We have been given this fabulously effective body, and it shouldn't be taken for granted.

Step 5: Develop Emotional Bonds with Others

Many of us, but not all, are fortunate enough to have loving family members. And at any moment in time, each and every one of us has the opportunity to bond with others as friends. We all need these emotional connections. It requires a give-and-take of trust to make relationships work, but it is well worth the effort. Welcome it and your world becomes a wonderful, loving place to live, a place filled with good, harmonious energy.

Stable and loving relationships have been shown to have a strong and positive influence on health. Those who have made the effort and commitment to develop close relationships with family members and friends are healthier than those who lack these relationships. If they do get sick or injured, they recover much faster than people who do not have a network of supportive family or friends.

Step 6: Think Positively in the Present Tense and Feel Its Effects

The power of your own positive thoughts helps balance your mental, physical, emotional and spiritual aspects. This balance empowers us, making us able to achieve our dreams and keep us healthy. Stay in the now, as the past is over and, although it is good to have dreams, fears about the future are futile.

Dream of what you truly love to do and do it. Only *you* can make a lasting change in yourself. By looking inward, it is possible to re-create yourself. Be aware of your feelings and your power to adjust and control them.

Put yourself into a quiet meditative state. Picture a three-dimensional holographic image of yourself. This takes lots of concentration and practice. Make it an exact image of yourself. If your eyes are blue, imagine the image of yourself having blue eyes. Visualize it. Concentrate on seeing your eyes exactly as they are. Work on perfecting this image until it is an exact image of you, exact in every detail. Even someone who lacks imagination can do this.

Once you have this clear image in your mind, repeat to yourself that you are all better and problem-free. Concentrate this beam of positive thoughts on the injured area. For example, if you have an elbow problem, project these positive thoughts like a laser beam toward your elbow.

Do not think of the problems. You do not have any problems in the image you have put in front of you. Think of the perfect hologram, one with no injuries. I know this can work for you because of what I do. I heal people with my ability to connect to their energy holograms. Once I connect to a person, I use my thoughts to perform the healing work that I do.

I understand that this ability to connect to a person's hologram is a gift. I also know that we all have the ability to make the connection to our own holograms and use the power of thought to heal. This does not come easily, but with the desire to learn and with some practice, you will succeed. By continuing to practice, you will find that it gets easier and easier, and that your ability to do this increases. Once you master it, you will find this an effective method of improving and maintaining your state of wellness.

Step 7: Understand and Appreciate the Connectedness of Everyone and Everything

Everything affects everything else in the entire universe in a web-like manner. Positive thoughts and actions taken by one of us affect everyone else. While the people most affected are those closest to us in the web—family, friends, workmates and acquaintances—the entire web is indeed affected. It is this interconnectedness that enables distant healing to take place.

Feel grateful for your life—it is precious. Be thankful for all the wonderful people who have connected with you along your journey. Look forward to the adventures that each day brings. We all face challenges, but our attitude as we face them makes all the difference. The positive outlook of each of us is contagious.

In order to get the most out of these seven steps, complete the quiz below. Understanding where you are currently is essential before you can move forward. How do you spend your time? What are your daily routines and your passions? Who do you spend your day with? Self-reflection is essential to understanding yourself. By answering these questions as truthfully as you can, you will be better equipped for your healing journey. Through the self-reflection this quiz will initiate, you will have many insights into yourself. This will help you on your journey as you explore the Seven Steps for Life.

ANALYZE YOUR LIFESTYLE
Habits
Smoking, drinking or recreational drug use: What triggers this habit of yours? Why do you want to smoke, drink or take drugs? What would happen if you quit?

Prescription and nonprescription drugs: Do you know what you are taking and why? Do you know the benefits of the drugs as well as the side effects? Pay attention to the messages your body is sending you.

Diet: Do you maintain a healthy and balanced diet? Try to see yourself as an outsider looking in. If you are overweight in spite of balancing all your food groups, eat smaller portions. A healthy weight results from a balanced equation of input and output: Calories in versus calories burned as fuel for the body's day-to-day functioning. Find your balance. Remember to drink lots of water.

Exercise: Do you have physical activities that you enjoy doing as a part of your daily routine? Do what you are able to and when you are able to. Find an activity you like to do. You will find it easier to integrate any good habit into your lifestyle if it is an enjoyable activity.

Attitudes

Stress: Do you feel weary from the stress of everyday pressures at home and work? Be in control of your stress level, rather than allowing stress to control you. Be aware of how day-to-day stresses affect you: your health, your relationships with others and your view of yourself. Reflect upon this. Eliminate that which affects you negatively.

Positive outlook: Do you see the glass as half empty or half full? Do others close to you radiate with the positive energy that you need?

Flexible: Do you look forward to change and the challenges that it brings? Do you enjoy keeping an open mind toward future possibilities?

If your answer to this question is "No," further self-reflection is needed. Examine why you feel this way. What triggers your resistance to change? Self-reflection is, again, your most useful tool in facing the future with a positive outlook.

Emotions

Useless emotions: Are you worried about your future? Do you feel guilt about some issues? Are you afraid to face some subjects head on? Do you feel angry with someone or something? What triggers these emotions for you? How can you imagine yourself avoiding these trigger situations? You are in control. Get in the driver's seat, learn to identify these hazards and steer clear of them.

Worry, guilt, fear and anger are emotions that serve no purpose, so get rid of them. Examine your reaction to events as they occur in order to understand your resistance to change. Becoming aware of your reaction is the first step to change. Stop yourself from reacting in your usual way and force yourself to react more positively. Just try it and see how it feels. You will consume less energy than if you are fighting change. Let this become your new way of approaching life.

Positive emotions: Do you consciously surround yourself with love and happiness? Love and happiness lead to self-acceptance and acceptance of others. What triggers these emotions for you? Endeavor to create an environment for yourself where these positive triggers figure prominently.

TELEPATHY, INTUITION AND INTENTION IN HEALING

The healing process involves telepathy, intuition and intention. Together, these allow for modifications to be made to the quantum information system of the body.

Telepathy is a form of communication that uses the transfer of images (thought) from one person to another. Once I am connected to a person, I am aware of subconscious and conscious responses of that person. Usually, a person's conscious thoughts dictate their actions, but this is not the case with people in comas. This makes telepathy especially useful in communicating with them. I have had amazing results by sending images to those who can "express" their ideas this way only, because of their infirm state of health. I was once contacted by the family of a man who had had brain surgery and had been in a coma for six months. At a prearranged time, I telepathically communicated with him when he was comatose. The energy treatment and telepathic communication immediately awakened him out of this state. After two sessions he was responding to his surroundings and able to see.

Intuition, as I discussed earlier, is another quantum attribute used in the healing process. Intuition is a sense of knowing something without needing to consciously reason about it. Sometimes intuitive information is not easily understood logically, but it usually has something to do with the healing task at hand. You need to learn how to interpret the intuitive data you receive when you are doing self-healing. This information is integrally linked to the healing process.

Intention is one of the most important quantum tools. The intentions of both the healer and the healee are what make things happen. Intention is the driving force that manipulates energy and information systems. When you have a large group of people, all with the same intent to heal someone, their combined intentions produce amazing results. Prayer is one example of an intentional group activity. There have been many studies showing that prayer works. Even if only one individual visualizes his intentions, the results can be amazing.

The intentions of the person being healed must be sincere in order for any significant change to happen. It is not a question of whether people believe in prayer or distant healing. They do not have to believe, but they do need to be open-minded enough to accept that it is possible. It is essential that one intends to get better in order to experience any changes.

Doctors often feel obligated to quote a specific amount of time remaining when confronted with patients they deem terminally ill. This may not be the fault of their training. Patients themselves demand to know. The irony is that many patients are planning their death when they should be planning to regain their health. The mind is powerful, and one's situation is very much controlled by one's beliefs.

There is no such thing as false hope. New directions are always possible. Many people who had been given a death sentence by Western medicine read my first book when it came out. Deep down, they knew I was not able to personally help all of them individually, but they were comforted by the book's message not to give up. They found new hope.

I believe that if we are all connected in life, then we are all connected after we leave our physical bodies. Death is an inevitable event that happens to every living creature. We cannot avoid it. What we can do is improve our health and happiness while we are alive.

Don't get hung up on any one ritual of healing. It is not necessary to jump up and down and click your heels together three times while repeating the phrase "There's no place like home." Healing is simple, and everything you need for healing is within you anywhere and anytime. If it seems like there are too many rules, and it is more complicated than it should be, then you probably have made it so.

Remember that you are always the person in charge of your own wellness. You are the driver of the car. You make all of the decisions—where you go, when you go there and how fast you travel. The healer is the navigator or map reader, advising you on the easiest route to your destination and assisting as required. Many other people assist—the mechanic who keeps your car safe and the gas station attendant who provides you with fuel. But you are always the driver. You ultimately have total control.

THE EVOLUTION OF SELF-HEALING

The wave of healing knowledge continues to build throughout the Western world. We have a long way to go, but people are beginning to understand and accept that we are all connected to one another and to every living creature in this universe.

We are able to feel empathy with someone who is experiencing sorrow or happiness. The entire world felt the pain of the victims of the 9/11 tragedy. A shiver went through my body when I saw the World Trade towers collapse. I believe that the sensations we felt were a result of our connection to one another. They are like ripples in the sea, which ultimately affects every molecule of water in the vast ocean. Our connection to one another is a vast pool of energy extending in all directions throughout the universe.

It is difficult to grasp the concept of our interconnectedness because of the boundaries we create in our minds. These boundaries are an extension of our limited five senses. If we can't see, smell, feel, hear or taste something, then it most likely doesn't exist—or so we have been taught. In other words, if it can't currently be measured or explained through scientific study, it isn't real. To go beyond these limitations would destabilize the very foundation of our current world view. Our entire physical existence is based on the concept of individual separateness.

Notice that we do accept as real some things not visible to the naked eye. We know that electromagnetic waves are all around us, even though we cannot sense many of their frequencies. Visible light is an electromagnetic frequency that we are able to sense. Radio wave frequencies exist, and they are also in the electromagnetic spectrum, yet we are unable to sense their existence until we tune in to a radio station. The existence of radio waves has been readily accepted for the last hundred years. Accepting our own energy systems will be the next big step. It is just a matter of time before science can measure and understand this phenomenon.

I often get the feeling that I should react to a situation one way, and yet I end up thinking about it and reacting differently. In retrospect, my first reaction was often the better choice. How can I learn to trust my feelings?
We have been taught to undervalue our feelings and place much value on the visible, material world. Society reinforces the idea that if something can't be accurately measured, then it should be ignored. We must relearn not to second-guess our feelings and, indeed, to trust them. As you have said, often our first instinctual reaction to a situation is pure, without rational weighing of alternatives. This may well be the better choice. Practice going with your gut feeling and you will gain more confidence in trusting it. We must forget what we have learned and remember what we have forgotten.

I have been told by my doctor that I have terminal cancer. How can I think positively about anything now?
How do you envision that thinking negatively will help you? We should all enjoy life while we have it, and now is more important a time than ever for you to be positive. Healing is more than improving the physical self. A true healing encompasses increased wellness and awareness in body, mind and spirit. It's true that death is an inevitable part of life, but nobody can tell you when you will die. It is important to look forward to each and every day, rather than marking the last one in your calendar.

Chapter 5

Group Healing

Your mind holds the wisdom to heal your body.

—ADAM

I receive thousands more requests for individual treatments than I am able to physically do. As I was trying to make sense of being given this healing gift yet having a limited number of hours in a day to use it, I made an incredibly useful discovery: It is possible to merge the auras of two or more people.

Every person's aura looks like a bubble of flowing energy surrounding the physical body. While watching energy demonstrations, I could see the effect that one person's aura had on another. Given that this interaction exists, I wondered whether it was possible to merge several auras.

I had always noticed that in sports the intention of a movement precedes the actual motion. When a basketball player is thinking about a move in a particular direction, I can see a spike in his aura indicating this intention. Intention is both powerful and visible. What would happen, I wondered, if I combined the intention and interaction of auras? I was eager to find out, so I asked my family to help me with an experiment.

My mom, dad and uncle were willing participants. I asked them to sit fairly close to each other so that their auras were touching. Although their auras still looked separate, they sort of stuck together when touching, just as I had seen happen to auras in a workshop I had attended earlier. Then I asked my parents and uncle to expand their auras by taking in energy from the universe. This allowed their auras to join through intention—like two bubbles in a bath that suddenly burst and form one larger bubble.

THE MASTER HOLOGRAM

Once my parents' and uncle's auras merged, I was able to connect them collectively as one to the universal energy field. (I explain this energy field in more detail in the next chapter.) What I call a master hologram immediately appeared before me. The master hologram contained and combined the information of everyone in the group.

Pleased with the results of this experiment, I was eager to take it a step further. If it was possible to merge auras and manifest a master hologram, could the single master hologram allow information transfers to bring about positive changes to all those present in a larger group?

In the past, I had helped several people with fibromyalgia, a chronic and painful condition with symptoms of muscle tenderness. At present there is no cure for it, so doctors typically prescribe large doses of painkillers to relieve it. How would this master hologram work for a group of people with a similar ailment such as fibromyalgia? I wondered.

It was easy to assemble a group of twelve people with fibromyalgia. Once their auras were merged as one, a master hologram appeared containing all the health information combined. What I discovered was that the master hologram allowed for the transfer of the information to all who were united in a common aura. The information is transferred in the form of energy patterns, of which I am the conduit. By doing the same type of energy transfer treatment that I do for individuals, I was able to convey information to improve the health of all the participants in the group.

This was a wonderful discovery for me and relieved the pressure of having to say no to so many requests because of lack of time and energy. In the fibromyalgia groups, most people noticed immediate and profound improvements in their health. Several participants stated that they no longer even had fibromyalgia. Their painful symptoms are gone.

These results opened the door to continued group treatments, but I wanted to be sure I was on the right track. I emailed *Apollo 14* astronaut Edgar Mitchell, one of my physics mentors, for his opinion and feedback on this breakthrough. This is his reply:

"Very interesting comments and effects. Regarding how it fits into the QH [quantum hologram] theory: Although each individual has a separate and distinct holographic record, you seem to have helped them resonate with each other and with you as a group, almost like an athletic team that is 'in the zone' and functioning as one. If they all have the same disease, then that disease has a distinct holographic pattern. Presumably, healing involves an inverse wave (or set of waves) to the pattern of the disease. It is interesting that you could have an effect on all just by focusing on the disease pattern. But, theoretically, no reason why not."

Edgar has been an invaluable source of information throughout the development of my healing abilities and I always appreciate his input. His scientific explanations ring true to me.

LESSONS FROM NATIVE CULTURE

Several hundred years ago, the Europeans conquered a medically advanced civilization in North America, that of the Native people. In Native cultures, people know how to use nature to heal the body. Many alternative healing methods ceased when these cultures were suppressed. The type of medicine that was practiced so effectively for thousands of years was outlawed.

My dad has Native American family on his mother's side. They belong to the Penobscot Indian Nation, based in the state of Maine. I have always been proud of my Native heritage and its connection with nature and the universal energy.

Native people accept the reality of spirit and energy interconnectedness. This makes them a pleasure to work with. The Cree language has one word, "mamaweska," to express a concept that takes seven words to express in English: "Our universal connection to everyone and everything." Visualizations and dreams are an integral part of Native cultures and have great meaning. We would do well to learn this connection to our inner power from our Native neighbors. Native people understand that energy is in and around everything. They are aware that it connects and influences everything. This connection with nature and its universal energy is regarded with the utmost respect.

It was shortly after I began my work in group healing that I was invited to be one of the ten healers at the Nekaneet First Nations International Healing Gathering to be held in Saskatchewan during the summer of 2003. The Nekaneet people, who are part of the Cree Nation, hosted the event. What an honor it was to be there.

Soon after our family's arrival, we were taken to the windswept grasslands where the Nekaneet people have lived for many centuries. Ten teepees were set up in a healing circle, with a fire pit in the center. I was given a choice of teepees to conduct my healings in. We had arrived fairly early, so only one had already been selected. It didn't take me long to choose one that backed onto a thick grove of trees. A constant breeze picked up the sweet scent of grass.

Then we quickly joined the others as they headed up the path to watch the youth riders approach on horseback. A horse and rider could be seen in the distance between the rolling hills.

Soon there were more than twelve, all riding toward us. It was a magical sight, surely reminiscent of centuries past.

An eagle staff was held high by the leader of the procession. The riders were greeted by the elders, who, by teaching their knowledge, are the link between the past and the future. A ceremony to honor the riders commenced. It was an awesome scene. The next morning, the gathering opened with the traditional healing dance around the fire, accompanied by singing and drumming. Then I started a day of healing in my teepee.

The Nekaneet people and others who attended the Gathering understood that the balancing of mind, body and spirit is what a healing journey is about. They were aware that spirit is the intuitive part of self. As well, there was an overwhelming sense that being in such a beautiful setting was therapeutic in and of itself; it was the perfect spot for reflection. I also had the honor of working with several shaman and learned to understand more about their traditional ways.

Native elders and organizers demonstrated the incredible dedication and enormous effort that has kept their culture and way of life alive. I will never forget the powerful energy and emotion I felt at this Gathering. The traditional healers were committed to helping anyone who needed healing. They spent long hours in the hot sun helping all who showed up, sharing their knowledge and healing skills.

With hundreds of people waiting in line for treatment, I felt it was best to try group treatments. Before this, the only group healings I had done was of people with similar ailments. Nevertheless, I proceeded with varied groups. My teepee held twelve people comfortably, so I treated four groups of twelve per day, in addition to a few individual healings. Everyone, either through their culture or their personal interest, understood the basis of energy healing, which made my introduction of the topic easy. The group treatments were very successful. One woman left my teepee after a session without needing her cane to walk. My dad found the cane and ran out of the teepee to give it to her, calling out, "I guess you don't need this anymore." Everyone had a good laugh.

By the last day of the Gathering I had a waiting list of over three hundred, so I decided to try something different. I asked permission of the elders to use the big open-air tent for a large group healing. They agreed, and it was announced over the PA system. Hundreds of people showed up.

I looked at the crowd that filled the tent and quickly realized that, although most of the people were familiar with energy treatments, many would be unfamiliar with the concept of grounding their energy, and that a group healing would not be manageable. So, instead, I asked that only the first two rows participate in the healing. This amounted to about eighty-five people. Everyone else had to move well back in order not to interfere with the energy of the participating group.

The results were fascinating—to me and to everyone else. We all felt that a powerful healing connection had been made. I heard numerous stories of changes in health-related issues when I spoke with the group after the treatment. Pain issues and breathing problems had the most immediate positive changes. I heard later from people with other health issues that their problems had also improved.

It was interesting that the visions people received during the healing had a common theme, which seemed to flow from person to person. A man in the center said that he saw vividly an eagle soaring with outstretched wings and wind in its feathers. Others on either side of him also saw feathers and felt wind on their backs. This vision gradually changed to a strong wind blowing from behind. It was incredible how people connected to one another in this state. Many were in tears, overwhelmed by the energy in the tent. This was a fabulous learning experience for me. Out of necessity, I had discovered that many people could take part in a collective treatment.

GROUP HEALING WORKSHOPS

Since I have come to the realization that group treatments are possible, I have held numerous group workshops across North America. My intention is to help as many people as I possibly can. In the process, I am continually learning more about my abilities.

The main point that I emphasize in these workshops is that everyone does have the ability to improve their own health. Specifically, I do these workshops to help people manage their own health issues, not to solve their problems for them. The group aspect of treatment provides a strong energy connection that enhances your own healing ability. After you experience this connection, healing yourself becomes easier. There is nothing that impacts our memory like experience itself. Feeling this connection is more powerful than any academic knowledge of it. This is what people take away with them from the workshops.

In the workshops I explain what I do as simply as possible and report the movement of energy exactly as I see it. I provide both the scientific explanations and the simple analogies of the healing phenomenon, which allows everyone to acquire a general understanding of the healing process.

Just as my abilities are evolving, so are the workshops. My first workshop had only twelve participants. The number at each has gradually increased to several hundred. The combined and focused energy of these group sessions is powerful. I still get many requests for individual treatments, and continually remind people not to underestimate the power of group treatments.

The workshops have proven to be an excellent step toward wellness for many people. Currently, each workshop consists of two group treatments, from which everyone can benefit, whether they have an immediate health concern or not. For people who are very sensitive to subtle energy, one group treatment may be all they need to return to their state of wellness. During these group sessions, attendees experience what it feels like to connect to infinite healing energy, for which I act as a conduit.

Once people feel this connection, they are able to return to it more readily and easily on their own to continue with their self-healing. It is like riding a bike. Once we master what seems an impossible balancing act, we gain an unforgettable lifelong skill.

STEPS IN GROUP HEALING

At the outset of a workshop, I teach the participants to, first, ground their energy to expand their auras and, second, join their auras with those around them. Although grounding is always helpful, it is only necessary to join auras for a group healing.

Step I: Ground Your Energy to Expand Your Aura

1. Visualize tree roots branching out from your feet. These roots branch out to more roots until the entire energy of the earth is engulfed in your roots (see Illustration 9).
2. On inhalation, pull the earth's infinite energy into you. Once you are supersaturated with this energy, your aura will expand naturally, since merely having this intention will make it happen.
3. On exhalation, push the energy now in your head down your body and out your feet, connecting with the earth.

Another method of grounding is to imagine that you are in a vacuum. On inhalation, feel the energy of the entire

Illustration 9: *Grounding your energy:*
Visualize tree roots branching out from your feet

universe being pulled into you (see Illustration 10). This will cause your aura to enlarge.

It does not matter which visualization you do as long as your intentions are to ground and expand your aura. Illustration 11 shows what your expanded aura might look like. (When auras are merged, they appear white or grayish as the group reaches an overall common frequency.)

Energy is easily influenced by intention. With the simple intention of taking in excess energy, one does exactly that: take in energy. Once you have become supersaturated with this energy, the only place that energy can go is out. As a result, the aura expands.

Step 2: Join Your Aura to That of Those Around You

When the aura is in an expanded state, it has the temporary ability to merge with other auras in the same expanded state. Now the group can join their auras as one.

Once you have allowed your aura to expand, shift your visualizing focus to connecting the auras. Visualize your aura merging with the auras of those around you—just as two bubbles in a bath merge into one larger bubble—until there are no divisions between persons. Illustrations 12 (a and b) and 13 show this process. A bird's-eye view of the room would be of one large aura that fills the room. When people are close together, their auras stick. They don't totally connect, but they adhere somewhat. If the participants' energy is grounded and super-energized, this adherence is more pronounced.

Step 3: The Master Hologram

Now the group is merged as one. This is the same oneness that is evident on a smaller scale within each of us. Your body is composed of trillions of cells, and every cell has its own distinct aura. On a larger scale, these cells are all resonating harmoniously

Group Healing

Illustration 10: *Grounding your energy:*
Pulling the energy of the entire universe into you

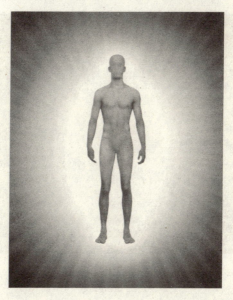

Illustration 11: *Grounding your energy:* Your expanded aura

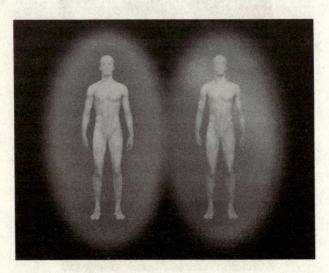

Illustration 12a: *Joining your aura to those around you:* Auras sticking

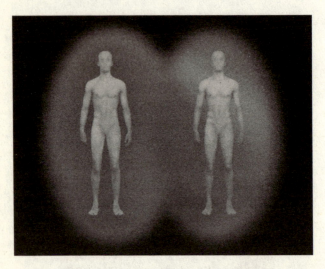

Illustration 12b: *Joining your aura to those around you:* Auras merging

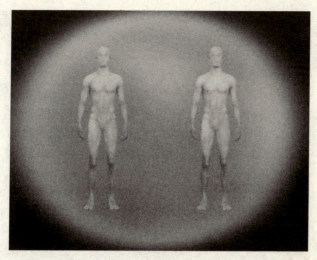

Illustration 13: *Joining your aura to those around you:*
Auras joined as one

together to form your own complete and uniform aura. Just as the auras of each cell within us connects and works together for our own benefit, each of our auras can be connected to benefit all within the group.

What appears before me is a master hologram—an image of a body with a collection of all the problems of the group. A change to the master hologram affects everyone in the group. With a group of several hundred people with various health issues, there is no way I can focus on every detail in the master hologram. What I can do is send as much energy through it as possible and, for many people, that is all that is needed for their problem to be corrected. It's difficult to portray what I see energetically and work with during a group treatment, but Illustration 14 will give you a general idea.

When the master hologram appears before me, there is an intelligent communication of energy information. This enables

Illustration 14: Energy at a group treatment

me to receive and deliver healing information to where it is needed. For example, if I receive and send information about adjustments needed for a person's back pain, only those who need back healing information receive it. In each group, I address as many areas of the body as I can during the twenty-minute or so session. (And, as I mentioned earlier, group healings are even more effective when everyone in the group has one common illness. When I adjust the master hologram for that specific illness, everyone in the group benefits more directly.)

At the same time that I am working with the master hologram, the group members are doing their individual visualizations in the manner that I've outlined to them. Everyone seems to know somehow where they need to send healing energy. Each person knows best what she personally needs. This is not necessarily a conscious thought, although people often come to the workshops concerned about a particular problem. I tell participants to just let the energy move naturally to wherever it is needed in the body, since energy healing is a natural process. Positive intentions will bring only positive results.

My experience during a group treatment is similar to that of an individual treatment. During any treatment, everything in the room goes dark and then I see a three-dimensional image, or hologram, in front of me. Next, the information appears before me in a format resembling a holographic computer screen. I can access the information in layers or subsets. I zoom in or out depending on what is needed to get the clearest and most helpful view. Then, with the energy of my focused intention, I can add or delete things to the hologram to initiate change. All the information is in a form that I can manipulate with my intentions.

What I am physically doing at this point is moving my arms, hands and fingers around. I became aware of this only after my parents told me that I do this and my dad filmed me. This movement makes sense to me: Verbal communication—body language—is often used to enhance what we are saying.

During an individual treatment, I connect to the person by allowing myself to resonate at her frequency. In a group treatment, once the auras of all the participants have merged as one, I choose a person at random and connect to her, just as I would during an individual treatment. For a moment I see only that person's hologram. An instant later, I see the image branch out to include everyone in the group; that is, a master hologram emerges, which I then work with.

Everyone has a role to play in this participatory group healing experience. I act as the conduit for the energy and as a facilitator by organizing and directing the energy to where it is needed. My primary role is to assist people in reaching the optimum resonance for accessing their health information. From this point, their own life energy takes over, and the information becomes intelligible to them. In this manner, I help people remember what they have forgotten. They become empowered to make positive changes in order to help themselves. The instruction to heal comes from you—your intentions—since your mind has the wisdom to heal your body.

If everyone joins auras, will I pick up any bad energy from others in the group?
I'm inevitably asked this question at every workshop. No, it doesn't work that way. There is no negative energy. There is no positive energy either. The energy is simply that which is directed through our intentions. It makes no sense to attach attributes such as "good" or "bad" to energy, as it reacts and moves according to your intentions. Keep every intention focused on healing and only positive results can occur.

Is a group treatment of fifty people more effective than one with five hundred attendees?
I am often asked this question, as many people think that the energy will be divided between all participants. This is not so. A healing workshop is filled with positive healing intentions. The more positive energy, the more everyone in the room can feel its intensity and effects. It truly seems to be a case of "the more the merrier."

Many studies have been conducted on the positive effects that a group of focused people can have as they create a collective consciousness. This common intention resonates throughout our interconnectivity to influence events far beyond ourselves.

Visualizations are focused intention. The workshops allow all participants to feel the power of energy and learn to direct it within themselves.

Why do you think that doing visualizations can positively influence oneself?
I know that visualizations can work because I can see the energy flow. When a person is directing his focused healing intentions through visualizations, I see the flow of energy interacting within him. A balanced and harmonious-looking flow returns as the body energy shifts to influence that person's wellness.

Chapter 6
The Physics of Energy Healing

Ill health is an imbalance of energy.

—ADAM

MATTER AS ENERGY

Einstein's most famous formula, $E=mc^2$, states that when you annihilate matter, you will get a certain amount of energy as a result. This means that matter is simply compressed energy and therefore everything in the universe is energy. When you throw a stone into a pond, every molecule in the pond is affected as a result of the ripple. Similarly, thoughts and intentions are a form of energy that radiate from you, affecting everything in the sea of energy—the universe.

As we zoom our focus in on matter with a microscope, it starts to look like Swiss cheese. The more we zoom in, the more we are able to see the increase in space within what formerly appeared to be solid matter. As magnification increases, solidity increasingly disappears and space expands. If we did find solid matter, it would be of infinite density, and that is impossible. There is no such thing as solid matter. The more you break things down, the more you find that everything is just vibrations. The bottom line is that everything and everyone is energy.

Once we realize that our bodies are all energy, we can appreciate the interconnectedness we have between every cell within us and between every living organism in the universe. Our thoughts, emotions and mental and physical energies emit outward in all directions. They affect others around and close to us in positive and negative ways.

Quantum string theory states that matter is energy, which is a frequency or a vibration. Everything in the universe is made up of energies that vibrate at different frequencies and in different patterns.

Ill health is an imbalance of energy. Energy imbalance manifests itself in the form of different ailments, depending on where we develop an energy blockage. Energy blockages, frequently first experienced as stress, manifest differently from person to person. Some people are more prone to headaches, for example, and others to stomach aches when under stress. A communication breakdown occurs when our energy systems are not flowing in a harmonious pattern. What I refer to as our pattern of wellness is the result of our energy systems flowing in a harmonious pattern.

The goal of every cell is to communicate in harmony with every other cell. On a larger scale, it can be extrapolated that every living being wants to be in harmony and communicate effectively with every other being.

The science behind a group treatment is the merging of these energy systems, the auras, into one large, vibrating energy system. My part is tuning the group to a coherent frequency that makes this merging possible—like an orchestra conductor. Then everyone in the group is resonating at the same frequency, commonly referred to as "getting in tune."

As a coherent energy pattern emerges, people feel this synergistic effect of resonating at the same frequency. Healing occurs when an energetic change or, more accurately, an information adjustment to one person in the group causes that identical change to everyone in the group. I act as a conduit, connecting the group to this energetic change. During a group healing, all the individual auras are connected with no divisions between individual auras.

Nature shows us examples of vibrating energies merging into one. Have you ever noticed that when a flock of birds is disturbed on the ground, they all fly away at the same time? Similarly, when you frighten a school of fish, they all turn away simultaneously, as though connected to a common grid, and swim in the same direction. Every particle in their bodies is connected to every other particle. The impulse to move, originating in one fish, radiates outward in all directions instantaneously. An inaudible alarm bell has rung out a simple message to all.

Another force of nature not to be overlooked is water. One drop is relatively powerless as a moving force, but lots of drops flowing together have reshaped our planet many times over. That's how group treatments work. The thoughts or intentions of many form the energy force that attracts and empowers the collective reality.

THE UNIVERSAL ENERGY FIELD

We all tune in to our various senses by picking up various energy frequencies. Our sensory system works like a radio tuner. Imagine the dial on a radio having words on it that trigger memories instead of numbers for stations. As you turn the dial, you tune in to what you recall of that memory, including sights, smells, sounds, tastes and feelings. Everything we pick up with our sensory tuner is information from the universal energy field (UEF). Everything that ever existed registers as information recorded in this field.

Every bit of information we hold in our minds is from the universal energy field. We all differ in our capacities to tap into this information. That is part of what makes us unique. Memory is the process of neurons in the brain forming and remembering patterns that help us connect to specific parts of the field.

To elaborate, when we have different thoughts, all we are doing is pulling the information out of the UEF. Our minds then organize, process and interpret this information so that it has local meaning—that is, so that it becomes meaningful to us in our physical reality. Of course, some people are more adept than others at accessing this information, just as some people are more naturally athletic than others.

Not all information is perceived by our five senses. It is much more efficient to bypass this sensory level and go straight to just knowing. It is a little like cracking an egg: You don't need to crack an egg to know what is inside; you just know from experience and trust in this. The brain's natural tendency is to process information in the most efficient way possible. Because of the interconnection we have with everything, the brain can use its quantum processing ability to interpret information with maximum efficiency.

OUR ENERGY LINKS

Living organisms share a common energy that links them together. The energy that connects us behaves in various ways at various frequency or vibrational patterns. As I mentioned earlier, it is for this reason that it is inaccurate to give attributes such as "good" or "bad" to universal energy. No matter which vibrational energy pattern is operating in one's body, it is not transferable to another person's body unless both intend for it to be transferred.

If two or more people meditate together or join auras in a group treatment, their brain wave patterns become synchronized to the most orderly and coherent energy pattern in the group. This can be compared to the body's cells working in unison to form the body's aura.

DISTANT HEALING

Many people tend to think of distant healing as the waving of a magic wand. That is not the case. First, participation from both the healer and healee is required. The healer doesn't directly do the healing but simply directs the healee's immune system to the problem.

The science or the mechanism of the healer's contact is still not fully understood within quantum physics. Space and time—that is, moving from point A to point B—has no meaning in the quantum world of energy connection. So, the healing connections do not travel so much as register instantaneously according to processes that we don't yet fully understand. What we do know is that the positive intentions of both people operate outside conventional notions of time and space. There are no limits to what can be achieved by accessing the quantum realm.

Many physicists now state that barriers separating us from each other are illusions. Understanding this is a step toward accepting that we are all connected. Then we will begin to see ourselves as part of an energy system that is connected to the entire universe.

I have heard of people connecting to "bad" energy. What would you tell them?
Do not think in terms of "good" or "bad" energy—that is, do not think about energy in any emotionally charged sense. It is just energy and is neither good nor bad. The intention is the driving force behind it.

Chapter 7

Skills for Self-Healing Visualizations

Trust yourself and your positive intentions.
—Adam

Visualizations are concentrated or focused intentions in the form of mental images. A visualization directs your immune system to the problem and guides its action. Visualizations should mirror reality as closely as possible in order to more accurately direct the immune system.

Strong visualization skills will provide you with a solid foundation for self-empowerment. You can enhance these skills by practicing specific strategies such as fine-tuning your ability to visualize, projecting a hologram and recalling details. Be sure also to address general improvements in your lifestyle and attitudes, as discussed in Chapter 4.

FINE-TUNING YOUR ABILITY TO VISUALIZE

One of the most important requirements for healing is being able to fine-tune the ability to visualize—to see vivid images in your mind's eye. An intention regarding a cut would be simply for it to get better. A visualization can and should be much more specific. For example, visualize the entire healing process taking place in your mind, step by step. First, see the blood platelets clot around the wound. Then imagine the entire healing process taking place, until there is no doubt in your mind that it is complete and that you are healed.

The most effective way to come up with suitable visualizations is to fully understand your problem that needs healing. Do research and learn as much about the illness and the anatomy of the injured area as you can. Because the mind is integrally linked to the immune system, having the visualizations as anatomically correct as possible will more accurately direct the immune system toward the specific problem. Know what white blood cells look like so that when you visualize them attacking the problem in their attempt to heal, your visual image of them is accurate. This will help you guide your healing intentions more precisely to the source of the problem. Also explore the mental or emotional aspects of the issue. It is important to make use of every tool available to you on your healing journey.

The better you are at visualizing, the easier it will be for you to heal yourself and others. When you are visualizing, it is important to know that it is going to work. In other words, if you convince yourself that your body is being healed, you will act on that belief by healing yourself.

Create a visualization. Continue practicing this visualization until you dream about it. Your body heals best when you are asleep or in a subconscious state. When you dream your visualizations, your body will naturally heal itself. In your dream state, you cannot distinguish between the visualization and reality; therefore, your visualization can become your reality.

Breathe energy into every cell. Every cell has a survival instinct; with this life purpose, cells communicate with other cells, passing on information about any changes within their immediate environment. The soul or total energetic body binds all cells into one functioning harmonious pattern of energy.

When using any visualization, remember to envision your healthy body. Your harmonious immune system is balanced and strong and you are resonating with it positively and confidently. Remember that your visualizations are limited not by the boundaries of your five senses but by your imagination—which is limitless.

PROJECTING A HOLOGRAM

An important skill for healing others and also in maintaining your own health is the ability to project a mental image or a hologram in front of you. When you use energy to heal someone, you must be able to mentally visualize that person. If you are planning to heal yourself, you can rely more heavily on feel, as you can do the visualizations directly on your body. You can also project your own image in front of you, or do both once you are comfortable with this concept. With practice, this becomes more natural. If you are not yet seeing this projection of yourself clearly, relax. With the constant intention of seeing this visualization, you will.

A hologram is a three-dimensional projection that contains all the information—past, present and future—of the person, place or thing to which it belongs. A person's optimum state of wellness is within his hologram. It is this specific information that differentiates a hologram from a simple image. (The two are not interchangeable, although for instructional purposes, I use the word "image" if it is most easily understood within the context.) Of course, it is important to understand this difference when doing healing on another person.

When healing others at a distance, it is necessary to project an image in front of you. As a guideline, this image can be the person's full body form projected in a two-foot-tall hologram. The size of the hologram is not crucial, as long as you can see the full body in your mind's eye. (I see holograms as an actual three-dimensional object, but for many people who are just beginning to learn to heal, it may be easier to think in terms of doing a visualization.) You will then see the modifications needed on this image.

Many people find it helpful to have a photograph of the person they are working with, even if it is someone they know well. Start with this simple two-dimensional image as a base for your visualizations. With practice and intuition, this data base will expand with intelligent information. Eventually, you will get to a comfort zone where a connection to the person's quantum information, or quantum hologram, appears.

Trust yourself and your positive intentions. Intentions and thoughts are natural forces of nature, just as gravity is. Once you are able to visualize a person's holographic image in front of you, the next step is to use your intention (along with their participatory intentions) to assist them with their healing.

Concentrate on the injured area. Visualize the problem being resolved in the hologram. At that moment it is literally being adjusted in the person's physical body. Know that this is happening.

Use your hands and arms to manipulate the thoughts and energies as you see best. Be sure that after you remove the energy blockages or unhealthy cells, you dispose of them into space. Remember that energy is dispersed according to your intentions. Create your own visualization of throwing unwanted material into a vacuum, the garbage or a black hole. Without a host organism, it will dissipate instantly.

RECALLING DETAILS

Have you ever thought about how you think? Think about it: How do you think? Do you think in images? Do you think in terms of your own voice narrating events and thoughts throughout the day? Would the transition from one thought to another make sense to anybody but yourself? How would someone follow the common thread between your thoughts? Spend a moment reflecting on this. It is important to be aware of how we process thoughts in order to be able to change them where necessary.

Telepathy is communicating through pictures or images, which convey richer and more detailed information than any words used to express that thought. A picture is worth a thousand words, they say. I refer to speech as "crude acoustical communication," as there is so much room for misinterpretation of words. We have all experienced such misunderstandings.

Telepathy is easier to have with animals than with people because the transition from one image to another is simpler. My cat, for example, appears to have only about three images: food, sleep, litter box. That's pretty straightforward.

How vivid are the images you create in your mind? In order to visualize more effectively, practice thinking in detailed images. Try staring at an image for thirty seconds; really burn it into your mind's eye. Would someone looking at your mental image right now be able to tell what it is? Most people find it very difficult to create vivid images in their minds.

To improve your visualization skills, learn to think in graphic images rather than in words. Changing our habits from thinking in words to thinking in images takes practice. It is like any other physical training we do: Practice makes perfect.

You will need to be disciplined in your mental training. People who have a photographic memory will most likely have an easier time, but anyone can train himself to remember more visual details. Concentrate on every little detail about a person. Remember her eye color, wrinkles, scars, nose shape, hairstyle, height, weight, physique, and so on. The more you practice this, the more natural and habitual it will become.

To help train yourself to remember more visual details, practice by looking at pictures of people and then trying to fix images of their faces in your mind. To form an image of yourself in your mind, stand in front of a mirror, then close your eyes and recall what you look like.

An easy beginning exercise is to visualize people you know when you are talking to them on the phone. Each time you speak to them, picture them in greater detail. Build an image of them in your mind's eye. Make it a habit. You will find that it gets easier with practice. This will prove to you that you can increase your capacity to recall details and visualize.

A woman approached me after a workshop saying that she couldn't visualize. I asked her if she was planning to attend my workshop the next day, to which she responded, "Yes."

"Do you know where it will be held?" I asked her. "Right here in the same room, isn't it?" she replied.

"Yes. So how will you find it?" I asked. "Will you need to ask anyone how to find the room, or will you rely on images stored in your memory of where you were today to find this same room tomorrow?"

That is when she realized that she does in fact visualize habitually. Visual information is stored solely in nonverbal images—there's no remembering a specific label or room number. This woman will know that the room is through the lobby and to the right. She will have an image in her mind as to the approximate size and shape of the room, so it will look familiar to her the next time she sees it. By becoming more aware of her natural visualizing ability and through practice, she can improve on something she does all the time.

We would be considered dysfunctional if we were unable to recall simple images without too much trouble. Everyone visualizes constantly; we just don't recognize this process for what it is.

Practice taking photographs in your mind's eye of people, places and events. Think in terms of being able to tell a story to someone using those images that you have "photographed." Every time you practice this, the story becomes clearer to the outside observer. More importantly, it also becomes much clearer to you. Imagine someone grating his fingernails on a chalkboard. I bet you have shivers up and down your spine from just the thought of it.

See yourself living your own personal shocking event, such as skydiving if you are afraid of heights. Feel the fear.

Imagine that you are in a tropical paradise. See the sun shimmering on the horizon; hear the waves crashing; feel the soft sand on your bare feet; smell the salt air in the breeze; taste the cold coconut drink on your lips. When you get proficient at this, your body does not know whether this actually occurred in physical reality or only in your imagination. In other words, eventually your body responds to your mental images as if they were physically real. That is the true power of visualization.

FOUR STRATEGIES FOR ENHANCING YOUR VISUALIZATION SKILLS

The next four strategies for enhancing your visualization skills are important reminders of issues I raised earlier about changes in your life. Implementing these suggestions will not only increase your powers of visualization but provide a foundation for self-empowerment. Remember that visualization and self-empowerment skills go beyond the visual connection. We must feel that we are intimately connected to ourselves and are at one with our goal of wellness.

1. Know Yourself

By guiding your emotions, intuition and memories of events (both past, present and future), you are fine-tuning your immune system to heal your body. Your mind has control over every bodily function, so use every tool you have to make all your body systems work for you in the best possible way.

Rather than reacting to emotional triggers with habitual responses, you will become proactive in the creation of new healthier thoughts and reactions. You will be choosing to take in only information that you need to improve your well-being.

Know that you can go beyond any limitations that you may have previously felt based on input from others. Reach confidently toward a new set of expectations of self-empowerment. Understand that you are responsible for yourself.

To understand yourself better, notice what pushes your buttons. What are your emotional triggers? When you understand this, you can control and then reinvent yourself. When we are in control of our conscious and subconscious selves, we are in control of our immune system and our health.

In your dream state (when meditating or about to fall asleep), synchronize your conscious and subconscious mind through visualization. Let your intentions and intuitions guide you. Trust yourself.

2. Improve Your Lifestyle

Get rid of any obvious poor lifestyle habits, including those that cause you stress and bring negativity to your life. The physical part of doing might prove to be the easiest: Work less and play more. Spend time with family and friends. While work is obviously still important, everyone needs to have fun and time to relax. Everyone needs nurturing human ties.

3. Balance Your Life

A basic principle of wellness is achieving balance in all aspects of life: physically, emotionally and spiritually. This is especially important for those who see their role in life as primarily one of helping. However, "giving all" by helping others can become a highly stressful burden when, in the process, you forget to take care of yourself. This can be a pitfall for a healer or caregiver, as the parable of the alcoholic-turned-healer I told earlier in the book illustrates. Achieving balance is everyone's constant challenge, not just the healer's. When imbalance occurs in any area of our lives, it always teaches us about ourselves.

Balance and counterbalance is the ever-changing dance of life. There aren't any specific guidelines for this, since our challenges are individual. Dance lessons can teach you basic steps, but ultimately it is enjoying the music, developing self-confidence and letting go of inhibitions that enable you to just do it.

4. Be Positive

Surround yourself with positive, like-minded people. Concentrate on what you enjoy. With circumstances you cannot change, learn to change your attitude. Find an aspect about the situation for which you can be grateful and dwell on that.

Monitor self-talk to ensure that what you are telling yourself is positive and reflects your personal goal of wellness. Your expected outcome must be synchronized with your goal: Be sure that you really expect your goal to manifest.

The following five steps will help you to become a more positive person.

Step 1: Eliminate Negative Feedback

Weed out all the negative feedback from your own self-talk and from those around you, and replace it with whatever you need to in order create your new, positive reality. Remember that self-talk is 24–7. This makes you the most influential person in your life. Monitor what you say to yourself about yourself. Once you become aware of this and the influence it has, you will be surprised at how easy it is to consciously dismiss your own subconscious views and attitudes. Change all the self-talk to positive encouragement. Be proud of the changes that you have made.

Step 2: Resist Self-Judgment
All day and all night, we listen to our own judgmental opinions of ourselves. Retire from the exhausting position of being your own judge and jury. Relax and step back as if you were an outside observer. We tend to be hardest on ourselves, so practice self-acceptance. Be your own guide through your best intentions. Approve of yourself through your new eyes.

Step 3: Resist Judgment of Others
Give others—and ultimately yourself—the benefit of the doubt and then move on. How could we possibly expect to judge another's thoughts, words and actions when it is often difficult to assess our own? It is not easy to forgive and forget, but the person holding onto the grudge does harm to herself. When you do this, you are letting an issue in the past grind away at you continuously. Forgive those around you, and with that you will forgive yourself and be free to grow. Forgive, and then forget. Relax and go with it. You will ultimately achieve what you desire.

Step 4: Leave Past Issues in the Past
Leave your personal baggage of anger and fear behind you and move forward. Whatever happened in your past has already happened. It can't be changed. Accept it, move past it. You can't change that the event occurred, but you can change your attitude toward it.

Step 5. Keep It Simple
In our society, we consider it necessary to consult an expert on almost every aspect of our lives. When faced with baffling calculations, we must see an accountant. We ask a lawyer to explain the meaning of a string of indecipherable words. When our body is sending us a personal SOS, we consult a doctor. Many

of us have the idea that whatever the situation, it must be complicated. Healing through your own intentions to return to wellness is simple.

Energy constantly flows within each and every one of us. We just need to provide it with some direction. There is no right or wrong way to do visualizations. My suggestions are simply meant to help you to focus more efficiently. Whatever works for you is the right way. It is an individual choice. Through intention, your wish is your command. This will become your reality. Your intentions or thoughts create your own reality. It sounds too simple to be true, but it is.

In the next chapter, I explain some general visualizations that you can use until your own creative juices kick in. Then you will have the feel of it and the confidence to customize your visualizations. Most important is your intention to return to wellness and your knowing that it is possible.

The general pattern to wellness is a healthy lifestyle reinforced by positive attitudes and specific visualization techniques. Remember the transition of the following statements as they apply to your wellness. This three-point belief system should help you reinforce your primary objective:

1. You think that you can be well again.
2. You know that you will return to a healthy state.
3. You are well again.

Visualize yourself in your optimum state of wellness. How are you feeling? What are you doing, thinking and saying? Imagine yourself being well and enjoy it.

I have difficulty visualizing. What do you recommend?
Visualizing is something that we all inherently do, but many of us are unaware of this. So the first step is to be more aware of your ability to do it. Take a mental photograph of the cover of this book as you hold it in your hands. Close your eyes and visualize it in your mind's eye as you recall the image, colors and any other details. Repeat the process again and increase the amount of detail that you are focusing on. With this intention in mind, you will expand your capacity to effectively visualize. Change the colors of what you see while holding your focus. Remember this process of challenging yourself until it becomes second nature.

How long should I visualize for?
There is no set time for the length of a visualization; it varies from person to person. Some people can visualize for hours while others can only do it for a few minutes. If you lose your focus and want to continue with your visualizations, just relax, refocus and start over. Do not push yourself. The idea is not to log a lot of time but to make the visualizations as real as possible.

Chapter 8

*General Visualizations:
Re-creating Wellness*

Visualizations are tools to empower you.

—ADAM

Visualization is more than using our sense of sight alone. We should be achieving a realistic feeling of actually experiencing the event. That is when we know that we are doing it right. Mastering visualization will give you the confidence that you need for self-empowerment. These are resources that we all have at our fingertips; we just have to tap into them.

Think of your new ideal self as your goal. Then learn that you can and you will achieve this goal. Your body has everything it needs to heal itself. Think of all your reasons to stay well and visualize them happening with you. Setting this goal and visualizing it will lead to your success.

There is a constant exchange of information between your quantum hologram and your physical body. Visualizations are tools to empower you to take control of this information exchange process. This is how you can direct your immune system to the desired location to maximize health benefits. It's that simple.

When you have a chronic problem, your body becomes so accustomed to it that it compensates for it. To put it another way, the body overlooks and ignores the problem; essentially, it no longer knows about the problem. And so, your immune system doesn't do anything about it.

Visualizations show your body that there is a problem. Your doing visualizations demonstrates to yourself that you are serious about making a change. Maintain the constant intention to make the visualizations work.

Visualizing involves integration and flow of your thoughts. It is very important to synchronize your conscious and subconscious intentions, since the more harmonious the intentions are, the more effective they tend to be. This means that the level of consciousness you're at when you can say out loud, "I know I can do it" is in harmony with that little subconscious voice deep inside you. Your outcome expectation must also be in harmonious agreement with your visualization and intention.

General visualizations are dramatic interpretations of how we are going to re-create our wellness. What these lack in specifics they make up for in dramatic impressions. Put as much realistic sight, sound and feeling as you can into each visualization, while holding your positive intentions and ultimate goal in mind. Strive to achieve a realistic feeling of actually experiencing the event. When you do have this feeling, you will have fully mastered the technique.

The following universal or general visualizations will benefit you regardless of the injury or illness. You may visualize these images directly on your physical self, or you may project these on a hologram in front of you, or both. These may also be done to a hologram of someone else, but not at the same time as you are working on yourself, as the energy gets dispersed, diminishing the effect. You can do the visualizations sitting, standing or lying down; just make sure that you are comfortable when doing them.

These are the stages for self-healing using visualizations:

1. Form the image (eventually the hologram) of yourself, or of the person you are healing, as described in Chapter 7.

2. Focus on your goal by using visualizations to:
    a. Exit your existing pattern of injury or illness.
    b. Reboot your system through intense visualizations (this will occur automatically).
    c. Reset your system to what is desired.
    d. Set your pattern of wellness in place.

You may find it helpful to practice saying the visualization steps out loud. The mere intention of visualizing will make it happen. Don't just say you will try: Do it.

There are five universal visualizations I recommend: Fire and ice temperature extremes, Lightning bolts, Smart Energy Packets, Explosion and Waterfall. The first four, including your personal adaptations, can be done in any order. Try them all and see which works best for you. Do all of them at various times, and you might find that a particular order works well. Use the waterfall visualization last in the sequence of visualizations you decide upon. This visualization calms, relaxes and cleanses your system: You have visualized the removal of your problem; now you must repattern or reprogram yourself.

Visualizations help maintain our healthy state as well. No matter what the health challenge was, you should continue to routinely practice your visualizations. They will ensure that your energy flows harmoniously without blockages long after your physical ailment has been addressed.

FIRE AND ICE
The temperature extremes of intense heat and extreme cold are useful in both nature and our visualizations.

Fire
The fire visualization is very powerful and is used for the same purpose as it has in nature. It is a renewal force. It destroys the

old and allows for fresh possibilities in the rebuilding of a new, healthy you.

Visualizing heat is useful for any problem, as the excessive heat attracts white blood cells to the area, and it is the white blood cells that will destroy the problem. It is a useful visualization for a tumor or cancer in one or more areas. It is also especially powerful to use when the problem is systemic—lymphoma, leukemia or a viral infection, for example—since you can visualize forcing steam through your entire circulatory system.

1. Imagine intensely hot flames roaring through your body. The force of the fire rips the problem from its roots.
2. Focus on the area where the problem exists. Some people find it easier to imagine being engulfed in flames (see Illustration 15).
3. Feel the heat and see the problem start to turn to ashes right before your eyes.
4. Incinerate the problem and watch it disintegrate. The ash blows away with the wind.

See the flames.
Feel the heat.
Hear the crackling.
Smell and taste the smoke in the air.
Make it real.

Another visualization using heat is that of the whistling kettle. It may help to have a whistling kettle in the background when you first try this visualization.

1. Imagine a whistling kettle at the location where you require healing. The steam is released with great, screaming force.

Illustration 15: *Fire visualization:*
Flames engulfing your body

2. The heat from the steam is a focused stream of heat.
3. Allow the circulation of its heat all around the problem areas, and see the energy blockages dissipate.

See the steam rise.
Feel the heat.
Hear the whistle.
Smell and taste the vapors.
Make it real.

Ice

Just as fire is a very powerful force in nature, so is ice. It too destroys the old and allows for new growth potential in its wake. With the ice visualization, the life force of the problem can be frozen and then shattered, and so is useful for problems such as tumors.

1. Imagine the problem area freezing over.
2. See the cold, blue ice form as if liquid nitrogen were flowing over it.
3. Visualize this icy image shattering or melting away the problem.

See the problem freeze.
Feel the intense cold.
Hear the cracking of the ice.
Smell and taste the frigid, pristine air.
Make it real.

LIGHTNING BOLTS

This visualization is effective for any neurological disorder, such as multiple sclerosis, motor neuron disease and peripheral neuropathy. It is also very useful for pain from injuries, arthritis and fibromyalgia, as it seems to overload the nervous system, forcing it to reboot. You can apply this to any area or organ requiring stimulation. That part of the body then has to start up again fresh and new, since it has been reset to its healthy state. The new you emerges.

In this visualization, lightning does strike the same location again and again.

1. Imagine that a lightning bolt strikes the top of your head.
2. It rips through your body, lighting up your entire nervous system with laser precision (see Illustration 16).
3. All the synapses of your brain fire off, sending intense pulses of energy down your spine, branching out until they reach the smallest nerve endings.

See the intense light of the lightning bolt.
Feel the energy ripping through you.

General Visualizations: Re-creating Wellness 245

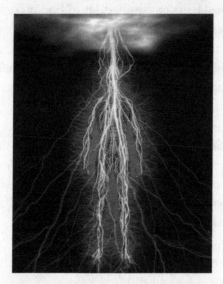

Illustration 16: *Lightning bolt visualization:*
A lightning bolt ripping through your nervous system

Hear its thunder.
Smell and taste its electrical charge.
Make it real.

SMART ENERGY PACKETS (SEPs)

Smart energy packets, or SEPs, are useful for removing a specific and localized problem. Visualize Pacman-like units circulating throughout your problem area. They orbit like swarming bees in a seek-and-destroy mission, yet spread healing energy in their path.

SEPs orbit and take a bite out of the problem, ingest it and then eliminate it from your system. It may help to visualize them as being Velcro-coated: As they make contact with the problem, they adhere to it. Removal is accomplished through exhaling (if it is a lung problem) or elimination of bodily waste for other issues. This stick-and-remove approach is easy to visualize.

SEPs also reproduce themselves and communicate with each other. This ability is useful, as they can send signals to each other to shock or jump-start the system. They continue to be effective long after you do your visualization.

You may want to make this visualization more realistic by turning the SEPs into white blood cells. Attract them to your area of need. Visualize all the arteries and other blood vessels in your body becoming more permeable to white blood cells. This allows and encourages them to surround what needs to be removed from your body.

1. Imagine a swarm of SEPs orbiting through your energy blockage area (see Illustration 17).

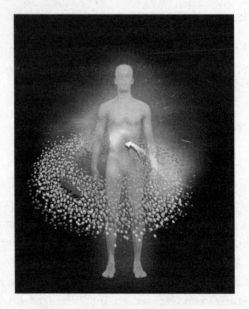

Illustration 17: *Smart energy packets visualization:*
SEPs orbiting the problem

2. Allow them to stick and grab onto the energy blockage in order to remove it from your body.
3. Allow the SEPs with the problem adhering to it to exit your body, and clean SEPs to enter your body.

See the smart energy packets orbiting.
Feel them sticking to the problem.
Hear them buzzing as they do their work.
Smell and taste the energy they are creating.
Make it real.

EXPLOSION

This is a powerful visualization for energetically ripping any problem out of your system. It can be used for anything from cancer to a stomach ache. For the best results, you need to visualize your problem as accurately as possible. Be your own health advocate and do the research required. Become familiar with its size, shape and location. The more detail you know, the more accurately you will be able to plant the explosive device in the most effective place. For those people who play computer games, it might help to imagine playing a game in which your health problem is the target.

1. Imagine that you are able to blast your problem out of your body.
2. Plant the explosive device right in the center of your problem.
3. The explosion sends ripples of energy out from the epicenter. All fragments of the problem are instantly vaporized. (See Illustration 18.)

See the explosion.
Feel the vibration of the blast.

Illustration 18: *Explosion visualization:* Energy rippling out from the explosion site as fragments of the problem vaporize

Hear the boom.
Smell and taste the burning matter.
Make it real.

WATERFALL

In this visualization, bluish-white liquid light energy cools, refreshes and cleanses your entire being. This visualization purifies you, and its intensity removes energy blocks, allowing you to exit the pattern of the injury or illness by overloading it. You automatically reboot; this is necessary to reset the system to your desired pattern of health.

1. Relax and imagine that you are standing under a waterfall of pure blue liquid light energy (see Illustration 19).

Illustration 19: *Waterfall visualization:*
Liquid energy pouring over your body

2. The energy is not only pouring over you but through you as it purifies. Its steady rhythm is soothing and relaxing, and it resets you.
3. Let the energy remove everything that it needs to in order to restore your health.

See the electric blue liquid light energy.
Feel it flowing through you.
Hear it cascading.
Smell and taste its refreshing qualities.
Make it real.

HOLDING YOUR STATE OF WELLNESS IN PLACE: THE PATTERNED ENERGY GRID

The waterfall visualization allows your energy to flow harmoniously in your new patterned energy grid. When you are in your optimum state of health, use the energy grid to hold it in place. This visualization can be done anytime—whether you are sitting on a bus or standing in an elevator. Your mind controls your body, and you control your mind. So work on keeping your mind-body healthy. We all have a perfect blueprint within us of our ideal health. Access it and hold it.

1. Visualize a three-dimensional grid in the shape of your body. The vertical and horizontal lines are perfectly spaced, or equidistant apart (see Illustration 20).
2. All your energy is flowing rhythmically, smoothly and harmoniously along these lines.

Through this visualization, the energy grid will hold your state of wellness.

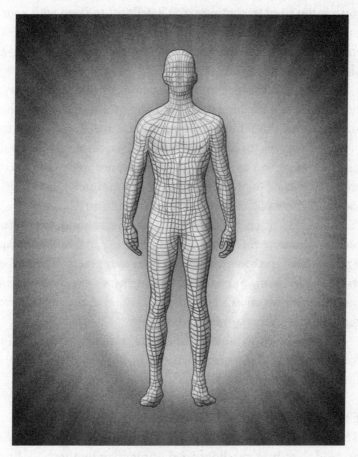

Illustration 20: *Patterned energy grid visualization:*
A three-dimensional grid in the shape of your body

WHEN AND WHERE TO DO VISUALIZATIONS

The best time to do these visualizations is right before bedtime; this is when they will be most effective. Keep doing them until you are too tired to continue. You'll drift off to sleep with your goals in focus. In your dream state, you are closest to the most effective state of consciousness for healing. You will heal at a phenomenal rate in your sleep.

You can also practice the visualizations throughout the day, aiming to integrate them into your daily routine. How long the visualizations should be done each time varies from person to person. Do them for as long as you can stay focused. This too varies from person to person. Most people are able to comfortably concentrate on them for about thirty minutes. Find a quiet location where you can relax and focus undisturbed.

If you find negative thoughts entering your mind, stop what you are doing, refocus and then start the visualization again. Through this repetitive exercise, you train your subconscious to be more aligned with your conscious thoughts. Over time, you will find that this becomes a natural process and that your positive thoughts have become more prominent.

Your goal is to do these visualizations until you are eventually having dreams about them. This is incredibly effective. Be a dreamhealer.

CUSTOMIZING THE GENERAL VISUALIZATIONS

The general visualizations I've outlined above are to be used as guides only. You should experiment with them to find what works well for you. For instance, if you find that the lightning bolt visualization is too intense, change the color of light that you use. White light is the most intense, so color it blue or red and feel the difference. Turn down the amount of electricity that you are using. Change the color of the cloud that the strike originates from. The important point to remember is to be creative with your visualizations and be aware of their effect on you. Modify and customize these guides to suit your individual needs.

You say that the best time to visualize is before going to sleep, but I always fall asleep before I really have a chance to try them. What should I do?

It is likely that as you are drifting off, you have this book in hand and have set a visualization in your subconscious through your intention to do so. You may be unaware of the impact that this has on you. I would recommend that you not try so hard, as this process will eventually become a natural state for you. Relax and go with the flow. Keep it up as a habit, and you will notice the positive effects. Our dream state merges our subconscious instinctive thoughts with the conscious rational part of our minds to create a cinema-like action of reality. Your dreams will put into action your path to wellness.

I have a drinking problem. Could you recommend a visualization that would help me with this problem?

The visualizations for fatigue and emotional problems have also been helpful for lifestyle habits and addictions. By bringing lots of energy into yourself and redirecting it, you re-establish a harmonious flow. The tree root visualization for grounding I describe in Chapter 5 is also very useful in rebalancing energy, and many people find that it helps with emotional difficulties. Develop your own visualization specific to your challenge. You have already examined the triggers that lead you to drinking. Now visualize what it is that you need in order to quit. What is it that you are gaining by drinking? You know that you alone have the power to quit.

Chapter 9

Visualizations for Specific Conditions

Visualizations are only limited by our own imaginations.
—ADAM

The specific visualizations I outline in this chapter can complement any treatment you may be undergoing through your doctor. These are visualizations that I have found to be effective for various conditions. There are many conditions that can affect, for instance, your respiratory system or your heart, so the first thing to do is see your doctor to determine which condition you have. The visualization strategies here incorporate very intensive and detailed information. While these skills are available to all, do not be surprised to discover that they will take a lot of practice before they are mastered. Many people have difficulty visualizing without precise instructions to follow. I want to emphasize that there is no wrong way to do these visualizations. You can use all the visualizations below, or you can use the ones you feel work best for you, or you can customize your visualization to be most effective for you or even create your own. It is up to you to try these various approaches and determine which are most effective for you. I do, however, suggest including certain anatomical facts to pinpoint the problem for your immune system. For instance, imagining attracting white blood cells to a cancerous tumor will make your visualization for cancer more effective than if you do not include actual anatomical features.

CANCER

Cancer occurs when cells become abnormal and continue to divide and form more cells, seemingly without order or control. Normally, cells divide to produce more cells only when the body needs them to maintain health. If cells continue to divide when new cells are not needed, a mass of tissue (a growth or tumor) forms.

Malignant tumors are cancerous. They can invade and damage nearby tissues and organs. Cancer cells can break loose from a malignant tumor and travel through the bloodstream or the lymphatic system. This is how cancer can spread from the original tumor to form new tumors in other parts of the body.

Cancer usually develops gradually and is affected by factors related to lifestyle, environment and heredity. We can consciously diminish risk factors, since many cancers are related to smoking, diet and exposure to carcinogens in the environment. Some people are more sensitive than others to these risk factors. Inherited risk factors are unavoidable. We should be aware of them but know that not everyone with a particular risk for cancer actually gets the disease; in fact, most do not.

You can reduce your cancer risk by making some simple food choices. Eat a well-balanced diet made up of foods high in fiber, vitamins and minerals. Choose your foods wisely. Eat five servings of fruits and vegetables each day and a healthy amount of whole-grain breads and cereals.

Early on in my healing work, I observed some interesting facts about cells, including cancer cells. I noticed that all cells communicate with each other. I see that, energetically, cancer is able to replicate quickly using what appears to be a sophisticated communications system. For example, when I use a particular visualization that works against one tumor, an adjacent tumor will not respond to the same visualization. It appears that the first tumor has warned the remaining tumors about the visualization. Through my connection and intuition I understand that this is happening.

The same mechanism that cancer cells use to send distress signals to other tumors can be used on cancer cells within a tumor to help destroy the tumor. When I did visualizations to break down communications within a tumor, the cancer cells passed on the message to all the cells in the tumor in a domino effect that was very useful in creating disorganization and disharmony within the cells of the tumor. I noticed that creating cell disorganization was more difficult when there were multiple tumors. I observed that as cancer begins to die, this communication between cancer cells slows down and eventually stops.

When doing visualizations for any tumor, the goal is to weaken it and direct the immune system toward the tumor. Your body should have more than enough white blood cells to tackle any problem.

I find that the most effective method of getting at the cancer is by attacking it from as many angles as possible. Do research about your particular health challenge. Visualization techniques can be tailored to address individual lifestyle issues, including stress, attitudes, emotions, diet, exercise and your social environment.

As I mentioned above, it is helpful to include relevant anatomical facts in your visualization to pinpoint the problem for your immune system. For example, a useful visualization for cancer is imagining the attraction of white blood cells to the region of the tumor. Here's the most effective way to attract white blood cells to this area:

1. Imagine all the blood vessels in the vicinity of the tumor becoming more permeable to white blood cells. Allow white blood cells to exit the blood vessel walls and surround the tumor. Illustration 21 depicts how you might visualize

the tumor, and then the white blood cells surrounding the tumor.
2. Visualize every white blood cell in your body being drawn to the tumor. Eventually, there should be so many white blood cells surrounding the tumor that they form a colony around it, completely engulfing it.
3. See the white blood cells that surround the tumor eating away at it. Essentially, the white blood cells grab the cancer cells, pull the cells inside them and then digest the cancer.
4. Visualize the white blood cells releasing substances that are poisonous to the cancer. See the tumor shriveling up from those toxins and from the white blood cells eating away at the tumor. (Note how detailed and physiologically precise these visualizations are.)

Illustration 22 shows first the white blood cells destroying the tumor, and then the area in the absence of the cancer cells.

The rate at which the white blood cells pick away at the cancer can vary. One factor is the temperature. The cells will eat away at the cancer at a far faster rate in warmer conditions. Therefore, you might also visualize flames raging underneath the tumor to apply heat to the area. Heat also increases the blood circulation, which speeds up the healing process.

A tumor needs nutrients to survive. Without a supply of fresh nutrients and without an exit mechanism for wastes, the tumor will die. Here's an effective visualization for this:

1. Visualize the blood vessels that supply nutrients to the tumor contracting to the point where there is no transfer of nutrients.
2. Visualize the tumor drowning in its own toxins and waste products. See this happen until the cancer cells simply die.
3. Visualize choking off what the cancer needs and simultane-

Visualizations for Specific Conditions

Illustration 21a: *Visualization for cancer:*
Cancerous tumor

Illustration 21b: *Visualization for cancer:*
White blood cells surrounding the tumor

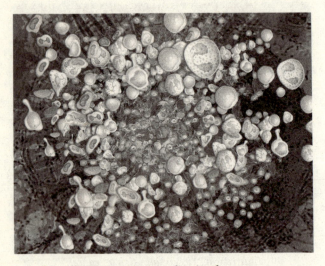

Illustration 22a: *Visualization for cancer:*
White blood cells destroying the tumor

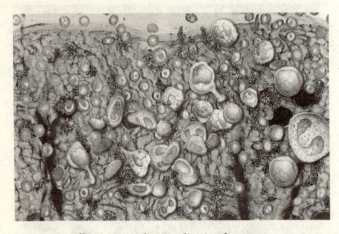

Illustration 22b: *Visualization for cancer:*
Normal cells prevail; the tumor is gone

ously attacking it in order to weaken the cancer.
4. As the essential needs of the cancer are being blocked, visualize the communication links between cells in the tumor (or between tumors) falling apart.
5. Once the communication links fail, visualize the cancer shrinking and losing its life energy as it becomes inactive.
6. Your body must now physically remove this tissue. Visualize a garbage disposal system working away 24–7 to remove the physical mass from your body.

LEUKEMIA

Leukemia is cancer of the white blood cells. These cancer cells are formed in the bone marrow—where all bloods cells are produced—and inhibit the production of normal white and red blood cells. The goal of any visualization for leukemia is to stimulate the bone marrow into producing a normal amount of red and white blood cells. Visualize lightning bolts going through the bone marrow one after the other until you can see a healthy number of red and white blood cells being formed. Keep doing this visualization throughout the session until you become confident in the process.

NEUROLOGICAL CONDITIONS

Neurologically based disorders include multiple sclerosis, fibromyalgia, chronic fatigue syndrome, head and spine traumas, central nervous system infections and growths, and peripheral nerve disorders.

I have held several workshops specifically for chronic fatigue syndrome and fibromyalgia, with great success. Many participants report that they no longer have these ailments, and many others note significant improvement in their quality of life.

Your nervous system has a direct effect on your immune system; therefore, virtually every health issue benefits from a positive change in your nervous system. Regardless of the health challenge you are facing, stimulating your nervous system will benefit you, whether you have an emotional or psychological issue or a physical problem. It is also useful in regaining physical energy, vitality and strength.

1. Visualize lightning bolts ripping through your entire nervous system (see Illustration 23). Remember that the goal of these lightning bolts is to reboot your nervous system.
2. Watch these bolts light up your nervous system, from your head, down your spine and to every nerve ending. After this "storm" passes, imagine calming ripples being emitted from your entire nervous system.

RESPIRATORY CONDITIONS

Many conditions can lead to breathing problems. Some issues, such as asthma, affect the air passages, while others, such as lung cancer, directly influence the function of the lungs. The first thing to do is see your doctor to determine which condition you have.

Asthma is a condition that makes it more difficult for you to breathe. When you inhale, air passes to your lungs through tubular airways called bronchi. When you have an asthma attack, the walls of these airways contract and become inflamed.

Factors that can trigger asthma attacks are smoke, dust, pollen, air pollution and allergies. Stress can make asthma worse. To me, asthma looks like a thick, sticky fog throughout the airways leading to the lungs. Lung problems often respond well to visualizations because there is so much circulation throughout the respiratory system. With this large amount of circulation in the lungs, the problem can exit the body rapidly. Most people with lung problems cough up a lot of phlegm after the treatments. Many people notice that breathing is easier and takes less effort. These differences are often noticeable quickly.

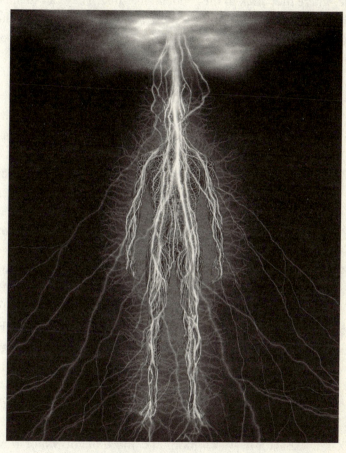

Illustration 23: *Visualization for neurological conditions:*
Lightning bolts ripping through your nervous system

Smart energy packets, or SEPs, are helpful with respiratory conditions, as they can be breathed in directly to your problem site, where they stick to the problem like glue. They can then be eliminated on exhalation (see Illustration 24). To enhance the realism of the visualizations, feel the problem moving out of your lungs with every breath.

1. Imagine bluish liquid energy filling your lungs (see Illustration 25). If you have asthma, visualize your airways—your breathing tubes—expanding as they soak up this liquid energy.
2. Watch your tubes expand, just as sponges do when they soak up liquid. The problem is absorbed into this liquid, which then evaporates into glowing energy.
3. Take deep breaths and absorb all this energy as deeply as you can.
4. Visualize a raging bonfire with flames burning underneath your lungs. See your problem shrivel up, vaporized by the intense heat (see Illustration 26).
5. Once your problem is completely vaporized, begin to take deep breaths. Imagine taking a deep breath of energized air into your lungs. This energy is absorbed down to the cellular level.
6. See your smallest capillaries light up and reflect this energetic boost. Every airway is clear and bright.
7. On exhalation, watch more and more of the vapor leave your lungs until they are clean and are a pinkish color (see Illustration 27).

HEART CONDITIONS

There are many conditions that can affect your heart, so the first thing to do is see your doctor to determine which condition you have. The visualizations in this chapter can be done

Visualizations for Specific Conditions

Illustration 24a: *Visualization for respiratory conditions:* Inhaling SEPs

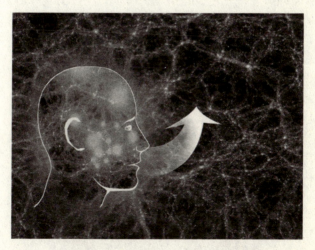

Illustration 24b: *Visualization for respiratory conditions:* Exhaling SEPs containing the debris

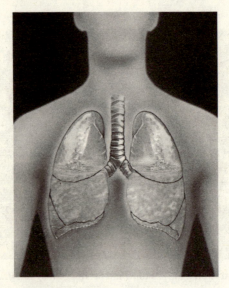

Illustration 25: *Visualization for respiratory conditions:* Lungs soaking up liquid energy and expanding

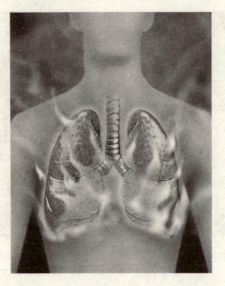

Illustration 26: *Visualization for respiratory conditions:* A raging fire vaporizing your problem

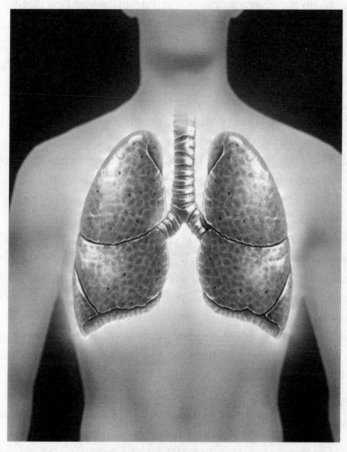

Illustration 27: *Visualization for respiratory conditions:*
Clean lungs

to complement any therapy, and you can modify them for your specific heart problem. Remember that there is no wrong way to do these visualizations. I am simply suggesting that you modify them to fit your diagnosis and therefore find what works best for you.

However, any heart problem is reflected in your breathing; this must be addressed:

1. Imagine breathing pure air so deeply into your lungs that it energizes the very functions of your cells.
2. Visualize this cellular impact of pure energy being absorbed by every fiber of your being. See every pathway being energized as all cells in your body bathe in this pure energy.

Blood Pressure Problems (Hypertension or Hypotension)
Stress is a major factor in high blood pressure, so it is essential that you relax in a comfortable position to visualize. Stay away from clocks that may remind you of the passage of time, which may cause tension. This is your time for yourself. Use it wisely. For those with hypotension, the purpose of this visualization is to regulate your heart's pumping ability, so be sure to relax and focus on this objective.

1. Visualize your heart filling up with a calming, pure, glowing energy (see Illustration 28).
2. Once your heart is filled, watch the glowing energy get distributed more and more evenly throughout your body with every heartbeat. Watch the glowing energy spread down every artery and every vein until your entire circulatory system is filled with this calming energy. Every tiny capillary is energized.
3. Watch your heart rhythmically pumping, until your heartbeat is calm, relaxed and regular. Visualize calming ripples of

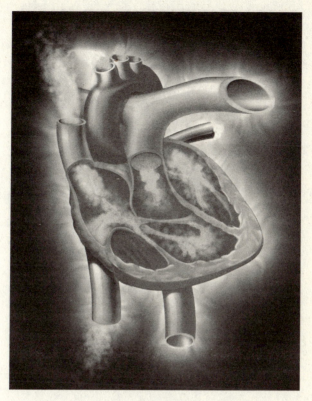

Illustration 28: *Visualization for heart conditions:*
Glowing energy filling the heart

energy emanating from your heart (see Illustration 29).
4. Breathe deeply, and enjoy feeling good.

When doing your visualizations, be creative. But do make sure that in the last step of each visualization for your heart, it is always beating at a relaxed yet steady rate. With each beat, feel the force behind each regular contraction.

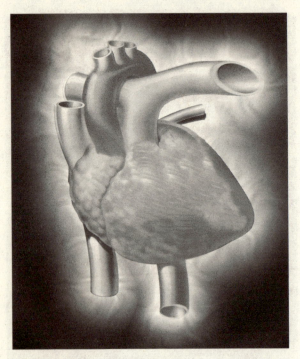

Illustration 29: *Visualization for heart conditions:*
A calm, relaxed heart

INFECTIOUS DISEASES

Many infectious diseases, including AIDS, HIV, hepatitis, cold and flu, are spread throughout the body. SEPs are a useful visualization tool for these types of ailments (see Chapter 8).

1. Visualize SEPs or white blood cells dispersing themselves throughout your entire body, engulfing the problem (bacteria or virus) cell by cell (see Illustration 30).
2. Visualize white blood cells permeating the blood vessel walls in great numbers, totally engulfing a localized problem area (see Illustration 31).

Visualizations for Specific Conditions

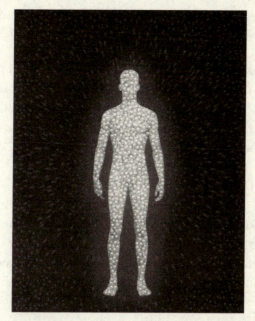

Illustration 30: *Visualization for infectious diseases:*
SEPs dispersed throughout the body

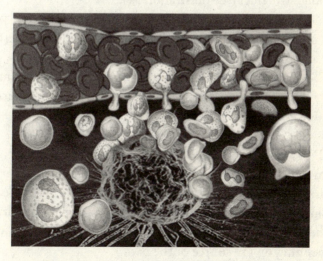

Illustration 31: *Visualization for infectious diseases:*
White blood cells attacking the problem

3. Visualize explosions in a specific area to address any localized problem. Think of comets or asteroids hitting where this is needed (see Illustration 32).
4. Visualize your kidneys filtering everything out of the dirty blood, or blood that contains the now inactive bacteria or viruses (see Illustration 33). Continue the visualization until only clean blood is going in and coming out of your kidneys, and white blood cells no longer have anything to "eat."

GASTROINTESTINAL CONDITIONS

Emotional issues and stress often aggravate gastrointestinal issues. Take time out to relax and visualize. One way to accomplish this is to sit down with a cup of green or caffeine-free tea before starting. Take a sip and move your awareness with the soothingly warm liquid. Be mindful of its calming effect.

1. Visualize pure light energy being absorbed all along your digestive tract (see Illustration 34).
2. See the unobstructed flow through your body from your mouth, esophagus, stomach, small intestine, large intestine and colon, and flushing out as waste.
3. See your entire digestive system working perfectly. Calming ripples of energy radiate throughout your system, nourishing every cell in its path.

PAIN ISSUES

Sometimes it seems as though there are as many different causes of pain as there are people living with it. Typically, mainstream Western medicine manages pain issues with drugs, rather than getting to the root cause. Visualizations vary depending on the source of the pain.

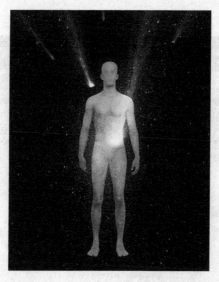

Illustration 32: *Visualization for infectious diseases:* Localized explosion

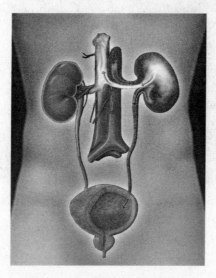

Illustration 33: *Visualization for infectious diseases:*
Kidneys filtering out dirty blood

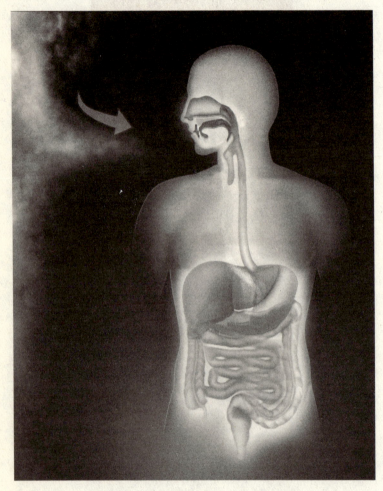

Illustration 34: *Visualization for gastrointestinal conditions:* Digestive tract absorbing pure energy

1. Imagine breathing in pure, warm sunshine energy deep within your lungs and heart area.
2. Form a concentrated ball of energy in the painful area.
3. Visualize this ball picking up pieces of pain like lint and radiating it out of your body in the form of sunshine. The warm rays carry with them everything that needs to leave your body. In its place is left glowing radiance. Feels good, doesn't it?

JOINT CONDITIONS, CHRONIC AND ACUTE

These visualizations are for any condition related to joints or mobility problems. Remember, you have the power to improvise your own visualizations.

The general visualization using lightning bolts (see Chapter 8) is helpful to many people.

1. Visualize lightning bolts forcefully moving throughout your joint until it is healed (see Illustration 35).
2. Imagine injecting a needle into your joint, dispensing a white liquid energy that totally surrounds all moving parts (see Illustration 36). This white liquid energy acts as lubrication for your joint.
3. Visualize gently testing the mobility of your joint by imagining many support wires at different angles holding your joint in place (see Illustration 37). Each wire adds support to various parts of your joint, and moves the joint or limb around like the strings of a marionette. Test your range of motion by playing in your mind's eye a sport you once enjoyed. Remember how wonderful it is to feel the breeze against your face as you hike, bike, play tennis or golf. As the mobility of the joint is being tested in your mind's eye, there is no pain at all. There is not even the thought of pain present. Remember how this feels and recall it often.

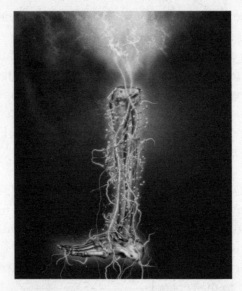

Illustration 35: *Visualization for joint conditions:*
Lightning bolt moving throughout the joint

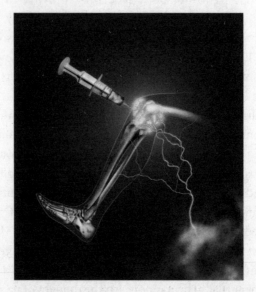

Illustration 36: *Visualization for joint conditions:*
A needle dispensing white liquid energy

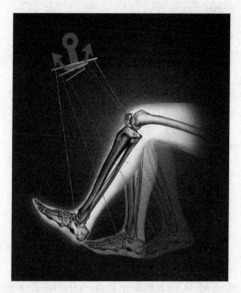

Illustration 37: *Visualization for joint conditions:*
Support wires holding your joint in place
as you test your range of motion

BACK INJURIES

Back injuries are very common. In group treatments this area is always addressed, as I haven't held one yet where this hasn't been an issue for many participants. Depending on the nature of your injury, it might be difficult to even get comfortable for a visualization session, but do your best.

1. Visualize a glowing white malleable rod going through the middle of your spine (see Illustration 38). This rod acts as a support.
2. Imagine that with every inhalation you are filling your lungs with pure energy. Create an energy flow from the top of your head through your spine and out through your tailbone. Visualize this pathway lighting up like a neon sign.

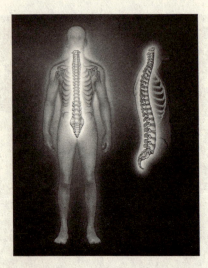

Illustration 38: *Visualization for back injuries:*
A glowing, white, malleable rod running through your spine

3. Visualize supporting your back while you are moving it around with great flexibility. The range of motion of your back is being tested through your imagery. There should be no painful sensation or even the thought of pain.
4. Visualize your back cracking into place as if in a chiropractic procedure. Your back is being reset to its optimum position.
5. In your visualization, flex your back to test its full range of motion until you have a secure sense of stability. Reach your comfort zone. You should then see yourself doing all the normal movements that have not been possible until now because of your back problem. See yourself doing these things with no pain or discomfort whatsoever.

As you experiment with your visualizations, continue to modify and develop those that work best for you.

MUSCLE INJURIES

Even if it is difficult to loosen up because of the pain, you must try to get in a relaxing position for your visualization session. Take a deep breath and begin.

1. Visualize a white spiral of calming liquid energy surrounding the problem area (see Illustration 39). See all your muscles soak up the liquid like a sponge.
2. Once your muscles become completely saturated with this liquid energy, watch calming waves of electrical pulses ripple out from your muscle. Feel the muscles relax as they bathe in the glowing energy (see Illustration 40).

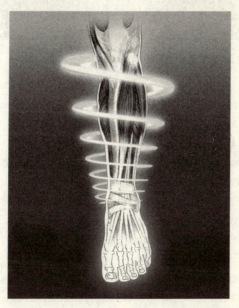

Illustration 39: *Visualization for muscle injuries:* Spiral of energy surrounding the injured muscle

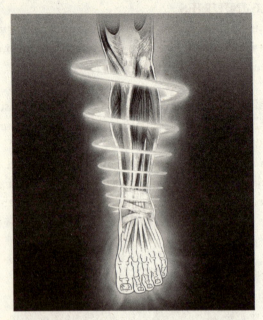

Illustration 40: *Visualization for muscle injuries:*
Glowing energy bathes the muscle

BROKEN BONES

Most fractures need to be physically set by a doctor first. The following visualization is intended to speed up your recovery. This visualization involves heat, which dramatically increases the rate at which every chemical reaction takes place, allowing an increase in blood circulation. This speeds up the healing process.

With multiple fractures, you can either do this visualization on one fracture at a time, or you can visualize healing the entire bone at once. Again, use whatever works best for you. There are no firm rules for what will work and what will not, as any visualization will direct the immune system to some degree.

1. Visualize a bright white light being absorbed into and then emitted from the inside of your bone (see Illustration 41). This bright light creates heat.
2. Imagine wrapping energy around your fracture.
3. Energy radiates outward as you flood the entire area with warm, healing light to speed up the mending process (see Illustration 42). Watch new healthy bone filling in any breaks, until there is no longer any sign of there ever having been a problem. Visualize the fracture as completely healed (see Illustration 43).

FATIGUE AND EMOTIONAL PROBLEMS

Emotional problems weigh heavy on our minds and this uses up a lot of our energy. By taking an emotional load off, we will feel lighter and have more energy to enjoy life. Bringing in energy helps accomplish this task. You may want to customize your visualization by seeing yourself actually taking that load off your back.

The visualization for fatigue or emotional problems is similar to the technique used to expand auras, as described in Chapter 2, "Bring in Universal Energy." Do this visualization whenever you feel exhausted and are in need of an energy booster. I have found this to be an effective tool in regaining energy after an intense workout. It is also effective in increasing the maximum amount of exercise you can do within your comfort zone. For example, I use this to increase the amount of weight that I can lift when working out in the weight room.

1. Visualize all the energy in the universe being pulled into you (see Illustration 44). Continue absorbing all this energy until you feel that your energy system is completely saturated. Mastering this takes practice.
2. Once all the energy is within you, imagine that it powerfully

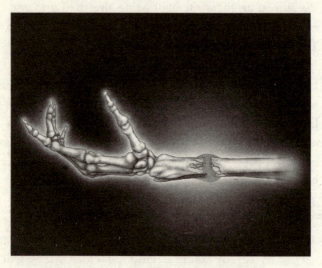

Illustration 41: *Visualization for broken bones:* The area of your fracture absorbing bright white light

Illustration 42: *Visualization for broken bones:* Energy radiating outward as you flood the area with warm light

Visualizations for Specific Conditions 285

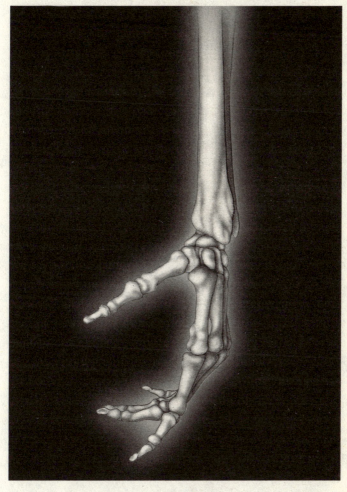

Illustration 43: *Visualization for broken bones:*
The fracture as healed

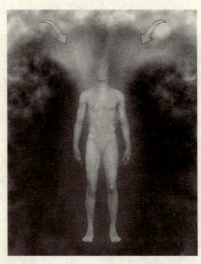

Illustration 44: *Visualization for fatigue and emotional problems:* Pulling all the energy in the universe into yourself through the top of your head

explodes in all directions (see Illustration 45). The shock wave of energy ripples out. When this has disappeared from sight, all that is left is a clear, pure white hologram of yourself, with no sign whatsoever of any problem.

Another effective visualization is of sending streams of laser light to loosen the knot that is holding you back from doing what it is that you want to do. Set yourself free.

CUSTOMIZING YOUR VISUALIZATIONS
It would be an impossible task to address in detail every possible visualization applicable to every ailment known. Not only is it unrealistic but it is unnecessary, as you hold the key to all visualizations. It is called imagination.

Be creative. Change or customize the visualization to suit you.

Illustration 45: *Visualization for fatigue and emotional problems:* Your abundant energy exploding outward in all directions

Never underestimate your own power in your health and healing. Visualizations are a tool for you to use. Your response to them is an individual process. So is what works most effectively for you. Some readers may have read this entire book and still be wondering, "Which visualization is the correct one for my condition?" If this is you, ask yourself these questions:

1. Have I researched my ailment as thoroughly as I am able to?
2. Do I know what the proper and healthy functioning of this area should be?
3. Do I know what this area should look like?
4. Have I practiced the general visualizations and varied them according to my specific challenge?
5. Have I practiced the specific visualizations that are most relevant for me and modified them accordingly?

All the visualizations in this book are designed to make you feel more comfortable as you explore what works most effectively for you. Becoming comfortable with yourself is the most important step toward self-empowerment. Trust yourself on your way forward.

Conclusion

If the material in this book has helped even one person with his or her healing journey, it has in fact helped us all. What appears to separate us is only an illusion. What we do for ourselves is ultimately what we do for everyone. Helping everyone is an unavoidable outcome of truly helping ourselves.

Stay tuned!

DREAMHEALER 3

The Quantum
World of Energy Healing

*In memory of my cat Gizmo,
my good friend*

Contents

Acknowledgments   295

From Outer Space to Inner Space   297

PART 1: HOW IT ALL BEGAN   309

CHAPTER 1   THE VISION   311

CHAPTER 2   THE ORIGIN OF THE UNIVERSE   321

CHAPTER 3   THE FIELD OF INFORMATION   331

CHAPTER 4   SYMPHONY OF LIGHT   347
    Auras   349
    Energy Exercises   353
    Biophotons   368
    Electromagnetic Frequency Interference   376

PART 2: WHAT WE MAKE OF LIFE   381

CHAPTER 5   CONSCIOUSNESS   383
    Aligning the Conscious and Subconscious Mind   392

	The Unconscious State: Coma	393
	Consciousness of Animals	398
	Collective Consciousness	401
CHAPTER 6	EMOTIONS AND ATTITUDE	407
	Achieving Emotional Equilibrium	415
	Addictions and Poor Lifestyle Habits	418
	Adjusting Your Attitude	420
	Packing for Your Healing Journey	423
	Taking Time Out	425
	How Humor and Gratitude Affects Health and Healing	426
CHAPTER 7	BELIEFS AND SPIRITUALITY	429
	Affirmations	436
	The Influence of Beliefs on My Healing Work	438
	Spirituality	450
CHAPTER 8	REINCARNATION	457
CHAPTER 9	KARMA	469
CHAPTER 10	THE SPIRIT WORLD	481

PART 3: HEALING VISUALIZATIONS — 489

Why Do Visualizations?	492
Strategies to Enhance Healing Visualizations	494
Speed Meditation	495
Maximizing Focused Intention	497
Exercise for Projecting a Holographic Image	498
Specific Visualizations	501
Reflection	517

Acknowledgments

Thank you to Doris Lora for her inspiration and patience. Thanks to Robert Stirling for his inquisitiveness. He brought forward lots of questions, which are answered in this book. Many thanks to Ivan Rados for his exquisite art creations. Thanks to everyone who has supported and helped me on this journey.

From Outer Space to Inner Space

I have been given the gift of being an energy healer in this lifetime. I have been drawn to healing people and to helping them achieve self-empowerment. My goal is to teach others how to use their innate energy resources and intentions to heal themselves and others. This has been the focus of my practice, my workshops and my two previous books. This book continues to focus on healing. It is about our beginnings and our characteristics and abilities as energy beings.

Concepts such as the Big Bang, biophotons, consciousness and reincarnation are all related to our health and healing. Although these concepts and others are explained in scientific terms in this book, it is not intended as a science textbook. Rather, *The Path of the DreamHealer* is a compilation of the information I have received and learned through intuition—part of my gift is being able to intuitively receive huge amounts of information that is normally acquired through years of study and research. Many people refer to this process of "downloading" information intuitively as channeling. I in turn have acted as a conduit in that these concepts have been channeled through me to you. All of the information I receive intuitively is in the form of complex scientific images, but here I have simplified the science to make it as accessible to readers as possible.

While it is not necessary to understand the details of quantum physics in order to practice self-healing, it is useful to have a general understanding of where energy comes from and how it works. I provide a general overview of this in Part 1, "How It All Began," which includes the story of my journey to affirm a vision I had. It is one of my most powerful examples of my unusual experiences and the one underlying the "downloading" of the information which is the basis of this book. So just how is the origin of our universe related to health and healing? As I discuss in Chapter 2, everything in the universe is energy, whether in the form of a wave or a particle. Moreover, everything in the universe originated from a common energy source. According to the Big Bang theory, the dominant scientific theory about the origin of the universe, the universe was created sometime between ten billion and fifteen billion years ago when a cosmic explosion hurled matter in all directions. Because of this, we are all energetically connected as one. We all have access to all of the knowledge in the universe; that knowledge is in the form of energy. This means we can access the information needed for healing. We do this through our intuition and intentions. The "library" of this universal knowledge is commonly referred to as "the field." In Chapter 3, I discuss the access that each of us has to this field, while the meditation exercises and self-healing visualizations you'll find in Part 3 of this book will help you tap into this universal field of information.

My gift was revealed to me in a variety of ways as I was growing up. As far back as I can remember I saw auras, the subtle light surrounding all living things. As I didn't know differently, I thought this was normal. It wasn't until my early teenage years that I realized this is an unusual ability. Furthermore, telekinetic events occurred around me that could not easily be dismissed as typical. When objects I reached for shot off away from me and my pencil flew out of my hand and hit the blackboard at school, I became very curious. (And it was nearly impossible to convince my teacher that I wasn't throwing things.)

Then one day, my mom was in excruciating pain from trigeminal neuralgia, an affliction caused by her multiple sclerosis. I told her to close her eyes and I placed my hand on her head. I wasn't thinking about anything in particular; I just didn't want my mom to be in pain anymore. I saw a throbbing bright green blob in her head. I grabbed it and pulled it out into me. "That was a horrible pain that you had," I said aloud. My mom was immediately pain-free, but I had taken on her stabbing headache. That was the last trigeminal neuralgia pain she ever had. By morning I felt fine, but my parents were very concerned. What had happened? Was my health now at risk? I too was baffled. Fortunately, through practice and some guidance, I soon learned how to influence another person's health without taking on his or her symptoms.

This started my most interesting journey on the path of healing. I didn't know how healing worked, but I knew there was much more to our universe than we can perceive with our five physical senses. Then I heard that Apollo 14 astronaut Edgar Mitchell was coming to town to speak at a meeting of the Institute of Noetic Sciences (IONS), of which he is the founder. On Dr. Mitchell's return journey to earth, he became aware of a deep sense of universal connectedness. Having had this transformational experience in space, he decided to devote his life to finding scientific explanations for unusual or little understood phenomena. At the time, I was aware that I could see health information about a person and that I could influence it, but I had no scientific terms for or understanding of what I was accessing. From attending the IONS meeting and afterward speaking to Dr. Mitchell, I learned that the information I was seeing was described scientifically as the hologram of the person's energy field. Furthermore, some quantum physicists were describing what they perceived to be a holographic universe, in which every part of the universe, including each of us, contains all of the information of the universe. This concept resonated with how I experience my healing work. My meeting with Dr. Mitchell was no coincidence, and he has been my science mentor ever since.

Shortly after, I started writing *DreamHealer,* which describes an experiential view of distant healing. Although the academic theory of quantum physics is discussed (in simple terms), the focus of the book is on self-discovery, and an understanding of our own awareness as we seek to achieve a higher level of consciousness.

Following the publication of *DreamHealer,* I became aware that readers want more information on how they can positively impact their own health. So I wrote *DreamHealer 2: A Guide to Healing and Self-Empowerment,* providing details on visualizations and other tools that will help readers practice self-healing. My step-by-step instructions show how to activate the immune system and return the body, mind and spirit to its natural balance and state of well-being.

When I look at someone, I see the person's body enveloped in energy of flowing colors. This is the outer reflection of the energetic system, or aura, which surrounds all living things. While playing basketball one day, I observed that intention affects a person's aura: When another player thought about passing the ball, this intention registered as a small spike on his aura in the direction he wanted to pass it. This allowed me to better anticipate my opponent's play and intercept the ball. This is when I fully realized the power of intention.

Some healing arts focus on the aura. In healthy areas of the body, the aura moves and swirls in a pattern and appears organized and in harmony: There is a flow. In an afflicted area, this flow is broken. Healers use their hands and minds to smooth and repair the energy blockages negatively affecting the body. I can get a great deal of information from the aura because it is evident from them where blockages of energy in the body are: These stagnant areas pinpoint the locations of existing or developing problems. But my vision goes much deeper than the aura. I have the ability to see energy fields at many different frequencies, which enables me to do a type of body scan on a person.

As I learned at the IONS meeting, a scientific concept that relates directly to how I practice healing is the hologram—a three-dimensional projection containing all of the information (past, present and future) of a person, place or thing, including, with people, their optimal state of health. This projection appears before me in the form of an image. Some scientists speculate that because the universe is holographic—meaning the universe is just information—our brains also operate and interact with the universal energy field holographically. Given our interconnectedness, we are all connected to this oneness of information.

You may be a little bit familiar with holograms if you have ever worn the three-dimensional glasses in a theater that project what looks like a holographic image of what is on the movie screen. You can see that images look like they are hanging in space. With holograms, every piece of that image contains all of the information of the whole image. This is typical of laser-created holograms, where each part of the holographic material contains the entire image, even if it is shattered into many pieces. So too in a holographic universe: Every particle of the universe, every cell of our bodies, every neuron in our brains contains all of the information in the universe. It's astonishing to imagine the resources we have at our disposal. It makes sense, then, when neuroscientists tell us that we use only a fraction of our brain power.

Each of us emits a hologram containing all information about us. Everyone is connected to the field of information by their unique body frequency—the frequency or resonance of the energy or light of their body. Like tuning a radio station to a particular frequency, I am able to tune in to a person's frequency within the field of information. At first, everything around me goes dark, then I "see" a holographic image of the person's body. I call this process "going in," as I can "see" an X-ray–type view in great detail. On this image, I can see areas of injuries or illness. When I am connected to the person, I also pick up a lot of intuitive information about the person, for example, what his or her attitudes and beliefs are. This helps me to see the energy blockages and, through my intention—that is, my intention to heal—manipulate energy to clear these blockages, permitting energy to flow harmoniously and, thus, allow the body to change. It is important to remember that we are all connected because we are all energy. If you view matter in its smallest manifestation, you would not find solid matter. Our interconnection to one another can be thought of as an ocean of energy. Like every atom in an ocean of water, every bit of energy is connected. If you throw a rock into an ocean, that rock and its impact will affect every atom in that ocean, as one molecule is connected to and influencing all others.

I also have the ability to zoom in to the hologram or access different layers to work on. For instance, if I want to look at the pancreas, I can go straight to the level where I can see all the fluids flowing within that gland. With my healing intention, I can tune in to and "see" any number of subsets of information contained within the hologram. Through my intentions to influence, I can control what information I receive about a particular health concern. This is similar to operating a remote control to access different television stations. My mind acts as a remote control that can adjust to different sets of frequencies, giving me different holographic views.

I can zero in on electrical impulses between neurons in the brain, or see specific systems of the body, such as neurological and skeletal, as well as that of the organs. The various holographic views of the body are like the various blueprints used in the construction of a building. There is a floor plan, electrical drawings and plumbing schematics of the same structure. Which view of the body is most useful simply depends on what part of the body or ailment I intend to focus on.

Through intention, I am able to create a resonance, or common energy frequency, between me and healing information I am projecting to interact with that person's hologram. Because our bodies are constantly interacting with their environments through the exchange of information, the person with whom I am interacting progressively reflects these healing changes.

An important concept that relates to my distant healing abilities is nonlocality, commonly referred to as quantum action-at-a-distance. A quantum object simultaneously influences its correlated twin object, no matter how far apart they are. This explains how energy can influence other energy elsewhere, and therefore why geographical distance or proximity is not a factor.

Photons, the smallest physical units of light, are capable of transferring information universally. Biophotons are the photons that are emitted from every living cell or organism. These electromagnetic frequencies (discussed in more detail in Part 1) are all energy or ways of describing energy.

In the quantum world, which is the world defined in terms of the smallest realizable units, the act of simply observing or interacting with a quantum object changes its behavior. Physicists readily acknowledge that they do not understand many of these aspects of the quantum world, but their mathematical formulas verify quantum theory. But what still perplexes physicists is why that quantum object's quantum twin simultaneously changes, no matter how far apart the quantum object and its twin are. Some refer to this connection as "entanglement."

Because of the connection of everything to everything else, our thoughts and intentions can influence events nonlocally. This quantum attribute of nonlocality helps me understand how I can facilitate a person's healing from a distance: I am able to connect to a person's frequency and see his or her hologram simply by looking at a photograph of that person's face.

When I do my distant healing, the transfer of information in the field is not affected by time and space. I know this because the clarity of information I receive from someone 5000 miles away is the same as if the person were in the next room. For example, I have connected to someone in China for a treatment and the distance made no difference to the treatment's effectiveness. In another case, my uncle showed me a photograph of a man and asked me what I saw. I had never seen anything like it. His skeletal holographic image was stretched and elongated. I told my uncle what I saw and asked what ailment the man had. My uncle replied that the photo was of a cosmonaut aboard the International Space Station as it orbited a hundred miles above the earth. No wonder that his hologram, when he was in reduced gravity, appeared a little peculiar to me.

How do we relate all of the information in the field to our present reality? I address this question in Part 2 by discussing the more personal and metaphysical aspects of this oneness and interconnectedness as it relates to our health. What role do our beliefs and emotions play? How does universal energy manifest itself in consciousness, reincarnation, karma and past lives? These metaphysical concepts help us understand more clearly our self-healing abilities. Chapter 6 includes exercises to help you access more effectively these innate healing skills that we all possess.

As an energy healer, I work with the properties of energy. You, as your own self-healer, can also learn to work with these properties. In addition to science mentors, I have had the pleasure of working with people from alternative healing disciplines, including qigong masters, reiki masters and shamans from many indigenous cultures. I've also worked with people who have discovered their healing abilities on their own. Every healer within each discipline has learned different ways to access a similar ability. What I have learned is that each and every one of us naturally possesses this healing capacity. Most of us just need some simple directions as to how to maximize our awareness of it and focus our intentions to guide it.

Throughout the book, I emphasize the powerful effect our beliefs and expectations have on our health. I have seen many people with varying beliefs as I go about my work. I feel that everyone is entitled to his or her beliefs, and my purpose is simply to respond to needs as I am able. However, in my experience, it makes a huge difference if the recipient of energy treatments understands what is happening and participates in his or her own healing. My objective in healing is to teach people how to effectively improve their own health through their own intervention.

Most people with paranormal abilities would love to find some scientific means of proving what they are experiencing. My parents were no different. They were eager to consult with experts who could answer some of their questions. They thought that contacting research experts at a reputable university would be a good place to start. This was the beginning of our experience as a family understanding the resistance that is found in the academic world. The professors we talked to were skeptics. We had hoped to find someone with an open mind who was willing to consider our questions about the paranormal with the intent of understanding rather than disproving these phenomena.

It is healthy to be an open-minded skeptic. However, those who proudly label themselves skeptics may be creating and reinforcing paradigms that prevent them from being open to understanding events beyond that of our five senses.

Since discovering my ability to influence health, I have been overwhelmed with requests for help. As I contemplated how to respond to such a great need, I realized that it is possible to join auras in a group of similarly intentioned people and affect change. From observing how intention affects auras, the idea came to me to do group energy treatments so that more people could benefit. This presented me with wonderful possibilities. I began leading workshops to teach people how to influence their health through intention.

Everything is connected at its most basic form of energy. We are all truly one. In group treatments, I act as the conductor in the symphony of merging frequencies. Participants have the opportunity to experience what an energy treatment feels like and can learn how to do energy treatments for themselves. Given some simple tools, all group participants can learn to feel, and even see, subtle energy movement within and around the body and become comfortable taking this knowledge with them to continue their own self-healing.

I also realized that when people participate in their own healing, a lasting change occurs. People feel incredible strength when they are empowered to do their own healing, when they realize that they have the tools to positively influence their own health physically, emotionally and spiritually.

When facilitating a group treatment, I am in a trance-like state of consciousness in which I am not fully aware of my physical surroundings. When returning to ordinary consciousness, my experience is similar to emerging out of a cave into brilliant sunshine. My pupils are fully dilated so my eyes take time to adjust to the light, even in a darkened room. Directing energy is energy consuming. After a group treatment, I find that my mind muscle has been thoroughly exercised. I rebalance myself by exercising my physical body.

Many people who have connected to me through the reading of my books or attending one of my workshops have written to me that they have visualized me when they are in a dream state. Upon meeting someone face-to-face, or even connecting at a distance, a bond is formed. We forge an even stronger bond if our thoughts and intentions are aligned. We feel this connection in a group treatment through our mutual experience and what we share. The barriers of individualism we have erected are nothing more than facades. A global shift in consciousness will erode these barriers as our evolution continues.

Many aspects of energy healing and other alternative disciplines have been seen as mysterious, shrouded in secrecy and ritual. My hope is that the discussion in this book of the energy concepts will help demystify the healing process. The self-healing strategies, in the form of visualization exercises, will help you learn how to heal yourself. The visualizations can be customized to meet your particular health challenge. Every one of us has different strengths and sensitivities. Our five senses vary in dominance. Some people are very visual, others are auditory and some feel everything intensely. We need to be aware of our individual strengths and use them to our advantage. You can tailor visualizations to your particular strengths and preferences, such as using primarily visual or primarily auditory input.

Just know that you have self-healing ability. The source of energy used in an energy treatment is the limitless energy of the universe. It is attracted by our boundless imagination and guided by positive healing intentions. Our thoughts and intentions, which are energetic phenomena, are unlimited. When you have a grasp of what science is suggesting about the origin of the universe and you understand your experiences as both a material (solidified energy) and nonmaterial (wave-like energy) being, you may be willing to open your mind to the power of energy and intention. I urge you to explore the ability that all of us have to influence our own health.

PART I

How It All Began

Chapter I

The Vision

The only limits that you have are the limits which you have set for yourself in your own mind.

—ADAM

Several years ago I had my first vision. It was an incredibly vivid dream where I was soaring above the ocean like an eagle. Then I found myself running very quickly through a forest. Suddenly, all motion came to a halt. Then I saw a big black bird sitting atop a mound of earth. I then got a strong feeling that I had to go to Nootka. I had never heard of Nootka and so had no idea where it was.

I told my parents about this vision and that I had a strong feeling that we had to go to Nootka. We went to the library to do some research. We discovered that Nootka Sound, also called Friendly Cove, is a remote area on the west side of Vancouver Island, in British Columbia, and is where Captain Cook first set anchor on his second expedition of the Northwest Coast. I found this particularly interesting, since I am related to Captain Cook on my mom's side. Through my dad, I am part Penobscot, a Native American band based on the east coast of the United States. Nootka Sound is a historical meeting place of both sides of my family roots: European and First Nations. The pictures of the Nootka region in the library books looked familiar to me. I recognized the landscape and, pointing to one particular picture, exclaimed, "That's where we have to go." My dad asked, "What will we be looking for when we arrive?" I replied that I had to find the big black bird which I had seen in my vision. Since summer was approaching, we decided to make a family vacation of this trip. We learned that Nootka Sound is accessible only by seaplane or boat. Then we learned that a converted minesweeper delivers supplies to the island lighthouse twice a week and also carries travelers back and forth for a day trip.

My grandparents and uncle heard about our trip plans and decided to join us. Although everyone except my younger sister knew of the many unusual events such as pencils flying that had occurred around me, I had told only my mom and dad about the details of the vision. But my grandparents and uncle knew I had had a vision of some sort and they understood that Nootka Sound was a place I needed to go in order to follow my vision. So we all got together with our calendars to set the travel date. The first date that suited all of us happened to be my sixteenth birthday. Without thinking, I said to my mom, "That's good because although it is going to be really cloudy in the morning, it will be sunny when we arrive." My mom did not say anything about my weather prediction but remembered it because, considering how variable West Coast weather is, it is hard enough to make an accurate weather prediction for the next day, let alone six weeks in advance.

During our planning for the trip, I noticed that two crows seemed to be always following me. They woke me up every morning and were more or less permanent fixtures in our yard. They followed me to the tennis courts and sat atop the fence. But I didn't spend any time trying to understand their presence. Then, several days before our trip, they were nowhere to be seen.

Our journey began with a two-hour ferry ride to Vancouver Island and then a four-hour drive inland to the town of Gold

River. When we arrived at our motel, two crows sitting on the telephone wire at its entrance cawed in greeting.

We didn't need to board the minesweeper that would take us to Nootka Sound until the next morning, so we decided to visit some nearby caves that had been known to the Native people of the area for centuries. As we drove down the long, winding dirt road back toward the town, after having explored the caves, one of the two crows guided us along. It flew only a few feet in front of our windshield most of the way back, leading us through every twist and turn of the road. We were all amazed.

In the late afternoon, we stopped at a sandy spot on the river bank to have a swim, since it was a hot, cloudless day. My mom reminded me of the weather prediction I had made weeks ago for the next day. It seemed unlikely to her that it would be cloudy for our journey, as I had seen in my vision.

The next morning we woke up early. Overhead, there was a solid blanket of clouds and it felt like a November day, even though it was July. We all bundled up in layers of clothing and headed out to the old minesweeper.

We boarded along with about fifty other campers, tourists and adventurers. The galley did a booming business serving steaming hot chocolate and chili to all of the shivering travelers on deck. I told my mom not to be concerned about the weather. As in my vision, it would be hot and sunny when we arrived. She looked up at the massive, dark clouds and said, "Whatever. As long as it doesn't rain, we'll be all right."

The scenery was spectacular as we headed through the ocean waters toward Nootka Sound. Half way to our destination, a single orca approached the boat. The whale followed alongside the boat for a long time, breaching and tail slapping. We learned that this male orca, which had become separated from its pod the year before, had been named Luna by some of the locals. The local First Nations people called him Tsuux-iit. Most passengers busied themselves taking photographs of the orca. I hoped that he would some day be reunited with his pod.

To the west, we saw a patch of clear blue sky. The clouds looked like a blanket being peeled back. A moment later we could see the lighthouse near the dock. Just then, brilliant summer sun emerged. We quickly stuffed our jackets and sweaters into our backpacks and prepared to disembark. I could see what appeared to me as a searchlight beam shining in the woods beyond the dock, and I was eager to begin on the adventure that was about to unfold. The captain announced that the boat would be leaving and returning to the mainland in three hours with or without us.

Even before the boat was secured to the dock, I leapt off and began running toward the light beam. My dad hurried after me. A path parallel to the water led us through an ancient Native burial ground. I was awestruck to think of the meeting of two such different cultures hundreds of years ago at this very site where Captain Cook first landed, but for now I needed to focus on my vision. Part way along the path I told my dad that we had to veer off the trail. This meant making our way through ferns and several feet of undergrowth in the dense West Coast forest.

After we ventured about a hundred yards into the forest, we stopped and scanned the area. My dad said, "There isn't anything here." I replied, "I know that it's here because I can feel it."

Then we saw the bird about fifty feet in front of us (see Illustration 1). It was four feet tall, black, with piercing black eyes, just like in my vision. We walked toward it until we were within twenty feet of it. As I locked eyes with it, it telepathically delivered complex scientific information to me in the form of images. The amount of information and the delivery speed were analogous to watching many hours of a video recording in just seconds. I told my dad that the human brain wasn't meant to take in so much information. Then the bird reverted from being the messenger to being just a bird again. This was obvious to me, as I began to telepathically receive "A day in the life of a bird" images, such as what it ate for breakfast.

Once my dad decided that I was okay while experiencing such an awesome event, he went looking for my mom, who was near by, walking along the shoreline. Dad led her to where I was and pointed to the bird without saying anything. My mom remarked at what an odd location it was for a totem pole.

As my mom got closer to the bird, she saw its eyes blink and she came to a halt. She shivered and all the hairs on the back of her neck stood up at the realization that the bird was alive. I knew that the bird did not intend to hurt us or it would have attacked already. It was clear to me that it was there for some other reason.

After a few minutes, my mom left and shortly afterward returned with my grandparents and uncle. All were rendered speechless by what they saw. We took some photographs. The bird remained in the same spot the entire time, only ruffling its feathers when someone got too close for its comfort. It was such a beautiful sight that we all were in awe. Then we had to return to the boat, as three hours were nearly up.

On the voyage back to Gold River, we found it difficult to even talk about what we had seen, as it seemed so incredible and beyond words. We were all stunned by the experience. What a sixteenth birthday it had been for me.

The next morning, my dad was chatting with the local Native chief and he asked him about the bird we had seen. The chief said he didn't know of any large black birds in the area.

Illustration 1: The black bird I encountered in the forest, just like the one I had seen in my vision.

He had seen some large ravens, but not as big as the one we described. On the drive from Gold River to the ferry back home, we stopped in at a Native souvenir shop. Near its entrance stood one fairly large totem pole. A figure of a large black bird was carved at the top. I asked the shop's clerk about the bird and its habitat. She told me that it was the mythical thunderbird.

The presence of this large black bird in the exact location that I had seen in my vision had huge significance for me. It confirmed that the extraordinary events I had been experiencing for several years were real; I myself was unsure of my experiences, but when my vision manifested physically, all my doubts were eliminated. I could trust myself on my way forward, and my family was able to justify their support of me. After the vision, I no longer had any doubts within me; this greatly amplified my healing abilities and made me open to receiving through intuition much more information from the field. It gave me the confidence I needed at that time.

I downloaded so much complex information from the bird into my consciousness that, several years later, there is still much that I have not been able to decipher. And it wasn't a finite amount of information that I received. Rather, the encounter with the bird opened a gateway in me that allows a more efficient connection to knowledge from the field of information. From that point onward, I have been constantly bombarded with vast amounts of information. This information comes to me in various forms. Sometimes it's words, sometimes images, sometimes thoughts, sometimes I hear a voice. It varies depending on the type of information.

Whether what I saw in the forest that day was a raven, an eagle or a mythical thunderbird is not the point. What is important is that the bird was there in all its magnificence, just as I had foreseen. I started believing in myself. This was the beginning of my journey, a journey that has taken me to write this book.

Did the bird make any sounds?
It made a clicking sound, something like the velociraptor in the movie *Jurassic Park*.

How far away were you from the bird?
We got as close as twenty feet to it. At this point, the bird showed signs of agitation: It made clicking noises and spread its wings slightly. We then backed away, as we didn't want to irritate it.

Did the bird move?
The bird stayed in the same location the entire time that we were there. It was there for at least an hour but eventually we had to leave because the boat was leaving.

Chapter 2

The Origin of the Universe

*We all originate from a common energy,
which explains our interconnectedness.*

—ADAM

After my vision I had the confidence to trust the information that I intuitively received. A lot of information that I was receiving was related to the science behind my unusual experiences. One day I felt compelled to write down some of this information that was pouring into my mind and distracting me from everything else. I went into my bedroom and within an hour had written down fifteen pages of scientific information which seemed to just flow out from me. That information now forms the basis of this chapter.

Humans have long sought to understand the origin of the universe and the origin and nature of consciousness. How did the universe originate? Has consciousness existed from the beginning, or has it evolved from something else? At first glance, a discussion about the origin of the universe may seem remote from healing, but in fact the two topics are strongly linked.

Imagine a time before the Big Bang, the cosmic explosion that occurred sometime between ten billion and fifteen billion years ago, hurling matter in all directions and thus creating the universe. All that existed prior to this event was energy constantly flowing in a seemingly random fashion, yet synchronized at some level. This simple state of energy had been flowing for an infinite length of time. With no physical matter in existence, there was an unlimited amount of empty space.

However, empty space is not really empty at all. Rather, it is a vacuum devoid of all physical matter but full of quantum energy fluctuations, that is, spontaneous movements of energy. Scientists have theorized that there is enough energy in one cup of empty space to boil all the oceans on earth. Energy is present in the form of waves, meaning it ripples outward like ripples in a pond, radiating in all directions.

Ripples or quantum fluctuations of energy have an effect on each other. Random pulses of energy interact as they bounce off or intersect with each other. Imagine watching ripples in the pond during a rainstorm. Sometimes the ripples converge and form a larger ripple. When ripples converge, the waves can amplify each other. Similarly, energy fluctuations accumulate at intersections, thereby increasing the concentration of energy in a specific area.

When there is a higher concentration of energy in a particular region of space, the probability of a quantum particle being manifested from energy fluctuations is increased (see Illustration 2). The probability of quantum fluctuations intersecting in the specific way necessary to produce matter is infinitesimally small, but there was an infinite amount of time before the Big Bang. When the fluctuations did intersect in a specific way, the first quantum particle was created, and the Big Bang occurred. Since the Big Bang occurred instantly, rather than being a long process, it is more accurate to say that we all originate from a common energy event rather than from a particle.

I have often heard people ask, how can something come from nothing? But this question implies that matter is something and energy is nothing. This could not be further from the truth. When matter is broken down, it is simply energy. Scientists have mathematically proven that a particle can be

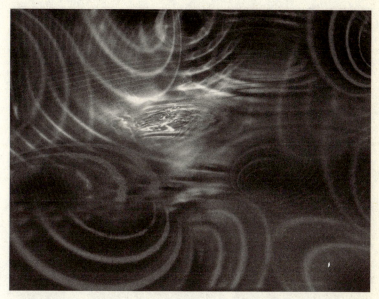
Illustration 2: Ripples of energy in empty space before the Big Bang.

manifested from the energy fluctuations in so-called empty space. Recently, physicists have demonstrated this theory by generating a particle solely out of such energy: They have shown it is possible to generate "something" from "nothing."

The mechanism that initiated and drove the Big Bang and that continues to drive the evolution of the universe is actually quite simple. The catalyst was gravity, which is the physical force that attracts particles to each other. With the manifestation of the first particle came the phenomenon of gravitational force (see Illustration 3). Although the first matter may have been only a tiny subatomic particle, its small gravitational field was enough to instantly initiate the Big Bang. Before this point, there was no gravitational field because there was no matter, and gravity doesn't exist without matter. As gravity attracted more energy, more particles manifested. As the

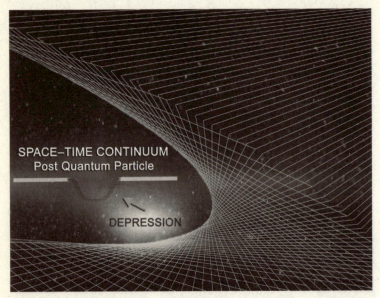

Illustration 3: The manifestation of the first particle of matter created a depression in the space–time continuum; the particle's tiny gravitational force was enough to initiate the Big Bang.

number of particles increased, so did the gravitational pull, attracting even more energy.

All matter is simply energy oriented in such a way that it forms a bend in the space-time continuum. Bends in space-time cause the attraction of particles and a distortion in time. Time passes more slowly around a strong gravitational field than a weak one. If it were possible for someone to go very close to a black hole, time would pass slower for that person than someone who was farther away from it. A black hole is such a concentrated mass that gravity prevents anything from escaping from it. Extreme gravitational forces distort time very noticeably. Even small subatomic particles distort time and affect gravity in a similar way, although much more subtly than a black hole.

Albert Einstein described gravity by using the analogy of depressions in a mattress. After the creation of the first quantum particle, the previously level space-time continuum had a slight depression, making it no longer perfectly level. The mattress analogy is very useful for understanding how gravity works. An object in space, such as a meteor, has a tendency to fall back to earth, just as an object on the end of a mattress has a tendency to roll toward the depression.

Energy has the tendency to collect in this depression in space. The energy collected there tends to take on similar properties to that of the original space-time bending energy when it comes in close proximity to it. This will in turn cause the small space-time bend to increase. The more the bend increases, the faster it collects more energy. As more energy collects around this particle, more particles are created, in a domino-like effect. As more particles are created, the bend or depression becomes deeper, attracting more energy.

This process happens at a phenomenal rate. When the particles are initially manifested, they are at a very high temperature. Because of this, they have a very high velocity, and so rapidly burst out from their point of origin. These escaping particles then initiate the same process over again. It is quite easy to see how this could accelerate exponentially. Newly formed particles start shooting out particles. When a particle gets forced out, it creates its own depression, thus repeating the process.

What ended the process the Big Bang initiated? As more particles are manifested, the empty space surrounding these particles slowly becomes depleted of its energy. This energy did not disappear, however; it was simply transformed into matter. Of course, empty space never becomes completely exhausted of its energy, but it becomes depleted to the point where it can no longer spontaneously manifest particles. This is why if I place an object in a vacuum, I am not going to initiate another Big Bang.

This raises an interesting point. The "empty space" within the known universe must be different from the "empty space" outside our universe. Logically, the empty space within the universe contains less energy because some of the energy has been converted to matter. The empty space outside the universe contains more energy, as it has not converted any energy into matter. I refer to this space beyond our known universe as virgin space. The border between these two types of space is very gradual, likely billions of light years. Of course, there is no known way to confirm that there is a difference in the two types of space until we find a way to travel to the edge of the universe.

While there is still much we don't know about our universe, the most important concept to understand about the origin of the universe is that everything is interconnected. If you were able to freeze time just prior to the Big Bang, you would see that for an instant only one common energy—one singularity—existed. Everything in the universe originated from this singularity, and therefore everything in the universe shares a connection to everything else. The result is our web of interconnectedness. The term for this web of interconnected frequencies connecting all of the information in the universe is "the field of information." Any change in one event in this web affects the whole web or universe; everyone and everything is linked. You are one with the universe.

This interconnectedness explains your fundamental ability to influence your life and consequently your health. Think of this interconnecting web of energy and information in a comforting way. Imagine the threads of interconnectivity forming a hammock in which you can relax. The webbing holds you and enfolds you easily and comfortably.

Why did nature produce a Big Bang in the first place?

One of the basic laws of the universe is that everything always seeks the state of minimal energy. The Big Bang occurred in an effort to reach minimal energy. It was energetically favorable for the Big Bang to occur as a result of a rare complex interaction from the energy in empty space before the Big Bang.

Can energy exist without matter?

Energy can exist without matter, as it did before the Big Bang. Matter is simply a form of energy. The quantum model of the atom shows that there is nothing tangible in matter: Matter does not exist but is simply energy vibrations. Energy did not magically appear at some point in time: It always was and always will be present in empty space. This energy keeps space stable.

Did time exist before the Big Bang?

Yes, time existed prior to the Big Bang; however, there was no matter in existence to reference time. All that existed was the energy fluctuations of empty space. Energy, of course, does not necessarily move in any predictable manner with regard to time. That is why it is difficult to reference time before the Big Bang.

Chapter 3

The Field of Information

*The field is a vast sea of information
without boundaries or separations.*

—ADAM

Often I spontaneously pick up information from the field. When I go into a person's holographic information in order to heal, along with seeing the health concern, I also intuitively pick up related data. For instance, I examined a man with severe back pain. He had been to see the orthopedic surgeon several days before and was considering surgery to fuse his spine. I told him that the problem was lateral instability and drew a diagram of the problem to illustrate it. He was flabbergasted. Not only was the illustration exactly the same as the one the doctor had sketched for him just days before, but "lateral instability" were the exact words the doctor had used to describe his back problem. This information was data I had intuitively picked up. The man decided not to have the surgery, and I continued with my energy treatment on him. Now, years later, this man's back has not bothered him since.

The field where I accessed this information is the cumulative collection of all information about everything in the universe and its connection to everything else. The field includes all places and all times simultaneously: It includes links to past, present and all possible future events; it therefore contains all possible outcomes. The field provides a template for this information exchange. Think of it as an infinite sea that transcends all space between matter, energy and time.

The field existed before the Big Bang, when only quantum fluctuations and no matter existed, but in a very simple form. With the occurrence of the Big Bang, this field of information became increasingly dynamic and complex as matter created more matter.

To again use the analogy of a radio, imagine your mind as a radio receiver that is tuning in to various frequencies. You are able to select from many stations, and which one you choose depends on your desire—news, weather, sports or music. You adjust the dial until the reception is as clear as possible. Once you have tuned into a particular station, you aren't able to hear the other stations, yet you know they exist. The field is similar in that all of the information you need is available to you; the information you access depends on your particular need. The visualizations I suggest in Part 3 are one way to access and use information from the field.

Usually, I access health information by using a face photograph of a person, connecting through the eyes. This is the most effective access point for me. However, information is everywhere. Some people make a connection through voice, such as a phone call. Sometimes I do too, although this is not a connection I can depend on.

My mom received a phone call from a man interested in my healing techniques. While she was on the phone with him, I walked in from another room. She asked me if I would do a treatment on the man. I asked for his name and when I got the reply, I blurted out, "The sciatic nerve is involved and that is why his leg is so painful. I don't see any more cancer though."

My mom didn't know at that point what the man's health challenge was, and she repeated to him exactly what I had said. For several moments he was speechless. Then he confirmed that he had just had a cancerous growth removed from his leg and it had been wrapped around his sciatic nerve.

We all have access to the same information. An infinite amount of information is passing through you at any given time. Your brain acts as the filtering mechanism by constantly selecting the information that it determines relevant. This is how we instantaneously decipher and analyze the incoming signals to obtain information that is useful to us. It must be decoded to be meaningful.

We all are equally connected to the field. This makes us truly one within this dynamic web of connectivity. A self separate from everyone else is an illusionary concept, created merely for our own purposes of human definition or for convenience. We must realize that we are all energy from the same source and that our individual realities are subjective. You can influence how you perceive your reality in any way you wish.

The field is the archive of universal information on both microscopic and macroscopic levels. It assists in the coordination of every cell within our bodies in order for the cells to exchange intelligent data. Even our growth and thought patterns are part of this communication, as well as memory, emotions and health issues. The field also contains all data about the planets and all celestial bodies in our universe, including the first quantum fluctuation. From the smallest subatomic particle to the immense, the field connects everything and everyone. One does not have to travel to a specific location to receive specific information from the field. The entire field is at all points in the universe at all times. This means that anytime or anywhere, you are always connected to all of the information in the universe.

Most psychic phenomena can be better understood utilizing this concept of a universal field of information. Because the field is everywhere at all times, any change in the field instantly influences the entire universe. This explains nonlocal influences, or action-at-a-distance, as I discuss in the Introduction. Some people are more skilled than others at focusing their connection to this information field; they are said to have psychic, telepathic or telekinetic capabilities. That is, reading information obtained nonlocally from the field is often labeled as paranormal. But the key word in the phrase "more skilled" is "more." We all possess these capacities, which can be developed further with practice.

I am fortunate to have been given the natural talent of being able to easily and selectively access intuitive information from the field. This includes the information in this book about the origin of the universe. It includes the ability to view the hologram—the three-dimensional projection containing all the information of a person—either locally or at a distance and thus facilitate healing. These are examples of intuitive perception that I am tuned to in my everyday life. Other abilities such as telepathy, clairvoyance, remote viewing and telekinesis seem to be part of or related to the same gift of being able to easily access the field. These abilities sometimes are referred to as a sixth sense.

Telepathy is the process of using mental images for communication rather than more commonly accepted means, such as writing and speaking. When both the sender and receiver are proficient at it, telepathy is an extremely efficient way to exchange information. Every one of us has the ability to communicate in this way, and it can be practiced just like any other skill. For people who have never tried this form of communication, it will seem like a huge challenge, similar to attempting to speak for the first time as an adult: One would not even have developed the facial muscles to enunciate words. Yet, with strong intention and focused practice, we can all become more aware of our ability to communicate telepathically.

Telepathy and healing operate essentially by the same mechanism. Healing is simply a focused, intentional kind of telepathy. In other words, telepathy in general is the mental transfer of various types of information, whereas healing is the transfer of information with the intent of influencing a person's health.

I have learned that there are two types of telepathy: local and nonlocal. Local telepathy involves sending and receiving mental images during a face-to-face conversation. Light emitted from one person influences the other person. Local telepathy (see Illustration 4) works via the field and also by an exchange of light locally, whereas nonlocal telepathy occurs solely by influencing the field of information. Light would not be able to efficiently carry information from one person to another over great distances without the field. When telepathically communicating with someone who is geographically distant, it is necessary to pick up and receive the images through your connection with the field.

I have occasionally met people with whom I can engage in

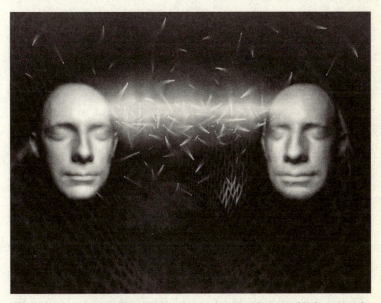

Illustration 4: Local telepathy involves a direct exchange of light emitted from one person and influencing another person.

a telepathic conversation. For instance, I communicated telepathically with a shaman at a First Nations healing gathering in which I was participating. If another person and I are particularly aligned—that is, if the light frequency we emit is similar—then information can be transferred back and forth easily. I have found that when speaking aloud afterward, speech seems a crude form of communication and an awkward means of exchanging information in comparison to telepathic imaging.

Telepathic communication is not limited to people with similar light frequencies. It is happening all the time on a subconscious level, whether you are emitting a frequency similar to the other person's or not. But on a conscious level, telepathic communication can be more difficult between different frequencies. With practice, all of us can improve our telepathic communication skills by paying attention to our subtle feelings and thoughts.

Clairvoyance is the ability to perceive things beyond the usual five senses of sight, hearing, taste, smell and touch. We have all heard of detective mysteries that are solved through the information provided by a psychic. The clairvoyant is proficient at connecting information in the field to the crime. Some clairvoyants access this connection through a piece of the victim's clothing. Others connect through names, locations, voices or photographs. Each psychic has his or her own way of working. The striking commonality is that a point of reference, or intersection of the information, must occur between the psychic and an object with which the victim had some attachment. This is how information becomes forever entangled from this meeting point on.

Remote viewing is the ability to "see" images or events in another geographical location by going beyond our everyday perceptual means and accessing the field. An example of remote viewing is observing a distant scene during an out-of-body experience. I have remotely viewed my dad's office during an out-of-body experience and correctly identified items in the room. I have also experimented several times with reading street signs remotely, with some success.

When I was fifteen, I tried to remote view my uncle's house. I found myself in an out-of-body experience and in the area of my uncle's house. While trying to figure out exactly where I was, I looked at a street sign. It said "Empire Street"—not a road that I knew. When I looked at a map of the area, I learned that Empire Street is a couple of blocks from my uncle's house. I tried to remote view his house again and eventually found it. I believe remote viewing, like telepathy and clairvoyance, is a skill that can be developed by any one of us.

Telekinesis is the ability to move objects by energetic means instead of physical means. When this has happened around me, it has been without any conscious plan on my part. In high school, my pen flew out of my hand many times. This occurred primarily when I was daydreaming and had no particular thoughts at all in my mind. On another occasion, I reached out to grab a nasal spray container. Just before I touched it, it launched into the air and hit the ceiling with great force. My dad, who was in the room with me, was shocked.

Some people are able to influence the physical realm remotely through intention. They can access information about an object from the field and modify that object's properties. For instance, Uri Geller, possibly one of the world's most famous psychics, bends spoons this way.

Accessing the field, especially nonlocally, also explains how distant healing works. The intention of one person affects the field locally, which then influences the other person nonlocally via the field. The field amplifies our every intent and influences changes accordingly, far beyond our conscious awareness.

When healing a person at a distance, I request a color photograph of that person's face. From the photo, I project the person's hologram in front of me. I don't understand exactly how this happens, but I instantly receive information on the person's health in the form of holograms, which appear before me.

To facilitate healing, I energetically alter the flow of energy to its optimal state, while paying special attention to areas where the energy appears stagnant, blocked or unusual. I describe to the person the problem areas as they appear to me. What I see depends on the subset of the person's internal information that I am exploring in the hologram. For example, if someone has chronic back pain, I would access the skeletal view of that person's health information. This view allows me to see where the pain originates. I am also able to get more detailed information at a cellular level should this be needed. With the information, I am then able to manipulate through my healing intentions the energy needed for that person's health to change. I mentally adjust the energy to its maximum potential for healing by removing energy blockages. The energetic change instantaneously influences that person's hologram, which in turn registers in that person's body.

How long the energy takes to adjust depends on the person and the ailment; it could be hours, days, weeks or even months. I get some sense at the time of treatment of how efficiently the person has received the new information, and it varies greatly. With some people, it appears to me, when I see how they react energetically to a treatment, that they have made the energetic shift, yet almost immediately they revert to their original health pattern. Their health challenge just bounces back. Changes sometimes seem to be very elastic, which is evident to me when I see their hologram again, perhaps for another treatment. They have energetically reverted to the energy pattern of their original health problem. This tells me that changes will likely not be lasting or permanent.

The Field of Information

The results that I get from my healings are directly related to the receptivity of the healee. This is why it is so important to review our openness to our energy and its healing possibilities. There are several possible reasons for achieving limited results in certain situations. We can be interfering in our healing potential by having self-limiting beliefs. Take the game of catch, for instance. Throwing the ball accurately is only half the game. To have a game going at all, the recipient or catcher must do his or her part. All the best pitches in the world won't lead to a game unless someone is there willing and able to catch the ball. Likewise, you must be receptive in order for energy healing to work. It is important to accept and know that energy healing will work. My hope is that by explaining the science behind energy healing, you are able to better understand it and work with it. Don't be afraid to catch the ball: You are in the game, whether you think you are or not. Learn how to be the most effective player you can be.

We may not always be consciously aware of what our beliefs are. If our conscious intent is not synchronized with our subconscious ideas, then we are sending mixed signals into the field. We ourselves must be clear about what we want and expect from an energy healing. Some people are very well read on energy healing and yet they still may be inflexible in accepting healing information that may help their situation. Embracing the new means embracing change. This may be the most difficult requirement of all, as change is often unsettling. It is important to sometimes approach something new by knowing nothing, yet feeling everything. That is, the paradigms that we have all learned through academia and life experience play a major role in what we can and can't accept; when we are able to truly let go of the conscious restraints that we place on ourselves, we will react to our gut feeling.

There are a small number of people I've treated with whom I believe I do have an energetic connection, yet it doesn't seem to be an effective one. Perhaps our frequencies are not working together coherently. Or perhaps there are conflicting energies, similar to when an energy wave and an inverse energy wave meet and cancel each other out, with a resulting nil effect. This is not because of any conscious effort on the part of the healer or healee, but nevertheless it does effectively block any energy healing attempts. I hope in future to have a better understanding of this so I may be able to connect more effectively in such situations.

In energy healing, as in life in general, the bottom line is attitude. Our attitudes stem from our beliefs. They guide us forward or backward depending on how we shape our reality: It is all a matter of one's perspective. The field responds to our every intention if we make it clear what that is. Ancient prophets and mystics were well aware of our connection to everything and the flow of nonlocal information that goes hand in hand with one's perspective. In many societies, the ruler—whether king or queen, emperor or empress, or chief—never made major decisions without consulting his or her prophets. Western cultures, in general, have lost respect for this way of knowing.

Many non-Western cultures are much more accepting than Western culture is of what exists beyond our five senses. Views within Western culture have become narrow and intolerant. We can readily accept that dogs can hear frequencies beyond our range, yet if humans hear anything that is beyond typical sensitivity, they are labeled odd or different. The same attitude prevails for unusual perception with any of the other four senses. Yet, all other animals rely heavily on the information they receive from the field. Many events occur in nature in which survival depends on accurately interpreting extrasensory information.

It seems to me that all of these psychic abilities—telepathy, clairvoyance, remote viewing, telekinesis and distant healing—are interlinked and interrelated. They all involve accessing the field of information for answers. If answers seem to come more easily for some, it is because those people are more focused when they ask a question. The field responds to what is asked of it.

You can influence greater change with your intentions by understanding how to clearly focus them in order to affect events. It is also possible to connect to more information by becoming aware of how you are habitually filtering the information which is continually running through you. By intentionally altering your filtering processes, you allow yourself to get in touch with more information vital to your well-being. These concepts are discussed in more detail in Chapters 6 and 7.

Our sixth sense—intuition—is similar to the other five senses in that we can fine-tune and sharpen it. Imagine someone who has never paid any attention to artwork critiquing a painting. Then imagine an artist evaluating the same painting. Who would have the most comprehensive perception of the painting? The artist. The master artist has developed his or her ability to see form and color. The sense of hearing works the same way. If you need a critical analysis of a symphony, a professional musician would be the best person to make an informed critique. Of course, the critique would be based on an existing knowledge base. The disciplined development of any of our five senses takes dedication and practice; our sixth sense is no different.

You can exercise your connection to frequencies from the field just like exercising a muscle. The more you exercise and use it on a regular basis, the more efficiently you can tune in to it. You can practice by paying more attention to your intuition, or gut instinct. When you feel very strongly about something, trust these feelings and act upon them.

Artists do not achieve mastery overnight. Some may

become aware of their talents at a young age, long before they begin formal study. Most musicians in a symphony orchestra, even though talented, must spend years studying and practicing to qualify for the job. One needs passion and perseverance for the development of any talent. At the same time, anyone can enjoy art or music, whether exceptionally talented or not. Self-realization is about making the most of our own special gifts and fully appreciating the special gifts of others.

Through examining your belief systems (a topic I elaborate on in Chapter 7), you can learn to have better control of the flow of data from the field to you. This is the essence of self-empowerment. Ultimately, your thoughts and actions are your responsibility. We all have the ability through intention to project this energy from the field into our physical world. Your thoughts can and do influence your reality. You are always an active participant in the universal reality.

The field of information extends to all inanimate objects as well. For instance, I always insist that water be present during my workshops. With the positive healing intentions of the five hundred people present, the energy in the room is powerful. I can feel that the energetic properties of the water are intensified. This is how I know that water is affected by the intentions, thoughts and feelings it is exposed to. In a domino-like effect, thoughts affect you and everyone around you, as well as the air and water near you. We are surrounded by lakes, rivers and oceans; our atmosphere contains water; we ourselves are composed mostly of water. This is why the impact that good intentions have on water will be present all over our water abundant planet.

Is the field "out there" or within us, or both?
Both. The field is all places at all times. The entire field is at all points in space at all times.

How can I receive information from the field more easily?
Is there any way to strengthen my connection to it?
The best way to get information more easily is to understand where you are picking up the information from—namely, the field. Just know that you are connecting to this source of information which is being funneled through you. If you accept that all of the information in the universe is running through you, it's then just a matter of using your intuition to choose which information is important to you and acting on it. Become aware of how you are habitually filtering the information that is continually running through you from the field. Pay attention to your hunches and act on them. The best way to strengthen your connection to the field is thinking of your intuition as a muscle. Exercise it until it's stronger.

Is just asking a question in your mind the way to ask a question of the field?
Yes. I like to clear my mind of all thoughts and then ask myself the question, and see what comes to my attention in this calm state of awareness.

Chapter 4

Symphony of Light

Every cell is influenced and directed by light.

—ADAM

At my workshops I often do aura readings on several participants. What I see varies from person to person, but in the vast majority of readings, what I see strongly correlates with the physical ailment that the person is already aware of. For example, in the auras of people with sciatic nerve problems, there are defined distortions over the sciatic nerve. I can see a jagged glowing or throbbing of light at the source of the pain. The pain radiates along the nerve pathway, sending the person's back into spasms. If I go in and do an energy treatment holographically, I see this light gradually dim in its intensity and become smoother as it sets into its new pattern of harmonious flow.

AURAS

The flow of energy in a harmonious pattern of light emissions is the basis of all healthy life forms. Light coordinates all life processes. Life is a veritable symphony of light.

Throughout history there have been people such as Edgar Cayce who have been able to see the light that is emitted from all forms of life; that is, the aura. Cayce (1877–1945) is best known as a psychic medical diagnostician and a reader of past lives. Many healers who can see or feel auras perceive a lot of information about the person whose aura they are viewing. The aura is subtle energy, a form of light at a particular frequency that is radiating from the living organism. Each of us radiates information through this aura. The harmonization of the light energy defines life itself, from the subatomic level to the cellular, to the whole organism and beyond. Subtle energy, the energy of life, is known by various names in different cultures. The Chinese refer to it as *qi* (pronounced "chi"), the Japanese as *ki* ("key"), and Hindus as *prana*.

Light is affected by illness—both disease and injury—as the body experiences change. Our bodies are constantly adjusting to differences, physical as well as psychological, in our well-being. I can see that through intentions we are consciously able to influence the light inside our bodies, which is in turn reflected and emitted outside of our bodies as an aura. Our bodies respond to every thought we think and every word we speak. We are directly affected physically by our feelings and intentions. Knowing this, each of us can maximize our well-being physically, emotionally and spiritually.

This light energy, or aura, connects us all to each other through information being communicated through it. Within our bodies, our cells use this vehicle of communication. By capitalizing on this concept, we are each empowered to re-create our optimal health. This, however, is just the beginning. Through this subtle energy we are all linked in a universal web of energy. Everything is just energy within a complex vibrating web. By helping ourselves through intention, we are positively influencing every other person and every other organism everywhere. Through manifesting our own empowerment, we naturally extend our awareness to a group consciousness, a global consciousness, and beyond these bounds to a universal consciousness. Thought has no boundaries.

Our thoughts and intentions create our reality by attracting what we are focusing on. Positive thoughts and expectations will bring positive results. For instance, I, like many athletes, practice positive thinking when I am weight training. When striving for a higher goal, such as benching a heavier weight or increasing the number of repetitions, I see the successful completion of the task in my mind's eye. The desired physical results are realized through intention of them. Of course, your goal must be a realistic one that you determine in increments. Expecting to win a marathon without adequate training is inconsistent with what your true expectations are. However, aiming to run five miles the first week, and ten miles the next week, increasing your endurance gradually, is a realistic goal. If you are already a marathon runner, wanting to better your race time is a realistic goal to work toward.

Learn ways to most efficiently access this ability to create your own reality that is within us all. Send yourself an intense message of what you want and focus on that. Be sure that your conscious thoughts are synchronized with your subconscious thoughts; this is analogous to making sure your goals are realistic. I explain this further in Chapter 5, on consciousness.

It is essential for people with health challenges to eliminate any underlying doubts or fears that they may feel about their way forward. Positive thoughts cannot be used to gloss over fundamental feelings of fear and negativity. Everyone's goal should be to replace nonconstructive thoughts and feelings with pure positive direction. Your body will reward you with a stronger immune system, more balanced emotions and a comforted spirit.

Every cell in the body responds to the subtle energy of light. Scientists typically view the body as a machine with biochemical reactions. In the future, science will verify what the ancient mystics knew: that energy is the most basic characteristic of life. These mystics had a deep understanding of many things for which there are no measuring instruments. Many of science's unknowns will be replaced by revolutionary knowns as measuring devices become more sophisticated. But whether humankind is capable of producing a machine sophisticated enough to measure the essence of life energy remains to be seen.

DNA is considered the basis of all life forms. It is responsible for the construction of our physical bodies and the replacement of cells as they become worn out. While DNA clearly is the blueprint of life for cellular reproduction, its information is dynamic, interactive and adaptable. Our DNA is not written in stone. I can see that our genetic makeup can be influenced through subtle energy. With every intention, you are emitting light that influences your DNA. Your intentions are constantly influencing your evolution.

In other words, thoughts and feelings can influence and reprogram our physical selves. By influencing our genetic codes, we are reprogramming its language and making adjustments to our holographic information. The people I have worked with on their healing journeys have taught me a great deal. In my first book, *DreamHealer,* I discussed the genetic holographic image, but I was uncertain as to how to work with it. I now have a much better understanding of it. As my learning has continued, I have had the opportunity to work with several people on their genetic disorders. I have learned that the information contained within DNA can be flexible. We can influence any aspect of ourselves.

Your genetic makeup influences how you react to your environment, but you still have a great deal of choice. DNA is dynamic and reacts to your environment. Intentions are part of that environment. This is the process that drives the evolution of all living organisms, including humans. For example, part of Nepal lies in the foothills of the Himalayas. One group of people who live there, the Sherpas, act as guides for the adventurers climbing Mount Everest. For many generations, these mountain dwellers have had to use oxygen more effectively in their bodies because of the high altitude where they live. Over time this trait has become engrained in the genetic makeup of the Sherpas.

How we react to our environment is dynamic. Our pattern of wellness, which is reflected in our energy, is also dynamic. It is easy to enhance the connection that we have with our own energy.

ENERGY EXERCISES

The following exercises will help you develop your skills in feeling and seeing your own energy, and then bringing in universal energy to your body.

Feel Your Energy

1. Rub your palms together in a circular motion. Feel the generation of heat. This is your own energy.
2. Now hold your hands about two inches apart, palm to palm. Push your hands toward one another without actually moving them. That is, visualize your hands pushing toward one another. Feel the resistance, similar to two like magnets repelling each other.
3. Spread your hands varying distances apart and feel the same resistance.
4. Establish the threshold distance at which your palms can be separated and you still feel your energy. With practice, you will be able to increase this distance as you become more sensitive to energy.

Illustration 5 depicts both the energy around your hands and the resistance you should feel when doing this exercise.

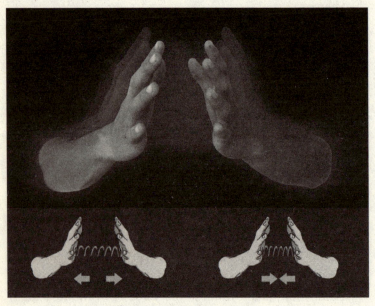

Illustration 5: Feel your energy.

See Your Energy

1. Against a dark background, hold your hands in front of you with your fingertips pointing to the fingertips of the other hand, about two inches apart (see Illustration 6).
2. Move your fingers slowly up and down and in and out. Think about the energy flowing from one fingertip to the other. You will see a faint line of energy passing between them. At first this may appear as a hazy band.

Practice this exercise against backgrounds of various colors. With practice, the energy flow will look more defined.

Bring in Universal Energy

1. Imagine all the energy of the universe circling above your head, available for your use (see Illustration 7).
2. Bring in energy through the top of your head and collect it in your heart area.
3. Send the energy from the heart area down through your right arm, through your right fingertips, back into your left fingers and up through your left arm and to the heart.
4. Continue to imagine this flow as an energy circuit: from your heart to right arm, right hand, right fingertips, to left fingertips, left arm and then to the heart.

At first you may see just a faint line. You will be surprised at how quickly, with practice, you will see defined energy flow.

How to See a Person's Aura

Look past the person whose aura you want to see. Concentrate on an area about two inches above the shoulders or head (see Illustration 8).

At first you may see a slight shimmering aura, similar to the one shown in Illustration 9. The aura may appear as a

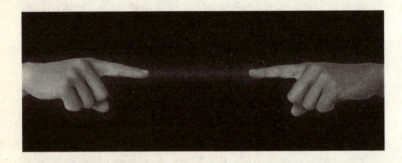

Illustration 6: See your energy.

Illustration 7: Bird's-eye view of bringing in universal energy.

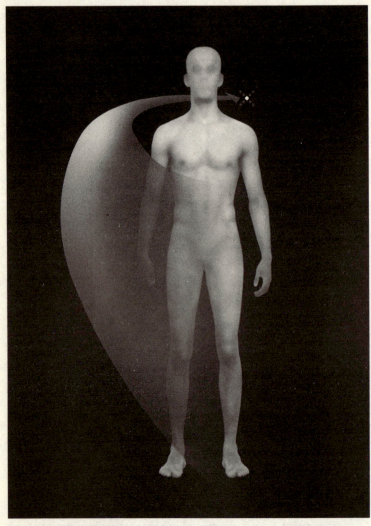
Illustration 8: Seeing an aura: Focus on a spot behind the person.

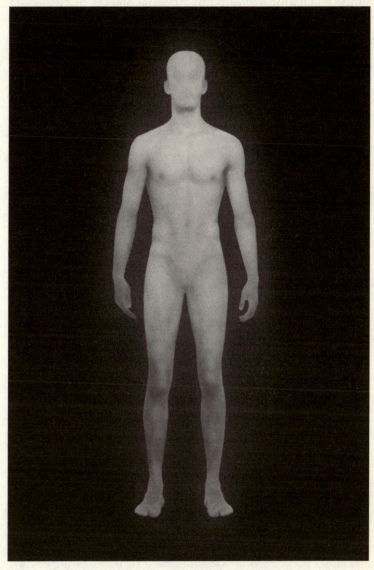

Illustration 9: A slight, shimmering aura.

subtle emanation surrounding material objects. Some people describe this as similar to heat waves, others as a misty fog. It will likely be far easier to see the aura after you've done a treatment using the visualizations discussed in Part 3 of this book. Few people will see the aura with the color intensity shown in Illustration 10, but with practice, you may see the defined flowing colors. Keep practicing!

How to See the Flow of Energy

A body without injury or illness would have harmonious energy flow. A body developing an injury or illness has energy that is beginning to lose its path or direction. A body with a fully developed injury or illness has a break in the energy flow, as depicted in Illustration 11, and can't find its way back to a harmonious energy flow, or wellness. Here is an advanced exercise to see energy flow; keep it in mind as a long-term goal.

1. Stand in front of a full-length mirror.
2. Relax your eyes by not focusing on anything.
3. Practice seeing and feeling your own energy flow.

Try doing this in both light and dark conditions. You can do this exercise with another person as well, practicing to see each other's energy flow. At first, you may be guided primarily by intuition—by feeling the energy. Soon you will be able to see it as well. As you develop this skill, you will find that your intuitive sense increases along with your healing ability. Trust that you can do this.

Everything that we tell our bodies through thoughts, words, emotions and beliefs is communicated through subtle energy, that is, through various frequencies of light. Subtle energies have a wide range of frequencies. Effectively connecting to this energy is a skill each of us can master by developing our inner processes

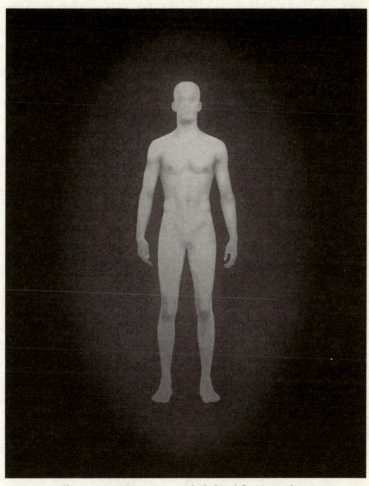
Illustration 10: An aura with defined flowing colors.

of feeling, "seeing" and knowing. It is up to each of us to recognize this communication skill that we can consciously access. Intention is the most powerful tool for this process. We must get in touch with our own awareness.

Reading Auras

As I mentioned earlier, usually at my workshops I call upon several volunteers and read their auras. What shows up in the auras is more than an indication of what is happening physically. The aura reflects a variety of information, ranging from the emotional makeup of the person to his or her thoughts and intentions. With all the movement of energy in the aura, it is generally not possible to pinpoint the exact location of the physical ailment, but it is possible to determine the general area of the problem.

Each illness looks slightly different in the aura. As well, every aura has many variations, suggestive of minor blockages or potential difficulties. So my challenge when reading an aura is not so much to find physical problems but to sort through all the blockages and potential problems and select the one that is likely to be bothering the person most.

Certain ailments have definite signatures on the aura. Problems with the sciatic nerve are generally easy to see, as they look almost the same on everyone. When an aura has a static look, similar to a blurry television screen, this generally indicates that there is a problem with the nerves, emotions or skin.

Anyone can practice reading auras by looking at an aura in a dark room. Many people will see what looks like distortions over certain areas of the person's body. These distortions will likely appear over a region that is bothering the person. However, do not be discouraged if the person cannot make sense of what you relate: The aura shows a variety of factors,

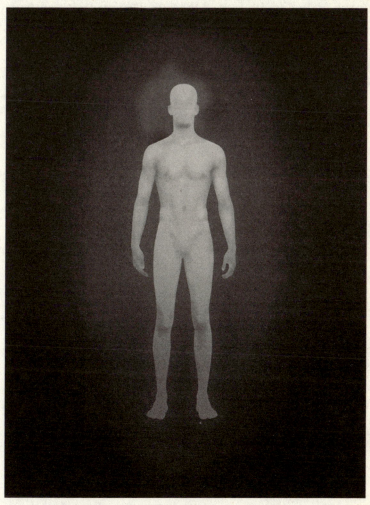

Illustration 11: A break in the aura, in the head area.

including old problems, emotional problems and developing problems. Medications tend to add a cloudiness, making it much more difficult to read the aura. Do not strain your eyes looking at a specific area on the person. Scan the entire body and pay attention to the information that comes to you. Practice this, and you will be surprised at how accurate you become.

Another point to keep in mind when reading someone's aura is that pain felt in one location does not necessarily mean this is where the source of the problem is. You might pick up on an area that seems unrelated to where the person experiences the pain, but they may in fact be closely linked.

If you are not seeing anything at all when trying to read someone's aura, practice relaxing and using your intuition. Ask yourself, what is wrong with this person? and the first thing that pops into your head may be significant. This non-analytical approach allows you to practice the development of your intuition.

The following Advanced Aura Reading Exercise will be difficult to master, and you might want to first practice the exercise on page 355, How to See a Person's Aura. This is an advanced exercise because it requires integrating left-brain activities, or logical thinking, with the holistic view of the right brain. You must be open-minded and try it without hesitation. The only thing holding you back is your own mind. Just relax and feel it. This exercise will help you trust your intuition. Once you master the skill of combining your left- and right-brain activities, it becomes easy.

Advanced Aura Reading Exercise
1. Visualize energy extensions coming out of your fingertips, similar to claws or chopsticks.
2. Put your hands several inches above the person's body and

physically comb the aura with your fingers, letting the energetic extensions of your fingertips penetrate deep into the person's body.
3. Run your hands along the aura very slowly and smoothly until you feel a dull pain, a sensation in your fingertips or a slight resistance similar to two like magnets repelling each other. At this point there is an energy blockage, which likely indicates a physical ailment of some sort.
4. Once you have identified the location of the blockage on the aura, attempt to remove the blockage. This is the difficult part.
5. You must keep pinching the blockage and pulling it away from the aura. Do not worry about these blockages affecting your health; they will not affect you if your intention is to not be affected by them. If you are worrying about this, then you likely have some subconscious intent to pull the energy blockage into yourself. Do not worry about it and nothing negative will happen. No negative outcome will occur when your intent is positive.

Moving your hands will help you in your visualization of removing the energy blockage. In your mind's eye, picture grabbing onto a problem in the aura and throwing it away. Simultaneously, physically move your hands on the person's aura. The aura will be physically influenced by your hand movements.
6. Dispose of the energy blockages by throwing them into the garbage, a vacuum or a black hole. Let your imagination dictate this. The energy of problems will dissipate without a host organism.

Combing Your Energy

Use this technique to give yourself a massage of light energy. Visualize light emitting from your fingertips as pure white light of pure intentions (see Illustration 12). Usually it can first be seen as smoke-like extensions from the fingertips or faint shimmering lines. Some people report seeing small bolts of lightning. Relax and let it flow.

1. Imagine that your energy fingertips are like a comb. Sometimes your energy, like your hair, gets knots and tangles in it. Use your energy fingernails to comb out these knots so that your energy flows smoothly again.
2. Start at the top of your head and "comb down" over your entire body, about two inches out from your body. No actual physical contact is necessary. Feel and see the energy. It now flows smoothly and effortlessly in a harmonious pattern.
3. Comb the energy down to your feet and out through your soles. Many people feel an immediate calming sensation when doing this.

It may be easier for you to feel rather than think about what is happening, making energy healing a more realistic experience for you. Try changing the colors of light emanating from your fingertips and feeling the variations. You will know what suits you best when you find what color (frequency) you resonate with most effectively: You will feel sensations such as tingling or heat. Always be ready and willing to alter your visualizations and techniques. Only you can assess what works best for you. Know that you are doing these techniques correctly and that you are on the right path.

You can comb someone else's energy as well as your own using this technique.

Children usually feel an intense calming immediately; I find it to be especially effective with hyperactive children. Pets love it, too.

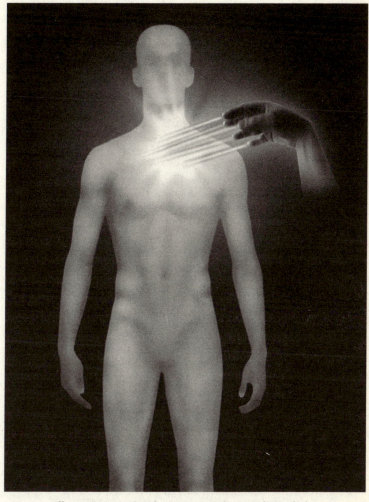

Illustration 12: Comb your energy by visualizing light extending from your fingertips; use it to give yourself a massage of light energy.

I believe everyone has the ability to heal themselves and others. This is built into our physical, emotional and spiritual natures as human beings. Some people are born with more innate readiness to use this ability than others. As with any talent, the time it takes each person to master reading auras will vary. Ultimately, it is a matter of motivation and practice.

In the realm of subtle energies, it is difficult to translate into words what is more of a nonverbal knowing. As you become more familiar with these exercises and skills you will become more familiar with trusting your feelings and your sense of knowing.

I have learned so much from working with many people who understand the power we all have to re-create our own health. Everything can be positively adjusted as we become tuned to the power of thought. I hope to be able to use this information to help others in many types of situations. One of my goals is to set up teaching centers so I can teach people some of my techniques. There are no bounds to what we can achieve in the re-creation of ourselves.

BIOPHOTONS

Biophoton emission is the scientific term for the communication and flow of subtle energy and information in the form of light between living cells and organisms. I offer the following brief scientific overview of biophoton emissions for those interested in the technical aspect. In your own healing, it is necessary to know only what you are going to change and how you plan to go about it. However, the science behind understanding healing may help some people put together the pieces of the puzzle.

Every time a chemical bond forms, light is absorbed in that

bond (see Illustration 13). Every time a chemical bond breaks, light is emitted (see Illustration 14). At any given point in your body, there are trillions of chemical bonds forming and breaking; therefore, light is constantly being absorbed and emitted in your body. This light plays an essential role in catalyzing or inhibiting various chemical reactions throughout the body.

Every chemical bond that forms has an ideal frequency for that specific bond. In order for that bond to take place, the surrounding light must alter its frequency to be more aligned with the ideal frequency for that bond formation. The closer the light is to the optimal frequency range, the more easily the chemical reaction will occur. For small molecules, the influence that light has on the reaction rate is immeasurable, but for large molecules such as proteins and DNA, these varying light frequencies have a great influence on the rate of reaction.

Everything emits its own energy signature. Every living thing coordinates all of its life functions through its unique pattern of energy frequencies. With every intention there are countless neurons sending pulses of energy to other neurons. Whenever a neuron sends an impulse to another neuron, there is a charge buildup between membranes. A spark then transfers the charge between the neurons, creating an impulse. This spark is quite visible, as it emits large amounts of light, which permeates the entire body, catalyzing and inhibiting various chemical reactions throughout the body. This is how and why I see thought patterns as light.

Every illness emits a signature frequency of light. The body recognizes this information and intensifies its immune reaction accordingly. This emitted light is visible to me: I see what I call "signature frequencies" for diseases. For example, when I see asthma in someone, it has the appearance of a thick foggy substance in the airways of the lungs. Every cell within the lungs appears contracted. As I'm doing the treatment, I see the fog

Illustration 13: Light being absorbed during the formation of a chemical bond.

Illustration 14: Light being emitted during the breaking of a chemical bond.

dissipate. I ask the person I'm treating to imagine burning the blockages out at the same time, until I see the air passages clear.

Some diseases, specifically some types of cancer, inhibit the release of light, so the body doesn't readily recognize the illness as being a problem. Our body's biochemical responses are initiated by the body's response to biophoton emissions; if this is blocked through the cloaking ability of the cancer, the disease remains invisible to the body's immune system, and it can grow undetected for some time. However, the light will intensify as the disease progresses, until the body becomes aware of its presence and responds. I have had some experience with this invisibility mechanism of cancer. Very rarely, I can't "see" cancer, but it shows on a scan. It is important to know that through the intention of the person, the immune process can still be stimulated. That is, the fact that a disease is cloaking the light energy does not mean that the body does not have a functioning immune system.

Energy treatments make use of the frequency signature, or wave, of disease. When I do a treatment, I reach a coherent resonance with the person's frequency and emit a wave inverse to that which the illness is emitting. This inverse energy wave neutralizes the frequency the disease is emitting. The person's body receives the signal, resonates with this new frequency and absorbs this energy as information. It then registers how to neutralize the problem and sets healing into motion. The basis of everything I see in holographic healing is light. Biophotons emitted from every process in every cell is the light that I see when I am doing a treatment.

Light can also help speed up chemical reactions in the body. Let's say I have a problem with my foot which I intend to heal. My healing intention simultaneously releases light and biochemicals. Light travels faster than biochemicals and so reaches my foot first and prepares foot cells to receive the body's biochemicals necessary to initiate the healing process. By the time the biochemicals physically attach to the cell, the cell is ready and waiting: All the biochemicals are aligned so that the process occurs efficiently. Although this chemical reaction may have a relatively small effect, cumulatively, these light emissions have a large effect on the organism.

The cumulative light frequencies emitted from a multi-cellular organism coordinate and unify all of the cells into one harmonious organism. Light coordinates life.

Remember, light from one organism (person) is capable of entering other organisms and influencing it. This is how your healing thoughts and intentions affect those around you. The light emitted from your intentions enters another person, influencing a series of chemical reactions that benefit the person's health.

For this reason, it is essential that you change not only your own intentions to be more aligned with healing but encourage those around you to be positive as well. If you are positive and everyone around you is negative, the light emitted from negative energy counters what you are trying to do. Likewise, if everyone around you is positive, their intentions will amplify your intentions.

Every thought you think influences light, which influences those around you, which influences life. That is why it is essential to reprogram your thought patterns in the direction of habitual positive thinking since it truly does make a difference.

I find it interesting that I can see by looking at someone's aura and looking at them holographically how light emissions are affected by drugs. This is because drugs—of any type—alter the biophoton emissions that are emitted by the body. When I look at someone who is on toxic chemotherapy, my vision is completely obscured, as though layers of clouds are blocking my view. Even over-the-counter medications change body chemistry and alter my ability to see clearly what is happening in the person's body. The good news is that even if you are taking medication, you are able to assist your own healing through your intention, which is your most powerful ally.

Distant healing and healing face-to-face both involve light emissions. Light emitted from a person's intentions does not travel by ordinary means. Rather, the connection works in a complex manner by influencing the field of information that we all share. The action is instantaneous and does not "travel" within the intervening space (see Illustration 15).

Since becoming a college student, I have been working primarily on short-term cases. Pain is usually remedied quickly with just a few treatments. For example, a fellow with a broken finger contacted me. He was in his first semester at university and had already missed ten days of school when we connected. The orthopedic surgeon used a pin to set his finger but in doing so inadvertently bent the nerve around the pin. The pinched nerve was causing the student excruciating pain. The doctor, unaware of the problem, prescribed high doses of painkillers, which made him too lethargic to attend classes.

When I looked at the student, which I did through a photograph, since we live 1000 miles apart, I could see that his nerve was pinched from the setting pin. The nerve appeared to me as white light, and I could see it pulsating. Pulsating white light is indicative of a throbbing pain. I could see that the white light of the nerve was bypassing an area near the pin. Through my intentions, I used energy to reroute the nerve. After one treatment, the student was pain-free, and once he cleared his system of the painkillers, he returned to his classes.

Modern medicine does not yet have the technology to examine nerves in such detail as this situation required. I can go in and holographically see the nervous system. It is obvious where the problem is because I energetically see the pain as it ripples out

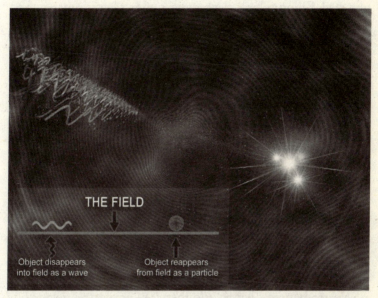

Illustration 15: A quantum object disappears at one location and by interacting with the field, it reappears at another location without having traveled through the intervening space.

from the source. Or, in the case of the student with the broken finger, I was able to calm the nerve and reset it into a new position. The student felt my treatment; he described it as "all tingly"—as though he were placing his hand near a sparkler. He reported falling asleep immediately after the treatment, even though he hadn't taken any painkillers, and he felt fine the next morning, still without having taken any drugs.

ELECTROMAGNETIC FREQUENCY INTERFERENCE

Recently, I had a very interesting experience with auras and electromagnetic frequencies. While I was visiting the Institute of Noetic Sciences (IONS) campus in Petaluma, California, Dr. Dean Radin, the institute's chief scientist, gave me a tour of the research facilities. What interested me most was a Faraday cage the institute had built for psychic research. Named after its inventor, physicist Michael Faraday, the Faraday cage was first built in 1836. It is designed to prevent the passage of electromagnetic waves through a type of shielding. Because there are no electromagnetic waves, and therefore no electric field inside it, it was useful in conducting electrical studies. Although it was not designed for the paranormal research it is used for at IONS today, it is proving very useful in that field.

My parents and I walked into this room with Dr. Radin and the door was closed behind us. It was amazing. I saw for the first time what an aura looks like when it is not being bombarded with unwanted electromagnetic frequencies. The auras looked clean, without any jagged edges or static-looking texture. All auras that I had seen up to this point looked frazzled. I was unaware of this constant impact of EMF, or electromagnetic frequency, which is the magnetic energy that is all around us. This was an unexpected revelation. Since I had never had the opportunity to see auras in this pristine form, I had no expectation of what they should look like. I am excited about the possibilities that the Faraday cage presents, and in the future, I hope to test the effectiveness of healing from within a Faraday cage. For instance, I wonder if a face-to-face treatment would be more effective in the cage, as the auras are so much clearer to me. Also, I wonder whether this clearness of aura would affect the efficacy of distant healing.

From this experience, it is clear to me what an enormous impact EMF has on our health and wellness. Several years ago, I underwent a brain-mapping test. I was curious to see if my brain wave activity changes when I access someone's hologram for healing. A cap placed on my head was wired with electrodes to measure brain activity as I connected to someone's hologram. It seemed like a wonderful idea until the mild electrical current, the electromagnetic field, was turned on. Immediately I felt uncomfortable and distressed. There was no way I could connect to anything or anyone in my agitated state. I also immediately got a headache and could not concentrate. The test was over none too soon. I had been unable to do anything during the entire test because of the pain and distress I felt. The headache stayed with me for the afternoon.

My physical reaction to the electrical current surprised me. The only conclusion I could reach is that I am sensitive even to very low voltage being applied to my head. I was concerned that it might have damaged some of my connection to the field, but the negative effects were temporary.

I have noticed that I don't feel well if I am near high-voltage power lines for any length of time. Also, I am always aware of my cell phone because I feel numbness in my body where I carry it. I believe that we all are affected by a variety of electrical currents that surround us in modern life. Apparently, I am just more sensitive than the average person to the effects of electromagnetic frequency.

Generally, the level of electromagnetic frequency interference that we are usually exposed to does not appear to be a major problem when I do aura readings. We have all grown accustomed to their existence. Electromagnetic frequencies certainly do have an effect on auras and may in the effectiveness of healing as well. I look forward to exploring that comparison some day.

When did you first see auras?
I have always been able to see auras, the swirling glow of varying colors around living things. When I was young, I knew that people on television were different from people I see in person because I was not able to see the auras of people on the television screen. Whenever we went for a drive, I was always the first one to spot animals in the bushes or on the roadside because it was their auras I saw.

Is the aura one of the various holographic views of a person?
The aura is not a holographic view. Rather, an aura is the light emitted from a person's body, which extends beyond the physical self.

Do plants have auras, and if so, how do they appear to you?
Yes, all plants have a colorless aura. This energy which surrounds them may appear as a shimmering clear aura. Intuitively, I know that this is because they lack the intense emotions that all animals possess. This is not to say that they do not have emotions but that they are unable to experience the range of emotions that the animal world can.

Is energy influenced by thought?
Yes, energy is influenced by thought, since thought is a form of energy. I am able to see that every thought is initiated by light and immediately followed by biochemical reactions. When you

have a thought, neurons are fired and light is thus emitted. Many things are influenced by thoughts. At the quantum level, quantum particles are being influenced by thoughts. Our thoughts influence things on the microscopic level and radiate to the macroscopic level, far beyond our conscious awareness.

You say that the harmonization of light defines life itself. Would you elaborate on this?
Basically, light emissions synchronize life itself. This synchronization of light is what keeps life organized. In a multi-cellular organism, all the cells are working together by synchronized light emissions. Any multi-cellular organism, even a single cell organism, depends on light to keep things functioning in a harmonious way, to keep everything coordinated.

What role does genetic predisposition play in a person developing a disease?
If you have a genetic predisposition to a disorder, you try to avoid the risk factors that increase the possibility of its manifestation. However, your thoughts and intentions play a significant role in whether the disorder is triggered. If you are worried about the probability of getting this illness, you are not intending it to manifest, but your thinking about it might have the same result. DNA is sensitive to light and DNA will react to light quickly (see Illustration 16), so the light emitted from your intentions will have an effect. If you are thinking about it constantly, the light emitted from those thoughts will increase the probability that you will manifest the problem or get that illness. DNA is dynamic.

Illustration 16: DNA interacting with and emitting light.
Energy as light information is dynamic; with every intention,
you are emitting light that influences your DNA.

PART 2

What We Make of Life

Chapter 5

Consciousness

Our consciousness, as energy, appears to generate spontaneous "thought links" to the field.

—ADAM

After my vision of the bird, any time a question popped into my head, I was bombarded with vast amounts of information that addressed it. Naturally, I had many questions about consciousness, especially how it relates to our health and healing. Each of us in our role as an observer creates our own reality. It follows that our own health and healing is part of this observation. Our individual consciousness is how we relate to every experience. By understanding more about the nature of consciousness, we will be better equipped to answer such questions as, what is my role in the universe? and, how can I create my new healing reality? By accessing the field beyond space and time, we are all able to influence our own health accordingly through our intentions.

The web of interconnectivity—the field of information—contains every possible event, past, present and future. From these potential events, the observer creates his or her reality. Each of us creates an order or pattern through the act of observing. Our thoughts, words and actions are expressions of what we perceive as our reality. Our reality is completely subjective. Objectivity is impossible, since simply by the act of observing an event we have an influence on it. There is no way we can understand or observe this theoretical objective reality in any way without making it subjective. To achieve pure objectivity we would have to be observing an event from outside our universe. Therefore, all of our perceptions are biased opinions—that is, subjective.

A person's pattern of observing things in life is a direct result of his or her life experiences. The way in which we individually filter information and process it for our own use is our individual consciousness. This is the foundation for our individuality, even though one's individual consciousness extends to everything that one connects to within the web.

The filters in our brains have been developed through all of our life experiences. For example, if we are distrustful of people as a result of past experiences, we will observe current events with mistrust and suspicion. At one of my workshops, I met a woman who said she was unable to form any relationships, either friendships or intimate relationships. She thought that everyone was "after something" and past experience taught her to trust no one. On the other hand, if we have found in the past that relationships are fulfilling to us, we will be more receptive to such incoming possibilities. (I discuss how we can change these filters for the betterment of our health in Chapter 6 in the section, Adjusting Your Attitude.)

Consciousness is everything we know to be real through our five senses and our intuitive sixth sense. Individual consciousness also can be thought of as the self-awareness connecting us to the universal field of collective consciousness. In this way, we are connected to everyone and everything in the universe. (I discuss collective consciousness in more detail later in this chapter.)

Which came first? The universe? The field? Or consciousness? We can only speculate. As I mention in Chapter 2, the first particle of matter was formed from fluctuations of energy. The field of information is the link between energy fluctuations, so it makes sense to say that the field preceded the Big Bang. It is possible that consciousness also existed before the Big Bang. If it did, it would not have been as complex as it is now, since it had no matter with which to form links. Consciousness would have merely existed as a probability in a sea of energy.

Is there a guide of some sort outside of us? Are our conscious thoughts guided by an external force? In theological terms, is there a god? What or who or even whether our thoughts are determined is certainly a subject for discussion (and I elaborate on it further in Chapter 7). Some would say that our self-reflective consciousness and search for meaning suggests the concept of a god. Many people refer to the collective consciousness of their particular religion, such as God, Allah or Jehovah, as the consciousness of everything in the universe influencing or interacting with everything else. According to most major religions, there was a consciousness that existed before the Big Bang.

I will leave the theological debate to others. What I will describe here is how I see brain neurons processing information. The brain organizes information in a way that is manageable and useful to the person. It does this by gathering informational frequencies into a resonant form that we can make use of. Subconscious thoughts are the result of spontaneous information that brain neurons pick up from the field. From this random information, the brain assesses what is of importance and sends this information to the conscious mind for action.

You are constantly receiving information from the universe. The process is spontaneous, and your brain is constantly filtering this infinite amount of information that passes through you. Your brain is a complex web of neurons with signals and responses. How you interpret the incoming information is a matter of your brain assessing what is important and what is not. That decision relates to your life experiences: Your life experiences determine what information is important to you and what isn't.

The brain is the physical organ of the mind. The brain filters information; the mind processes it. The individuality of the mind lies in how a person is uniquely interpreting information from the field that we are all receiving. Even if we all witnessed the same event, each of our minds is interpreting it uniquely. Each of us sees only what we expect to see based on past experiences. The rest of the information that we receive will stay as a subconscious stream of unused background data.

Everyone picks up on different information at different times. The process is dynamic. What information the brain picks up and how it picks it up is constantly changing with our environment. For instance, if we are in a noisy, chaotic setting, we will find it impossible to focus on and process every action and sound. If we are in more subdued surroundings, it is easier to concentrate on one event at a time.

There are many frequency levels—or, one might say, levels of consciousness—even within the same person. Your brain is always sorting out these different frequencies. When you are sleeping, you are doing so at a particular frequency. When you are awake, you are functioning at another specific frequency. When you meditate, you are operating at yet another frequency. These various frequencies allow you to make connections to the universal energy field in various ways, but still within your own frequency spectrum. A good analogy is measurements. One might use various angles and lengths to describe an object. Alternatively, it could be characterized in terms of its weight or density. These are all expressions of the same object, and simply represent it in different ways. All these frequencies are vibrations at the subatomic level, and are part of a complex array of frequencies. Certain information is available at a particular frequency, and other information at another frequency. There is no hierarchy of vibrations—no higher or lower vibration—just *different* vibrations.

There are millions of neurons in our brains, each with its particular frequency that enables us to explore several thoughts simultaneously. If you have several neurons all at different frequencies then you are connected to several different sets of information simultaneously. It is therefore possible for your brain to process several thoughts at the same time. This ability to be multi-focal is essential in our fast-paced society. It is referred to as multi-tasking. When we are in an altered state of consciousness, such as a meditative state, more neurons are on the same frequency. That is what we seek to achieve in a calm, meditative state. This allows less interaction with incoming information.

We are capable of receiving enormous amounts of information, but we are limited in our capability to decode it. Imagine that, rather than focusing on the specific information that you usually process selectively as you need it, you are acutely aware of everything in your surrounding environment—every detail of every sight, sound, smell, taste and feeling being processed at the same time. Think about what that would really involve. At any point in time, we have a finite number of neurons in the brain available to decode this information, so we must have a selection process as to what we need. This is our consciousness.

Many of us think of consciousness as residing solely in the brain. However, every atom, every cell, every subatomic particle in the body has some form of consciousness as a result of connecting to the field. Each of our cells can react with its environment, and live or die independently of the body as a whole. The cell makes all of these functional decisions through the use of its cellular memory. What was successful for it will be a repeated behavior, and what was unsuccessful will not be repeated.

The brain is capable of coordinating every cell in your body into a resonant frequency, organizing them so that they work together. When they are at a common energy frequency, you will be able to make a more effective connection to the field. As cells resonate together, this allows them to function as a whole entity, rather than as separate parts. If you are thinking about a past event, your brain is making a specific connection to the pattern of frequencies making up the memory of that event. The brain can sort out an enormous amount of data from the field and make it manageable so that we are not overwhelmed. It does this by organizing the incoming information into a pattern that we understand, and then signals the other cells accordingly.

To again use the analogy of a pond, the universal energy field is like one huge pond, with people the many ripples in that pond. Focal points of individual consciousness are the spots where the ripples originate. Every time you think a thought, the thought links to a piece of information. Think of it as the thought reaching out to grab a piece of information from a common field of consciousness—the pond. By grabbing this information, it affects something else (the piece of information) that is also in this field, causing a ripple in the pond. This ripple initiates a domino effect.

Think of each individual consciousness as a pebble. With every thought, your pebble (which represents your uniqueness) is being dropped into the pond. Each of your thoughts is represented by the same pebble. Another person's thoughts are a different pebble, which also causes a ripple when dropped into the pond. All the ripples in the pond interact. Everything makes a connection to everything else.

We are making connections all the time, whether we are aware of it or not. From our subjective point of view, we are each making unique connections according to our personalities and insights. Every experience in life is subjective, based on our perception of reality using our individual sensory input. From a scientific or objective perspective, our thoughts are all energy. So, while every living organism makes a unique connection to this field—that is, everything makes a connection through a different frequency—it is all the same energy.

After you die and go on to the next life (I discuss the concept of reincarnation in detail in Chapter 8), your energy, or essence, is the same pebble but in a different body. Your frequency patterns are the result of light emissions similar to those in your previous life. You are the same energy and the same vibrations; you simply reside in a different body. And while you are the same original conscious energy, this energy is constantly evolving. It does not change just when you die; it has been constantly changing since its origin. All matter continuously taps into this field and is constantly evolving.

If we can't make sense of the information we receive, it is possible that someone else may decode it for us. That is, their point of consciousness, or their brain, decodes the information, then their "ripple" in the pond interacts with our ripple. This is a natural process of information flow. We can pick up the information about any organic or inorganic thing in the universe—a bird, a plant, even a rock—because they are connected to the same field. It takes practice to do this. We are more complex than a rock because we are actively, dynamically and intentionally directing energy and thought patterns.

The flow of energy as information and our access to it are constantly evolving and changing. With continued evolution, we will all be able to access information from the field more easily. Our intuitive abilities increase as our skills to listen to them are developed. I call this tuning in. Most people have experienced this to some degree and know it as intuition. You are constantly receiving information subconsciously in the form of hunches, ideas or images. People who are visually oriented will tend to receive pictures; those who are more auditorily oriented may hear voices. The data you receive is not only from yourself and your own body but is information being emitted by others. In fact, all objects—animate and inanimate—emit information.

Tuning in to and deciphering this data is a survival mechanism. For example, you may get a feeling that you shouldn't eat something, and it turns out to be poisonous or that you are allergic to it. I always knew that I shouldn't eat kiwi fruit, yet I had never even tasted it. When I was about eight years old, my dad made a milkshake for my sister and me. He added kiwi without telling me, knowing I would refuse to taste the drink if I knew it contained kiwi. He thought my dislike of kiwi had no basis. Within a minute of swallowing the milkshake, my face became itchy and started to swell. Even as a small child, I had connected to the information that I shouldn't eat kiwi.

ALIGNING THE CONSCIOUS AND SUBCONSCIOUS MIND

As I mentioned earlier, it is important that your conscious and subconscious thoughts and intentions be synchronized. Make certain that when you consciously say, "I know that I can do it," this thought is in tune with the subconscious voice deep within you.

Synchronizing your conscious and subconscious thoughts is a skill that can be developed through practice. It is like playing the piano. Playing a tune with your dominant hand is pretty straightforward. Adding the accompaniment of the other hand seems almost impossible at first. You feel as though you need to keep track of two separate actions simultaneously. But with practice, coordination of both hands becomes second nature.

To synchronize your conscious and subconscious mind, you must become aware of your subconscious thoughts. One practice strategy is to quiet your mind. In the stillness, ask for information about subconscious blocks and wait quietly for answers. Then consciously intend to let go of subconscious blockages. Do this regularly. Your goal of creating harmony within your intentions will make your visualizations more effective.

The game of golf is also a good example of coordinating conscious rational thoughts with intuitive knowledge. In golf, as in any sport, you must focus on numerous details while at the same time allowing yourself to just feel the connection that you are making to the game. As I watched golfers on the course, it looked like an easy game. How complicated could it possibly be to swing a club and hit a little white ball? During my first lesson, the pro had me grasp the club in a certain grip, stand at an exact distance from the ball, position my front foot precisely and then move the club behind me in a certain way while rotating in a specific motion. Now came the easy part, or so the pro said. I just had to relax and swing. What he was saying was, "You now have the information and the clear intention to hit the ball properly; just get out of the way and let your subconscious do the job."

THE UNCONSCIOUS STATE: COMA
I have been able to communicate with many people in comas, with some wonderful results. However, time is of the essence when working with those in comas. Immediately after the trauma, body memory in light emissions is still prominent. The biophoton emissions are evident to me, which makes stimulating them more straightforward. This light fades over time, making the reversal of the injury more difficult. When the biophoton emissions dim in intensity, it is as though memory fades. After this point, the person must relearn each forgotten skill, such as cognitive and communication abilities. The neural pathways (see Illustration 17) do not instantaneously transfer

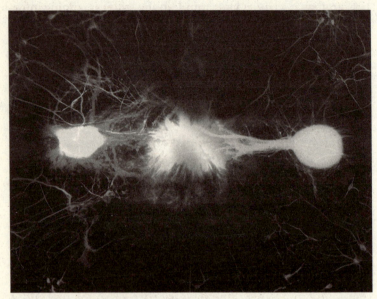

Illustration 17: Thought as light being transferred along neural pathways. Thought interacts nonlocally as it radiates to and absorbs information from the field.

information as they did previously. As time passes, healing becomes more difficult, but it is still possible. Neural pathways can be regenerated but it takes energy and time.

In preparation for a treatment on someone in a coma, I ask the relatives to email recent photographs of family and of happy events and gatherings. This is because the comatose person will recognize those in the photograph and will want to regain consciousness to join them. As well, any details about the accident are helpful, including the circumstances of the injury. With this information, I start to update the comatose person about what happened. This sometimes sparks the wake-up call.

A factor that I have noted when treating comatose people is that I can see that they receive the messages that I send without any judgment: They process it just like any other incoming information. I don't need to be concerned about their belief systems and past experiences interfering, as they are not actively filtering out what they think they don't need. The part of their brains that guide their awareness is not functioning properly. This part usually filters through all incoming information, streamlining what they think is needed for processing at any given time.

One teenager I worked with had survived a head-on car crash. She was unconscious and at first it was questionable whether she would live. Then her family faced another hurdle: They were told that if she lived she would have severe brain damage. Fortunately, her parents contacted me immediately after the accident. Her mother was active in the healing arts, and she understood what was involved in energy healing.

Although the daughter was comatose and couldn't verbally respond to me, she could understand when I sent information telepathically. I applied as much energy to her as possible through distant healing, concentrating on her brain and the intracranial bleeding caused by the impact. Energetically, I helped the girl stop the bleeding, and after several treatments, I could see that light was sparking along the neural pathways in her brain. It was apparent to me that she was coming out of her coma. The doctors told her parents that she would still have severe mental impairments, but I saw that she was going to be fine. Six months after the accident, the girl was attending university.

Another teenager's father got in touch with me immediately after she had fallen nearly sixty feet, hitting her head hard when she landed. Amazingly, the girl survived. However, she had extensive head injuries, and the doctors expected her to be severely brain damaged or even brain dead.

I started distant treatments on her right away, bringing into her brain and running through it as much energy as I could. I focused on stopping her intracranial bleeding and attempted to get the neurons sparking with light again. Her father was at her bedside during the first treatment. The girl was comatose and motionless. Immediately when the treatment began, her eyelids fluttered. This first movement since the accident demonstrated to him and to me that a significant connection to this healing had been achieved.

By the second treatment, I could see that there was some light activity in her brain, so I continued to bombard her brain with energy. It was clear to me that her neurons were regenerating and reactivating rapidly.

Doctors at the hospital left the family little hope for the girl's recovery. They reported that scans showed half of her brain to be dead. Paralysis to her left side seemed certain, and her right side was thought to be impaired as well. This was, of course, devastating news. But I did not agree with the doctors because what I saw energetically was increasing electrical activity in her brain. She was coming back.

After several treatments, I could see that the girl wanted to speak and was ready to do so with just a little energy stimulation. I focused on her speech during the treatment, and she began talking. Her first words were directed to her grandmother. She held her grandmother's arm and asked, "What happened to me?" It was no wonder she needed to ask this. It is exceptionally frustrating for injured people to find they are unable to communicate, especially at a time when they need to express their emotions about the traumatic event. It was a great relief for the girl to have this limitation removed from her life. She continued to improve as she regained both her mental faculties and physical movement. One month after the accident, she was sitting up in bed, eating, talking to visitors and going to physiotherapy. She had no paralysis.

It is encouraging to work with young people, as they have a

powerful ability to regenerate after sustaining an injury. This is because of their youthful and strong physical selves, which are often accompanied by open-mindedness. One can often achieve results more quickly than when working with an older person.

Sometimes I can connect to the comatose person, but he or she is unable to return to a state of conscious awareness. I can only imagine what life is like from the perspective of people in comas. What we perceive as normal states of consciousness must seem so far removed from them. It seems as though they are in a very deep sleep, but unable to awaken from it.

I did a distant healing on a woman who was in a coma for five years following a car accident. Her infant son was unharmed in the accident. Her family was at her bedside when I did the treatment. I telepathically sent images of what had happened since the accident, as well as a current photo image of her son, which her family had sent me. As I sent her the images, tears started to roll down her cheeks. She understood, yet she just couldn't wake up.

A man had been in a coma for over thirty years after a car accident. Now age fifty, he had been nonresponsive since his late teens. From a distance of 2000 miles, I telepathically sent him images, and his family reported that he seemed to enjoy them: He smiled and appeared to be listening intently as if hearing music he liked. His father was thrilled when the man smiled directly at him. The man was unable to wake up into a conscious state, but that loving response was a heartwarming experience for his devoted family. His family also reported that during the treatment he moved more than he had ever done in the last thirty years.

I was contacted by the family of a man who fell into a coma during brain surgery. After six months in hospital, he still had not regained consciousness. I asked the family to be at his side during my treatment so they could report any changes during my distant healing. At the exact moment when I began the treatment, his eyes opened and he became conscious and responsive. He still wasn't able to see, as it had been so long since he had used his eye muscles. During this treatment, I sent into him as much energy as possible, and I could see sparking in his brain, as though the energy might be stimulating him. Sometimes it seems as though the treatment will produce results, but then the light fades or dissipates entirely soon after the treatment. Only in a subsequent treatment can I tell whether the brain has been activated enough to spark with light on its own.

The next evening I did another distant treatment, and I could see that the man was producing his own light in his brain. The family was once again at his side during the treatment, and they reported that this time he was able to see. The man has since attended one of my workshops, and his family is thrilled to have him back with them.

CONSCIOUSNESS OF ANIMALS

Some people have difficulty accepting that organisms other than humans have a consciousness. The idea that consciousness is something special, reserved only for humans, is quite arrogant. A great part of consciousness is perspective, and from an animal's perspective, the animal itself is more important than you or I.

Although I regularly read my cat's intentions telepathically, I never pick up any telepathic messages from her suggesting that she is searching for the deeper meaning of life; but this does not mean that she does not have consciousness. Consciousness is simply being aware of one's own presence. I am sure that my cat is well aware of hers. Just because she can't communicate in the same manner as a human doesn't mean that she is without conscious awareness.

All living creatures work within the same knowledge base

and natural communication system as we do. Their cells communicate through subtle light energy just as ours do, and they are linked to all other animals and ourselves in the same way. Larger animals have more information than smaller ones because of their greater number of cells, which must be synchronized with the flow of data. The more highly evolved the animal, the more complicated the information is, since it contains both emotional and physical data.

Animals are acutely aware of information that they receive and process from the field. Their awareness is commonly referred to as instinct. Humans over time have learned to ignore most instinctual information and override it. We tend to concentrate instead on our conscious programming, which involves the societal concepts of time and space that we have learned about ourselves, our work and our relationships. Animals receive information from the field and act on it. What they process is pure, unadulterated guidance, free of the analytical clutter humans have. The field has always provided an organized flow of information to every organism.

Emergency workers who were first on the scene of the December 26, 2004, tsunami in Asia were amazed that no dolphins, whales or other sea life were washed up on shore. Many animals managed to escape this natural catastrophe because they can sense danger beyond the limitations of humans' five senses. It was reported that all of the elephant trainers were spared in this disaster because they were chasing their elephants as they ran to higher ground. Many people also were unwittingly saved as they ran after their dogs to higher ground. When an animal gets the danger signal, instinct takes over and all else is secondary; the fight or flight for survival takes precedence. Animals instinctively receive clear messages about what they need to do to preserve their lives, and they do not hesitate to act on it. This instinct is similar to the signaling that coordinates the movement of a school of fish when all the fish turn simultaneously and flee from danger. Every fish gets this signal at the same instant.

A disaster of the magnitude of the Asian tsunami radiates the intense energy of its danger signal over a great distance. The animal kingdom heeded the danger signal, which can be described as a collective consciousness resulting from this information resonating from the field. Those people in the vicinity who were sensitive to the disturbing energy patterns that radiate out from an earthquake must have experienced headaches, stomachaches or otherwise felt unwell. Yet, these feelings were likely dismissed because of the many obligations and distractions in their lives, as well as the social pressures that overrule these gut feelings.

You may know your own bodily signals better than you think. Everyone has a body area that pays the price when we feel tension. For some people, it is a pain in their neck. Others get stomach butterflies or migraines. Whatever the malady and wherever it strikes, we can learn to know our own signals. Listen to your inner voice, which takes the form of bodily signals. Then act on that information rather than overriding it.

Our connections to animals can be as meaningful as our connections to humans. Some time ago, a man sent me a photograph of one of his race horses. It had been ill and the veterinarian could not figure out why. Out of interest, because I have never connected energetically to a horse, I took a look at the photograph.

I could tell that the horse had eaten something that did not suit it because I saw excess light emanating from the stomach area. I also noticed that its upper back lit up as a problem area. I told the owner what I saw. He reported that some months earlier, the horse had injured its back while playing, and the problem in the stomach area could possibly be explained by a recent change in the horse's feed. The owner informed the veterinarian, and the horse was treated for these ailments. Shortly afterward, the horse owner emailed me to tell me that the horse was once again participating in equestrian competitions.

This demonstrated to me that connecting to animals, even nonlocally, is done in the same way as with humans. I was able to access the horse's hologram through a photograph just as easily as if it were a person, and its aura and light emission was no different.

COLLECTIVE CONSCIOUSNESS

Within the oneness of universal collective consciousness, each of us is unique. Although each of us has a distinctive energy frequency or vibration level, essentially, we are all one: a universal collective consciousness composed of the entire spectrum of frequencies. Every living organism (not just humans) is part of this. Everything, even inorganic material, is tied into a single conscious web of energy. However, nonliving substances are not as dynamic as living systems. Living organisms have a much more complex connection through the exchange of information. This is because they are constantly at chemical disequilibria. This means that all biochemicals are constantly being adjusted and readjusted, which defines the dynamic processes of life itself. Only at death does a living organism reach a state of equilibrium.

It is possible for cells and complex organisms, such as people, to adjust to surrounding vibrations. This is essential in healing to get all of the cells working together. Each cell in our body has its own frequency. When all of our cells are working in unison, they collectively form a common frequency. During the group treatments at my workshops, after merging auras, a common frequency is reached among all participants: All frequencies are merged as one into a coherent pattern of energy resonance, and we all resonate at a common frequency. It is as if I am conducting an orchestra, creating harmony out of a chaos of musical notes. All of the individual holograms of information are merged into a collective hologram. The collective hologram functions as a group consciousness with healing intentions.

When I am doing a distant healing, I am aligning myself to another person's frequencies in order to make an intentional connection to the person's unique connection to the field. As I've mentioned, I do this through a photograph, which enables me to connect to the person's frequency and, from this, access the person's holographic record. When I focus my intention on a person at a distance, I connect to that person's hologram and decode it into useable information for health and healing, which allows me to change it and positively influence the person's health. By "decoding" I mean interpreting the information that I receive into an understandable form.

It is important to recognize that our consciousness extends beyond our individual selves to a collective consciousness, which links us to everything in the field. The more extensive the scope of this link, the more information is contained in the connection. It is like a camera being opened to a wider aperture. We get the broader prospective of the big picture, a more expansive focus.

When more conscious beings are connected to the same focused intention, a stronger and more intense bond is formed in our collective consciousness. This synchronicity of group consciousness can be strengthened by a common focus or intention. The wonderful possibilities that lie ahead will be chosen from all the positive outcomes imaginable. I believe that this is the same principle that will eventually help us realize a true global consciousness. Imagine the possibilities if millions of people in the world merged their auras as one. When we talk about the world reaching a higher level of conscious awareness, it is the result of many people merging their frequencies as one into a coherent pattern of resonating energy. Energy resonates as a singular unified conscious intention. The realization that we are all one will heal the world.

I believe that consciousness is becoming more complex all the time as the collective consciousness rapidly evolves to higher levels. People are becoming more aware of how consciousness functions and are making better use of it. They are deliberately manipulating their intuitive abilities to access information and therefore are developing stronger intuition, better mental telepathy and increased self-healing ability. Awareness increases the ease with which people can connect to the field. If a person is deliberately paying attention to their intuition, he or she will find it easier to make a connection to the field.

Each of us is unique insofar as the specific way in which we access the field of information, but the process is the same for everyone. For example, someone who thinks faster than someone else makes a more rapid connection, or someone who thinks more about a particular subject or object than others will have a stronger connection to that frequency of information. The combined energy of our interests, abilities and inclinations is our particular essence, you might say. What we focus on and what we are interested in gives us a greater understanding of what makes us who we are. It defines our uniqueness—our energy essence.

Our next step of awareness is global consciousness, where we all understand that what helps one of us helps us all. Only then can we understand that healing the planet is an extension of healing ourselves. We can actively participate in this evolution by understanding that our intentions affect things far beyond our conscious awareness. Individual consciousness, collective consciousness, global consciousness and universal consciousness are all the same. Here or there does not exist. Everything is here *and* there. Before or after does not exist. Everything *is*.

Would you elaborate on how our intention can manifest things in our lives such as finding a parking spot or getting a job?
By having the intention to get a job or even find a parking place, you are interacting with the field. You are part of the collective consciousness. This collective consciousness can influence events in ways that seem coincidental. Nevertheless, the collective consciousness is the interaction of every living organism's consciousness and aligns similar energy patterns.

Does the collective consciousness of all organisms in the universe have a tendency to influence events?
Yes, although the influence is subtle, rather than dramatic. Events are influenced in small and seemingly coincidental ways. When you look back on your life, think of all of the situations in which you noticed coincidences. You will begin to think that things happen for a reason. Part of what made events line up to produce coincidences is this collective consciousness.

Within this collective consciousness of all minds, how would you describe individual minds—my mind, your mind? Are we individuated somehow?
Yes and no. The intentions of everyone combined are functioning as one consciousness. This consciousness in turn influences everything else as we collectively form a web of connections. Imagine throwing a handful of pebbles into a pond. Even though every ripple from each pebble has a point of origin, the ripples will all connect and affect each other in countless ways. The ripples become one. So you could say we lose our individuality in how we affect other things. Every one of us and everything is affecting everything all the time. Yet there remain points of origin.

Is the collective consciousness past, present and future?
It is current, with the past definitely having some influence and the future being just a series of probabilities. When tapping into information about a future event, you are tapping into probabilities. All probabilities are in the field.

Chapter 6
Emotions and Attitude

*Emotions can work for you or against you.
You can choose how they will affect you.*

—ADAM

I've been asked many times what the root cause of disease is. Is it emotional, physical, spiritual or karma based? All of these aspects may interact to produce a health challenge. Emotions play an important role, one that we can influence.

Everyone reacts differently to events and experiences. Everyone experiences a range between happy and sad emotions. It is healthy to have a range of emotions. However, habitual negative feelings often contribute to physical illness. Many people whom I have worked on have a very strong emotional component to their physical ailment. In a great number of cases, the source of the problem is emotional: The health challenge is the physical manifestation of emotional baggage.

Just as emotions can intensify a health problem, they can also be used to alleviate many issues. Use your intentions to guide your emotions for the betterment of your health. I have noticed that some people who attend my workshops show signs of depression. The physical ailment may be at the root of the depression, or physical symptoms may be manifesting as a result of depression. Whichever the case may be, depression is intertwined with one's emotions, and emotions are inseparable from the physical body. It is important to realize that we can influence emotions and our reaction to them. Rather than spending time trying to decide which challenge appeared first, use energy to improve your state of mental and physical well-being.

I see depression as static patches of energy surrounding the head and shoulders. The patchy areas block the free flow of energy to the brain and nervous system. By resuming a harmonious patterned energy flow, the symptoms of the person's physical disorder or illness often lessen quickly. Just knowing that one has control positively affects one's emotional outlook. Mental and physical health cannot be separated in sickness or in health.

Attitudes about our health and healing are paramount to our wellness outcome. What we think and how we think about all experiences affect what we choose to do with our emotions. A woman I know attends every workshop I hold within 1000 miles of her home. When we first met, over two years ago, she had been given a terminal diagnosis by her doctor: Her cancer of the pancreas had spread to her lungs, liver and spleen. She was emotionally shattered. Since then, as a result of her diligently practicing the exercises given in my books and workshops, she has come to realize the influence she has on her own healing. Emotional and attitudinal self-reflection and change was a significant aspect on her journey to self-empowerment. A recent scan showed no evidence of any problem in her lungs, spleen or liver. Even the pancreatic tumor has shrunk. Knowing that her health has improved through her own doing makes her very proud. While the workshops help her to focus and stay on track, she feels self-empowered. Self-confidence radiates from her.

In this chapter, you'll find steps that will help you balance your emotions in a positive way. Doing this is an integral part of healing.

What are emotions and what purpose do they serve? How do they interact with the field of information? Emotions are feelings associated with intentions, thoughts and memories. The process emotions initiate is somewhat circular. Emotions function as the fuel for thoughts, or the fuel *of* thoughts. An intention, thought or memory stimulates neurons to emit light emissions—a specific frequency—which then connects to the field of information. This connection to the field instantaneously triggers the release of biochemicals; this in turn results in the manifestation of a specific emotion. The emotion expressed is specific to the particular frequency of light emitted (each of our emotions has a preset frequency that varies slightly from person to person), which in turn has a specific connection to the field. The manifestation of the emotion completes the circle.

Although emotions fuel and influence your intentions, they do not do so to a degree that overrides the intention. Intention remains the primary mechanism behind an action. Your intention activates neurons in the brain to send impulses from one neuron to another. This creates an electromagnetic field that resonates at a specific frequency. When you think a thought, a neuron resonates at a frequency that connects to the particular part of the field also resonating at that same frequency. In the body, the emotion related to that thought and the instantaneous connection to the field release biochemicals that fuel the expression of that emotion. From a subjective or experiential perspective, you feel the emotion as a sensation; by you feeling it, others around you can sense it or observe your expression of it also.

Emotions and their corresponding frequencies are complex. This complexity is due to the variations in a person's biological and chemical makeup. Our various types of measurements at present cannot measure emotions. We attempt to measure behavioral responses, breathing rates, biochemical levels and memory recall. Despite all these measurements, what remains most important is the attitude and interpretations we bring to this data. We have more control over these processes than we think.

Some people believe that emotionally charged intentions and their connection to the field figure prominently in the creation of our own reality. There is a lot of truth to this, particularly in the idea that we can influence our own physiology. You will tend to manifest those things on which your mind is set. Your attitude and focus not only will connect you to the field but will influence what actions you take in your everyday life.

Emotions can be a powerful healing tool when directed properly toward healing. They fuel our intentions, which activate physiological changes, of which the biochemical ones are the most well known. Each emotion triggers the release of different biochemicals. Certain biochemicals have opposing effects and so cancel out each other: When one molecule binds to another molecule with an opposing effect, any effect that either of those molecules alone would have caused will be nullified. This is the manner in which we can neutralize any unwanted effects from unproductive emotions. Through our focused intention of responding to emotions in a more balanced way, we can bring a healthier equilibrium to our biochemical systems. This is a vital part of what it means to be aware and to know yourself. This happens not by suppressing your emotions but by retraining your responses to them. You'll find steps to help you do this in the section Writing Your Own Ticket to Emotional Freedom, on page 416.

Because emotions have chemical correlates and specific energy patterns, they affect your physical health. The chemistry and energy of the body are entwined. Energy precedes the chemical reactions. Having a variety of emotions is healthy for the body in terms of energy, as balance is always the goal. It is human to have a wide range of emotions, rather than feeling an extreme of either anger, sadness or happiness all of the time.

Indeed, we almost never experience one single emotion at a time. Even when an emotion is intense, other emotions are present. We can feel anger, sadness and happiness during the same event. All of us develop our own range of emotions that we are comfortable with. As we grow and change, our median point of emotional equilibrium will change.

Emotions are neither good nor bad in a moral or ethical sense, although some of them certainly make us feel bad. Emotions just are part of who we are. They come and go in a way that feels as though we have little control. But we do have control. Our thought patterns are the key to which emotions we feel. In addition, we can change or control how we react to our emotions. We can rationally decide how to evaluate and respond to our emotions in a balanced manner. It is important to become more aware of our emotions in order to recognize how we actually feel. Then we can decide how to react to the situation. Decide what your intentions are in that moment and that is how you can exercise control.

Health challenges often arise if a person gets stuck in negativity. Negative emotions will manifest into an unbalanced aura, or energy system. The healthy, flowing pattern of light emissions is being altered. This aura imbalance is a warning of physical problems. It indicates that detrimental chemical changes are occurring in the body because of toxic thoughts and emotions. With emotional challenges, such as depression, it is important to understand that you can influence control over your emotions and health.

Severe psychological and emotional disorders take particular forms in the aura. Schizophrenia usually appears as an aura with a sluggish-looking flow of light energy accompanied by spikes protruding and disappearing at random spots around the head. Once I began to work with this disorder in more depth, I noticed a particular energetic dysfunctional pattern. The initiation of a thought, which I see as a spark of light in the brain, gets derailed before it completes its path to form a completed thought, which I see as a pattern of light. This results in fragments of light shooting off in random directions. Thoughts get interrupted before they are completely processed.

As I mentioned previously, I see depression as patches of a static pattern of energy, similar to the snowy picture on a television screen when it is not tuned in to a station. These patches effectively block the free flow of energy.

Because emotions are feelings associated with intentions, thoughts and memories, they greatly assist us in recalling memories. When we experience an event, many neurons form a connection to the associated thoughts or pattern of thoughts, emitting light at certain specific frequencies. We have feelings or emotions about each event. Recalling an event simultaneously triggers the emotional association to it. Because of this, emotions can be used precisely in healing. Each emotion makes a strong connection to a particular region of the field. By being in control of your dominant emotions, you are controlling the information you are connecting to within the field. This in turn affects which frequencies of light remain prominent in your body and, consequently, which biochemicals are released to optimally affect your health.

Emotions of others also have an effect on us and on the wider collective energy of a group of people. This is why group healings are so powerful: The collective healing intentions and emotions of everyone in the group make the environment perfect for healing.

Suppose you are feeling neutral and not experiencing any strong emotions. Then someone in the room becomes angry with you. There is now a difference between your emotional state and that person's. Consequently, either you, or the other person or both of you will experience a shift in your feelings.

You may not actually feel angry, but you will feel the difference between your frequency and that person's frequency. Many possibilities could occur at this point. You might become angry also, which results in the anger vibration level intensifying. Or you might intentionally move to a calming frequency level where you could influence the other's frequency to become more tranquil. Eventually a state of equilibrium will be reached. The two frequencies will tend to balance out or neutralize each other. Similarly, a non-angry person walking into a room of angry people can neutralize the intensity of the anger by emitting a calming emotion. This equilibrium will happen naturally with the introduction of a different vibration to the environment.

ACHIEVING EMOTIONAL EQUILIBRIUM
It is clear that emotions powerfully affect health. Take charge of your emotions. Only you have the power to do this. In this way, you can heal emotionally based problems. Everyone has emotional issues from their past, such as regrets involving relationships and forgiveness issues. It is how we handle them that impacts our daily lives. The past is over: We must leave it there as we move forward. We live in the present moment and are guided by our intentions, which are focused toward creating our future.

A woman I met was divorced many years before and had lost contact with her only son. As a result, she was emotionally unable to move forward. Although she remarried and had three more children within a stable, loving relationship, she was always thinking about her son. What was he doing? What was he thinking and saying? Would he ever question the negative stories about her that she was certain he was hearing? Would he ever try to find her?

Years ago she also developed fibromyalgia, a painful disorder causing stiffness and tenderness, so physical pain accompanied her psychological anguish. She attended one of my group workshops and found that as she gained control over her physical challenge through the use of positive intentions, she came to an understanding about her son. She practiced positive thinking as she imagined meeting her son as a young adult and getting to know and love him. She felt that he would feel this and respond in kind to her positive intentions.

A year later she attended another of my workshops. Through her tears she explained that she was no longer in any physical pain from fibromyalgia. And out of the blue her son had called her. They had met and now are catching up on the years that they missed together.

It is important to stay positive in order to project healing intentions accurately. This is not easy if you have recently received a negative medical diagnosis. Some people have told me that they found staying positive absolutely impossible. But nothing is impossible.

Start with imagining that you are in a positive frame of mind. Make a conscious effort to be optimistic and, before too long, it will become a habit: You will be naturally thinking this way. Don't forget to give yourself a pat on the back as you begin to notice changes in your perspective.

Writing Your Own Ticket to Emotional Freedom
This exercise will help minimize the impact on your daily life of all of the emotional difficulties you carry with you from your past.

1. Create a list of all the negative emotions your thought patterns tend to revisit. Make sure that you really have made an effort to dig deeply so that you leave no emotion buried.
2. Underline any themes you notice, as well as the repetitions of issues with no apparent solutions. You will be able to

identify such issues by the negative self-talk phrases you habitually use, such as, "I always have trouble in relationships."

3. Now close your eyes and reflect on the issues and recurrent themes you have noted. In self-talk, what ideas do you reinforce? Question why you habitually have the thought. For instance, in reflecting on your use of the phrase "I always have trouble in relationships," you may not be sure whether this thought is a result of past events or whether your reality has been influenced by your negative thought.

4. Next, reflect on how your self-talk phrases and ideas can be expressed as positive changes. Identifying these issues is only the first step. Now you must actively work on modifying or eliminating them. The phrase "I always have trouble in relationships" leaves no room for positive change. Reword it in a positive framework, such as, "I am forming positive relationships with others."

5. Keep this list and, the following day, review each emotion and theme one at a time and reflect on it.

6. Think of what triggers this negative emotion in you. Then think of healthier ways to respond to the trigger event. When you hear yourself say aloud or in self-talk the same old line, "I always have trouble in relationships," catch yourself. Review what made you relate events to this statement that reinforces your negative thoughts and emotions.

7. In your mind's eye, re-create your reaction in this positive manner as realistically as possible. Set this new response as your emotional equilibrium goal. For instance, imagine the scenario of meeting a new person who shares many interests with you and may become a friend. Leave yourself open to new possibilities, rather than maintaining the old habit of shutting the door before you see who is there.

8. Draw a line through each listed emotion that you have dealt

with as you master your reaction to it. Enjoy the feeling of satisfaction and freedom from thoughts and emotions that don't serve your best interests.

Or, instead of trouble forming relationships, take road rage. In our time-challenged society, road rage sets many into irrational anger. If someone cutting you off in traffic sets you off into a rage, the next time this happens take a deep breath before reacting. Then imagine that the person in the other car is in a hurry to get to a friend at the hospital, or another such scenario that morally excuses the behavior. Chill your trigger by changing how you are going to react.

ADDICTIONS AND POOR LIFESTYLE HABITS

Our emotional reactions are a combination of two factors: our genetic makeup and environmental influences. Both are dynamic systems. We have all been raised in different environments, environments where our developing thoughts and emotions are guided by parental influences and everything else that we experience.

For some people, part of the explanation for health challenges lies in their first emotional experiences. In some family environments, it is expected that emotions be suppressed. If you were a boy, perhaps you were not permitted to cry. You may have been told to "suck it up" and "take it like a man." Some of us may have been told that we were stupid, or undeserving of what we wanted or needed, and thus we may be suppressing emotions of embarrassment, inadequacy or guilt. Addictions such as alcohol, drugs and smoking often can be tied to these denied emotions. And it is clear that physical symptoms and emotional reactions are often intertwined.

Addictions of various kinds are epidemic in the world. Addiction has physical, chemical and emotional factors. The pattern must be broken and the software reprogrammed to your benefit. In the long run, it doesn't matter what first caused the situation, as all the causes are intertwined. What is more important is analyzing the trigger, so that you can revise your reaction in order to negate those unwanted impulses. For instance, if stress sets off your smoking addiction, explore ways to decrease a specific stressor.

If a parent has a negative outlook, that energy influences everyone else in the household. Through the child's act of observing this behavior, he or she may develop poor emotional habits. The same may be said of any habit, such as smoking, drinking or overeating. Children can emulate the physical behaviors that they observe. You might be from a family in which all of the adults smoked. You can either accept this as being the norm, or reject it on the basis of what you have learned elsewhere. These are emotionally charged environmental factors that are obviously beyond your genetic makeup. Excessive stress and poor lifestyle habits can be deeply ingrained. One can have poor emotional habits as well as physical ones.

Your goal is to achieve and maintain emotional balance by retraining your responses to them.

Poor lifestyle habits can often be an underlying cause of health problems. Make it a priority to notice any issues that contribute to bad habits. The first step is to admit the existence of a problem. Understand what led you to a harmful habit or reaction so that you can retrain your responses at the emotional level. Reflect on emotional issues that go to the root of the problem. For example, if you overeat, ask yourself, why did I start overeating? Why do I let myself eat this way when I know it is unhealthy? Meditation may help you focus, with the intention of finding the answer.

Moving forward is not easy. First you must make peace with your past. Understand why you are currently facing this challenge.

Learn from it so that you can effectively leave it where it belongs: in your past, not in your present or future. What feelings do you have to let go of in order to move forward? Do you need to forgive someone, or forgive yourself? Be honest in your self-reflection.

Your thoughts, emotions, words and behaviors determine the frequency of light you emit, and hence, all of your biochemical reactions. Your biophoton emissions react to your intentions; emotions fuel your intentions. Change is a complex process. However, you are ultimately in charge. Just know that you *can* influence your emotions to achieve the level of wellness that you seek.

ADJUSTING YOUR ATTITUDE

If you doubt your ability to heal yourself, you must work on changing your attitude. It is important to realize that we are all healers. In this way, healing is demystified because each and every one of us embraces its power. We must become responsible for our own well-being. The mind, functioning as our computer, must know that we not only are serious about making changes but *are* making changes. Being honestly and consistently self-reflective is not easy in our chaotic modern society where there are so many distractions and so many potential stressors.

Many of us have grown accustomed to quick fixes as the solution to every difficulty that we encounter. For our health, we expect that there are pills to aid us. The same instant gratification is associated with having money. Even having a baby is sometimes viewed as the key to fixing a relationship. We are constantly searching elsewhere for the instant solution to our problems. With health and healing, look no further than yourself. You can make the difference.

A quick fix should not be your motivation for pursuing energy treatments. Imagine that you are given a prescription for an antibiotic that should be taken four times a day for ten days.

After taking two pills, you feel no different so you stop taking them and declare that the antibiotic doesn't work. Yet, you haven't taken the whole course of antibiotics. It is important to follow directions in any treatment, whether conventional or alternative. It is pointless to judge the outcome if you haven't followed through on the process.

Or imagine that you become ill after drinking contaminated water, so you take all of the antibiotics your doctor prescribed. Immediately after finishing the course, you drink water from the same contaminated source. As a result, you become ill once again. Is the treatment to blame if you haven't changed the habits that contributed to your illness in the first place? Keep this in mind as you follow your chosen healing path so you don't repeat what created your health challenge.

When illness strikes, it is natural to feel worried and fearful. This results in a lot of anxiety. Family members and close friends also feel the stress. This can lead to further complications that prolong the negative impact that the health challenge has on you. Well-meaning family members and friends may find it difficult to be positive even when you want to make changes for the better. It is very important that those around you be supportive and positive with you. Their intentions will affect yours. Be genuine when deciding to empower yourself. You know the difference between being truly positive in your outlook and sugarcoating a negative attitude.

Remember that you can change yourself. You can change your thinking patterns. Fear blocks the flow of helpful information needed to initiate your transformation to wellness. Go forward, leaving any doubts and fears behind.

Your level of education is not a factor in your ability to become self-empowered and develop your potential to change. I have spoken to many people well educated in mainstream Western medicine who have a hard time changing their attitudes and who doubt a person's ability to really change. It is important that you are able to feel and know that change is forthcoming. Our challenge is to forget what we have learned, and remember what we have forgotten.

Steps to Achieving a Positive Attitude
1. Notice your attitude toward change. Decide to expect change, then welcome it and enjoy it. As with any experience in life, there is a direct relationship between what we put into it and what we get out of it. Be willing to modify your unproductive attitudes.
2. Forgiveness is an essential part of cleansing negative emotions and removing unproductive attitudes. This includes forgiving others as well as ourselves. Past mistakes should be left in the past. As the forgiver, empower yourself to let go.
3. Live freely in the present. Learn from past experiences, and dismiss as nonhappenings any worries of possible future events. Concentrate your energies on the here and now and make the most of it. What you do now creates your future. Focus on thinking, feeling and being in the present moment. Step up to the challenge.

We all have different filters through which we perceive our experiences. Sometimes these filters so totally block the incoming information that they become blinders. I call this "an intellectual block," as the person—either consciously or subconsciously—is not receptive to new incoming information at that time. For such a person, self-reflective work is required before he or she can be receptive to change. Rather than thinking about the change, it is more effective to *feel* the change. The next step forward is knowing that you are on the road to recovery. The *mind* is programmable by word and thought, and the body will follow.

We all have receptors that can receive these subtle energies, but they must be ready to receive, connect and vibrate as they absorb new information. Even harmless, innocuous distractions can interfere with tuning into subtle energies. Some people are preoccupied with watching their favorite T.V. shows, to the exclusion of all other shows. We can only effectively watch one program at a time, so by watching it we effectively block all other incoming information. We must be ready and willing to shed old habits in order to allow ourselves to receive and process new incoming information.

I recently attempted a distant healing requested by a woman with impressive academic credentials. She was extremely well read in alternative healing. I was puzzled when she felt minimal effects after the treatments. When she told me a third time how she thought she had got her ailment, a light dawned. Apparently she saw herself as a victim. She was blaming someone else for being responsible for all of her health problems. But her victim mentality was not serving her well. Blame undercuts self-empowerment. A me-versus-them perspective not only is a futile attempt to separate oneself from others but it shifts responsibility away from oneself. This woman's attitude left her with nonproductive negative thoughts that interfered with her self-healing.

Once you have done your emotional clearing and have let go of outdated beliefs, step away from your rational, analytical role and move to an awareness of feeling your energy. Analysis, with all of its argumentative chatter, causes resistance to the natural course of information as energy. Just let the energy flow.

PACKING FOR YOUR HEALING JOURNEY

Dealing with emotional and psychological baggage can be a daunting task. A relatively easy way to tackle it is to imagine you are packing for your healing journey. You have one backpack to carry with you, so it would be wise to bring only the essentials you need along the way. Examine carefully what you are taking. Be selective. Take only what you need. What you are leaving behind is every emotion, thought, feeling or memory that you do not need. Think of these as bricks that only weigh you down. Bricks can also create a wall, which may be comforting in its familiarity but will hinder your journey forward. What you don't need must be left behind—or rejected and deflected away from yourself.

If you find that your backpack is too heavy to carry, open your mental backpack and take a close look to see if it is weighed down by negative emotions such as:

- Doubt about your own ability to influence your health.
- Uncertainty about the power of subtle energy.
- Hesitation about your commitment or that of those around you on your path to wellness.

Every one of these thoughts is a stone in your backpack, weighing you down. Assess each belief or thought that is holding you back from achieving your goal:

1. Pick up one stone (i.e., negative emotion or attitude) at a time.
2. Identify the belief or event that is causing you to express this emotion or attitude.
3. Say out loud what it is and why you don't need it anymore.
4. In your mind's eye, throw the "stone" as far away from you as you can.
5. Turn away from where it lands. Turning away leaves every stone isolated and powerless.
6. Repeat this process until you are no longer carrying any unnecessary baggage. You will soon realize that all you need

to pack for your journey is universal energy and your own imagination. In fact, what you need is both limitless and weightless, so you don't really need a backpack at all.

If emotional issues are not dealt with, then an energy treatment will be like stretching an elastic band. It seems as though the person is accepting the energy, but he or she is unable to process the incoming information. The person is not receptive to receiving. The elastic stretches, but it retracts to its original shape and there is no lasting benefit from the treatment. This is why it is essential to focus on emotional issues that may be blocking your way forward.

How effectively you can do this emotional clearing depends on how flexible in your thinking you are. A woman contacted me for advice on energy healing, and I suggested this exercise to her. She considered herself already well informed in energy work and when I asked her what she would pack, she told me that she planned to take along some of her favorite books for her healing journey. It seemed to me that she was using these books to find emotional comfort in familiarities from her past, an attitude that did not lend itself to an open-minded approach to her future. She became incensed when I suggested that she might need to be more receptive to change in order for her healing path to lead to lasting benefits. While her academic knowledge base could have been valuable background information, her rigid dependence on it had become a block against moving forward.

TAKING TIME OUT

Without even being aware of it, we all can become preoccupied with the daily routine of our lives. Sometimes it is beneficial to step back and take stock. Evaluate where you are in relation to your goals. Take time out to relax—or play basketball. Give yourself permission to just hang out. You don't need to justify every waking moment on some sort of linear productivity scale. Take a break from your schedule.

Relaxation is vital to our well-being, so it is important to find leisurely pastimes or exercise routines. Many people find meditation a wonderfully stress-reducing exercise. It relaxes our minds and bodies by resetting our conscious awareness. Whatever you find to be an enjoyable way to unwind, set aside time for it. Many of us feel that we don't have enough time as it is, so how could we possibly set time aside for "doing nothing"? Change your thinking on this, because downtime should be a priority in our busy lives. Grab your calendar and schedule more relaxation time. Restructure something in your life so you are free for this essential activity.

HOW HUMOR AND GRATITUDE AFFECTS HEALTH AND HEALING

Humor is necessary because it reminds us to view life on its lighter side. There are many documented cases of people improving their health just by adding humor to their lives. A few laughs a day are wonderful medicine for the soul. Even something as simple as watching a silly T.V. show after dealing with the more serious issues in life will be beneficial.

And finally, be grateful for life. Learn to be content with what you do have, rather than dwelling on what you do not have. This applies to material objects, relationships and health. Appreciation brings happiness. Life should be enjoyed. Being continually grateful is perhaps life's greatest challenge. The simple act of saying thanks before a meal is a good way to express gratitude for what we have. Another simple act is to every day acknowledge one thing for which you are thankful. Each morning say aloud what aspect you appreciate about that particular day. Another part of gratitude is returning positive energy to others. Did you go out of your way to make someone else's day a better one?

Practice gratitude until it is habitual. Before you realize it, you will have established a new attitude. Then you will be able to attract into your life everything and everyone that you need. The shift to this balanced attitude toward life is in your hands.

Reset your goal of overall health to its maximum potential. Absorb into every fiber of your being what you need to achieve this. You will feel changes taking place as this shift toward healing starts to happen in your mind and body. Deflect outward by throwing away what you don't need on the path toward this goal. Now you are ready for your journey.

When you put emotion into a thought or intention, does that always give that thought or intention more influence on your reality?
It depends what the thought and the emotion are. If they are aligned with each other, then the intention is being amplified, sometimes very powerfully. In that case, the influence would be greater. However, if you have an intention with a conflicting emotion and they are not working together, the intention is less effective. For instance, your intention is to remain calm in traffic. But you get cut off and you react in anger. As you become more aware of your trigger to anger, your intention to react calmly will become more effective.

Does fear block the flow of information?
Nothing can actually block information. Fear can divert your attention. Fear might deflect or redirect other information from coming to the forefront, making more important information seem less important. For example, if you are afraid of snakes, that fear will be your singular focus if one is near you. This might prevent you from noticing that you are dangerously close to a moving car while trying to get away from the snake. As a result of fear, you might not pick up on what is more essential for you at that time.

How do we know if our healing intentions are sincere when we are assessing our emotions and attitudes?

Sometimes it is difficult to know if we are sincere in our intentions. Subconscious conflicts that might undermine a seemingly sincere intention to get well could be common issues such as economic or social concerns. No one knows you better than you do. Pay attention to how you think; notice your habits, attitudes and the emotional patterns in which you think. Try to understand your subconscious mind the best you can. In a relaxed meditative state, ask yourself, are these intentions sincere? Reflect honestly on your answer.

Do animals have emotions?

Pet owners swear that their pets have emotions. At least, pet owners read into their pets' behavior a wide range of emotions. Domestic pets constantly interact with the actions and emotions of their owners. This is why we become so emotionally attached to our pets: We carry on a constant emotional dialogue with them. Humans are not unique when it comes to having emotions. We simply express them differently than most other animals.

Chapter 7

Beliefs and Spirituality

Intention and expectation of outcome guide our reality.

—ADAM

𝒯hree years ago, I started working with a woman who had pancreatic cancer. She traveled from the Canadian province of Ontario to Saskatchewan to see me at the First Nations International Healing and Medicines Gathering in which I was participating. At this gathering I had my own teepee in which to conduct my healing groups. It held twelve people at a time. I began working with the woman in the group setting of my teepee. Doctors had told her the cancer was terminal and estimated that in a few months she would be in palliative care. We worked intensively in that week of the Gathering, but I told her that she would need to assume responsibility for her own healing. I could guide her occasionally, but I would be unavailable to do individual treatments with her when I returned to school that fall.

Since then, she has made many changes in her life. I emphasized to her what I teach everyone. It is imperative to examine every aspect of your life and undertake major destressing. Allow only positive self-talk to filter in. She now does qigong, yoga, meditation and positive visualizations and affirmations. She has made it her full-time preoccupation to get well, and this attitude has paid off.

Before we met, her oncologists said her pancreatic tumors

were growing rapidly and that her next scan likely would show that they had spread to the liver. Instead, the next scan showed a 25 percent reduction in tumor size, with no metastasizing. More than two years later, the tumors have almost disappeared. She feels wonderful and maintains her own self-healing program.

Everyone has the ability to self-heal; we just have to learn how to use it. Healing of body, mind and spirit is true healing. Energy healing requires flexibility for change and participation.

Every one of us views our world subjectively, that is, from within our individual belief systems. We form our opinions through life experiences, religious beliefs, and spiritual and cultural views. Our beliefs and disbeliefs act as filters through which we view everything. They set the limitations that guide our thoughts, words and actions. This is true of scientists, too, of course. Their reality is based on their subjective biases. This is an important point to understand, since scientists play a major role in shaping society's accepted theories of reality. Most often what scientists conclude in experiments is based on the pre-existing and accepted theories that are part of the subjective viewpoint of the scientists in the first place. In other words, they prove what they already "know" to be true.

As children, we see life only in the present moment. Consequences for our actions can be envisioned only as some obscure possibility in a vague and distant reality. Children feel a certain way and react intuitively in the here and now. They have not yet developed an analytical process which interferes with intuition. By the time they are adults, they will have had years of societal training which limits imagination and dictates acceptable beliefs and behaviors. This is achieved through parental role modeling, the school system and other cultural, social and religious practices. These influences mold our reality. Prior to this conditioning, everything and anything is possible.

We have all been young children—that is, spontaneous beings—at one point in our lives. It is important to regain that boundless imagination that we all still have within us. The ultimate in flexible thinking is allowing ourselves to know this. The most important aspect of remembering our spontaneous selves is, as with our emotions, to forget what we have learned and remember what we have forgotten.

Each of us faces challenges in life. Most of us are not very old before we have some sort of health concern to deal with. There are many other things in life, such as relationships, school and work, that require our attention as well. Beliefs are fundamental in each of these. We all know someone who approaches any challenge with a positive outlook. Time seems to reward these people with an etched-on, permanent smile, rather than a worried frown. It is not that they have traveled through life unscathed. It is that they see every event in its most positive light. Our outlook and expectations stem from our beliefs.

In health issues, expecting to get better is a huge step toward recovery. Imagine two patients who are facing the same dire health challenge, one in which a statistical survival rate of 50 percent looms over them. One of the patients is almost always optimistic, seeing the proverbial glass as half full, and expects to be one of the patients who fully recovers. The other is usually pessimistic, seeing the glass as half empty, and doubts whether she will be one of the patients who survives. Which person would you expect to survive if all other factors are the same? Most of us would expect the optimist to survive, because he expects to.

This optimistic belief is often described in an almost mystical sense as the will to live. What exactly is the will to live? It is a self-declaration of the intent to survive. It is the unwavering belief that this will happen. When you expect a positive outcome, you send that intention within yourself and beyond yourself via biophoton emissions, initiating a cascade of biochemical reactions in the body that will maximize the possibility of this event actually occurring. Your thought has set everything in motion to achieve what you expect to happen. And guess what? Your positive thinking does influence events.

We all innately possess this limitless power within ourselves. Our bodies do listen to what we tell them. All we have to do is ensure that we are sending out the optimum signal for our wellness. The constant reinforcement of our beliefs does impact us by either setting a healing pattern in place or by emphasizing and strengthening an established negative response.

Think of your mind as a computer that can be programmed to enhance your growth and well-being to their optimum. Maximize the functioning of your immune system by programming yourself to ensure your healthy future.

Before this can happen, you have to want to change. It sounds easy. Of course you want to get better. But it has to be more than idle talk. Your mind and body will recognize whether or not you are ready and willing to make changes. If you are not, the intentions are not sincere and will be viewed and dismissed by your body as background noise.

If you are attempting to feed yourself the same old unproductive self-talk and thought patterns—and just sugarcoat them—think again. For instance, if you are telling yourself that right after summer vacation you will start an exercise program, what you are really saying is that these changes are not important enough for you to start now. You are attempting to fool yourself, and that will never work. You are too smart for that. Who knows you better than yourself? You can't fool yourself, but you *can* change yourself.

Your sincere intention must be your singular focus. This can be accomplished by becoming self-reflective and totally honest with yourself. Your conscious desire must be synchronized with your subconscious thoughts and beliefs. Ask yourself, "What do I want?" Limit yourself to one desired outcome. If your answer is that you want to be healthy again, say so. If you want to live, say it aloud. Shout, "I want to live!" Let it resonate within you that this is your intention. This is what you expect. Change any habits or patterns that are not in synchronicity with this new program. Let yourself know that you are seriously focused on the path toward change.

When doing your self-healing work, you must maintain your focus on your positive intentions of change. While doing so, you may wonder if what you are doing is working. If you are practicing the following four steps, your self-reflective work should bring you answers right away:

1. You make time to reflect on your goals and intentions in a relaxed state of mind.
2. You make time for the emotional equilibrium exercises outlined in Chapter 6.
3. You reflect on your healing beliefs during relaxation.
4. You do the affirmations outlined below.

Must a person believe in energy healing in order for it to work? It certainly speeds along changes if you do believe that you can be well again. You do need to be positive and have an open mind. A positive attitude is very important for any type of healing process to be successful, whether you pursue conventional or alternative treatments, or both. It is a skill to achieve this level of control of one's attitude. But remember: A closed mind is locked from within. Like everything else in life, the shape of your future is ultimately your decision and your choice. Now you have belief and intention directed toward healing. You can now expect change to happen. Everything is set into motion, and you know that your positive outcome will occur.

Change is a choice. This responsibility is our own. Most adults understand that they are accountable for their own actions, including habits. What is more of a challenge is recognizing that we are responsible for every thought, word and belief as well. Go beyond any blame, whether it is focused inward at yourself or outward at someone else. Blame and guilt are totally unproductive.

Imagine the process of change already taking place within you. Practicing the appropriate visualizations for you (see Part 3) will help you actualize this shift. Your imagination is limitless, so use it to program change. Make the time to do visualizations: They are an essential part of reprogramming. No matter how busy you are, make reprogramming a priority. Programming for positive change is your decision and your doing. Take responsibility and you will receive all of the resulting benefits.

AFFIRMATIONS

Affirmations are short statements of belief which can be said aloud or in your thoughts for the purpose of empowering yourself. They help change existing beliefs that may be holding you back from reaching your potential—in any aspect of your life. Affirmations also reinforce positive beliefs that you may need to strengthen. On your path to wellness, they help you realize your maximum healing ability.

A major health challenge can be overwhelming. It may be the first time in your life that you can't be healed by a quick visit to the doctor and a prescription. A crisis calls for change. Whatever the ailment, it has been brewing for some time before it is evident through symptoms or diagnosis. Once the symptoms manifest or the illness is diagnosed, it can no longer be ignored.

This call for action can be a positive life-altering experience. How you react to your health challenge is your choice. Be proactive rather than reactive, and embrace necessary changes. Look at it as an opportunity to take charge of your life and health. Create affirmations of self-acceptance and self-empowerment; I've given you some examples below. As with visualizations, your affirmations are particular to your needs and challenges. The more you customize these examples, the more effective they will be.

Set aside a specific time in your day for doing affirmations. If you do them first thing in the morning, they will set a positive tone for your entire day. Look into a mirror and make eye contact with yourself. You expect others to look you in the eye when they are addressing you, so extend the same courtesy to yourself. Focus on the words as you express them aloud with feeling:

I love myself.
I love others and others love me.
I am happy with who I am and what I think, say and do.
I feel wonderful and am full of healing energy.
Today is a marvelous day full of new opportunities.

Those of you saying, "Yeah, sure, but I don't really like myself," do this anyway. Intend to begin liking yourself. Practice self-forgiveness and monitor your behavior as you begin to change.

The power of the mind over functions of the body is widely acknowledged. The power of the mind over the body has been observed in medical studies to measure treatment efficacy: Patients often improve even when the pill they are taking is only a sugar pill. This is because they believe the pill they are taking will heal them. This phenomenon is known as the placebo effect. In fact, in drug trials, the health improvements in the placebo group are often as significant as those in the group receiving the actual drug.

You undoubtedly have heard of people who have a dissociation disorder that results in multiple personalities. One personality may exhibit totally different characteristics from another. Therapists who work with these patients report that one personality is able to have a medical condition independently of the others. For example, an allergy, eczema or even asthma exhibited in one personality may not exist in another personality. Each personality believes it is a separate person to the extent that each has separate physical characteristics, including medical conditions. The existence of varying medical conditions in the same physical body illustrates the incredible power of beliefs and expectations of our minds, as all personalities are within the same physical body. We all have this level of control of our mind-body; we just have to harness its benefits.

Because beliefs are so powerful, healing must be participatory. Give yourself positive affirmations. Meditate and reflect. Regain harmonious balance in your life. Having supportive people around you is important, but the bottom line is that you yourself must be ready and willing to make the necessary changes to improve your own health.

THE INFLUENCE OF BELIEFS ON MY HEALING WORK

Years ago, a loving mother contacted me seeking help for her teenage son. He was diagnosed with obsessive-compulsive disorder (OCD). People with this affliction often overemphasize perfection and a need for orderliness. They engage in repetitious compulsive behavior, such as constant hand washing because of fear of germs, or constant checking of electrical appliances to make sure they have been unplugged. Repeated blinking and facial tics are OCD symptoms of anxiety. In severe cases, the person is unable to function in society because the behavior rituals consume the entire day. Leaving the house for an errand can be as challenging as planning a climb to the top of Mount Everest.

Recognizing the complexity of the disorder was a good start in helping their son, and the teenager's parents were certain that he would be receptive to my suggestions. I had never seen what OCD looked like on the energetic level, so I was eager to take a look at his photograph to see what I could do.

I could see that OCD appears on the aura as loops of information that are never fully processed. This loopiness is an intuitive feel I got from the aura more than it is an actual appearance. I realized that the boy would benefit from doing a calming visualization and meditation, which would allow the repetitive information loops to synchronize into smoother energy flow throughout the aura. The goal would be to tune the untuned behavioral habits by regaining a more orderly flow of thoughts.

When I replied that I would work with the young man, his response was unexpected. The parents were more surprised than I was. Their son was not interested in distant treatments. His disconcerting response was that he was afraid of losing the OCD. Despite the challenges it presented, it was a known quantity. He defined himself through the disorder and had learned to wear it somewhat comfortably. Obviously, he was not open to change at that point.

This young man's belief that his affliction was an integral part of him raises an interesting point. Every one of us must take an objective look at ourselves and ask, how does this illness serve my needs? It sounds like a ridiculous question until you answer it honestly. Does this ailment give you permission to relax more, or to get out of obligations that you would otherwise have to face reluctantly? Does it serve any purpose in your relationships with others?

People with addictions often view their habit as being an integral part of themselves. Such beliefs are intensified and compounded not only by how we perceive ourselves but by how we believe others view us. This can make change even more of a challenge. Yet, each of us has the ability to accomplish anything that we set our minds to. Do not fall into the trap of labeling yourself or living by a label imposed by others. Move beyond it. Only you can decide your future, through the choices you make.

Another belief that blocks healing is that of being a victim. A man who came to me with Lyme disease repeatedly told me the sequence of events leading to his contracting the disease. He blamed a friend who owned the cottage where he had been bitten by the infected tick. Yet, before being bitten, he was constantly thinking about being bitten and was desperately afraid of contracting Lyme disease. It didn't occur to him that he was attracting the course of events through his focused thought signals about being bitten by a tick and getting ill. He repeatedly imagined himself being bitten, and his belief in the outcome contributed to it becoming reality.

In his mind, however, he was a victim. He was not interested in changing any of the beliefs he had, as doing so would threaten his position as an innocent bystander who was wronged. He believed that he needed rescuing, and he wanted someone else to heal him. This belief kept him stuck in the past because he couldn't get beyond the "if onlys": If only he had not been invited to the friend's cottage; if only he had been informed about the prevalence of ticks in the area.

When I spoke to him about how he could change his perspective on what occurred, he became defensive to the point of hostility. He considers himself a victim. This man will experience the help he needs when he becomes open to a significant change in his beliefs. When he is able to accept responsibility for his own choices, and forgive his friend and himself, he will be able to move forward. Only then will he be able to make any significant progress in his own healing.

Many people have been injured in car accidents when someone else was driving. The driver didn't have the intention to harm anyone. If this is your situation, you must try to leave the establishing of fault to the lawyers and courts. Concentrate on getting well. Make sure that being a victim is only a legal term, and not an emotional state for you.

Life consists of a series of choices. The book of "if onlys" is the longest book on the shelf. Leave it there gathering dust. Those possibilities did not occur. One cannot dwell on the past and fully focus on the present at the same time. Let it be, and move on into the present. This is a choice that you make with every thought, word and deed.

It is important that you understand the participatory nature of healing; that is, your role in your healing. I have held many workshops across North America in order to teach self-empowering techniques for healing. My emphasis in these workshops is how you can better manage your own health concerns, rather than how I can solve them for you. Each workshop session has at least one group energy treatment. This enables all participants to feel the connection to our universally common energy source. Feeling this energy shift is often what is needed for someone to believe that a change is possible. I suggest tools, such as the visualizations in Part 3, that enable participants to continue their healing process independently. The workshops are intended to strengthen the self-confidence needed to assist in self-healing.

I cannot emphasize enough how important it is to become aware of your recurring thoughts and your beliefs and to be open to new information and change. You will attract and experience whatever it is that you consistently expect to manifest. As I mentioned, in my workshops I often do several aura readings, on volunteers among the participants. The accuracy of the aura readings is usually immediately confirmed by the participant. It is interesting to note some of the exceptions. Once again, one's focus, based on one's beliefs, enter into the picture. The aura of one particular man showed a problem with his sciatic nerve. When I pointed that out, he did not concur. He had prostate cancer for which he had undergone surgery. Later, however, he told me that he has experienced severe sciatic pain on and off for over thirty years. He had forgotten about that ailment because his singular focus was on the prostate cancer: He was so preoccupied with the possibility that the cancer would show in his aura that he could think of nothing else.

Another man's aura showed a problem in his abdominal area. He told me that he had diabetes and that I hadn't correctly identified his health challenge. However, he is taking insulin, so his blood sugar levels appeared normal. The aura is simply an external reflection of what is happening inside the body. An aura reading gives general, cursory information. I can more specifically see a problem with the pancreas when I "go in" for a treatment, a more involved process than reading the aura. Even though the pancreas is in the abdominal area, where I said a problem was indicated, the man expected more detail than the aura provides. He had one answer in mind—diabetes—and heard nothing related to or beyond that.

Outside of the workshops, I have worked with people in comas who are unable to communicate their wishes and beliefs. At this point, the wishes of the closest relatives must be respected, and so their beliefs and expectations play an important role in the healing process. A supportive family who accepts energy healing will, through their positive intentions, amplify the healing intentions that I send during a treatment. In this way, others play a direct role in the process of healing.

Sometimes our limiting beliefs stem from the statements of health professionals. It is traumatic enough to be diagnosed with cancer. To be told it is terminal is devastating. This news can become a self-fulfilling prophecy. We might see our situation as hopeless and mentally set ourselves on a course toward death. While we are all going to die eventually, the question is when—and how we choose to live until that time. We all can improve our quality of life through attention to mind, body and spirit.

I treated a woman who had been diagnosed years earlier with multiple myeloma. She has consistently worked on influencing her health through visualizations and energy treatments, and now tests negative for cancer. When her test results first showed that there was no evidence of cancer, this wonderful news was quickly dismissed by the doctors. She was told, "The cancer is gone for now, but it will be back." It is difficult for a person to stay with their program of positive self-healing intentions when faced with dire predictions. Remember that nobody knows for certain what the future holds for any of us. There is no doubt that you have more to do with your own future than anyone else does. Her doctors now refer to this woman as their miracle patient.

Another woman with pancreatic cancer has been working on influencing her own health through visualizations and energy treatments at workshops. Over two years ago, she was given a terminal diagnosis: The cancer was growing rapidly and was by now evident in her liver and lungs as well. A recent scan revealed that her liver and lungs were clear and the pancreatic tumor had shrunk, but her doctor told her that the radiologist did not include this fact in his report. Within his framework of beliefs, the tumor could not have shrunk, and therefore it had. If the woman's positive health result had come about through Western medical intervention rather than a patient's own energy work, the radiologist probably would have been more inclined to believe what he saw. The results were actually so positive that her doctors have spoken to her about rewriting her medical history as a possible misdiagnosis in the first place. I congratulate all of those people who have achieved this level of improvement.

Many times I have observed how beliefs can influence diagnoses. For some health practitioners, it is easier to change the diagnosis than it is to change their beliefs. The goal posts can be moved. Most people see the medical diagnosis they receive as an indisputable and unwavering fact. Yet, the diagnosis often seems to be flexible when a condition improves by means other than Western medicine. In cases where energy healing produces positive results, I have heard responses from skeptical health professionals such as:

- We were wrong about it being terminal cancer in the first place, because the patient has survived.
- It wasn't cancer at all. It just looked like a malignant tumor. But it couldn't have been because its behavior is not consistent with that diagnosis since the tumor has shrunk or disappeared.
- The spinal cord wasn't completely severed as was previously thought. It must have been only partially severed, because some feeling and mobility has been regained.
- Pain is a subjective experience and therefore we cannot possibly determine whether it has actually decreased or not.

- The brain damage could not have been as severe as we thought or a full recovery could not have occurred.

I am no longer concerned about these medical interpretations. What matters is that a person's physical, emotional and spiritual health improves.

If you have been diagnosed with a serious illness, make sure the diagnosis is not blinding everyone, including yourself, to other unrelated illnesses you might also have. For example, I knew a woman who had pancreatic cancer but died of an untreated bowel obstruction. Everyone treating her was cancer-blind: They couldn't get past this six-letter word on her chart in order to consider other conditions she might also have.

Patients themselves can do better at informing their health providers of all healing disciplines they are involved in. Many people don't bother discussing alternative therapies they are using with their medical doctors and, conversely, the naturopathic practitioner doesn't always hear about the allopathic (Western) medical choices a person faces. This fractured health care system, which has not optimally served the needs of the health consumer, is slowly changing.

Despite the fact that many health professionals continue to view the body as made up of separate mechanical parts, I have been encouraged by the opening of minds I have seen within the medical community. Patients want a doctor with two ears—one to hear the holistic needs, and the other to hear the allopathic needs—so that their health needs can be addressed without conflict. As enlightened consumers become more informed and demand change, health professionals are seeking to better understand our mind-body connections and thus are beginning to reflect a holistic awareness.

Alternative and complementary medicine is beginning to integrate with allopathic medicine. This is known as "integral medicine." The mainstream media is reflecting this change with increased coverage of healthy practices such as meditation, positive attitudes, improved diet and exercise. As with most change, it will take time and patience, and we still have a long way to go.

Edgar Mitchell, the Apollo astronaut and IONS scientist, has not only been my science mentor, but I have helped him with his own health challenge using energy treatments. Because of Edgar's past personal experiences with cancer, as well as his work in the science of consciousness, he understands the concepts of energy healing. Says Mitchell, "The story of my life is an account of being hit on the head with astonishing experiences, which drove me to find an explanation."

Years before we met, Edgar Mitchell was healed energetically of prostate cancer. Then, a couple of years ago, he was diagnosed with a cancerous tumor in his kidney. Doctors wanted to operate, but instead of opting for surgery, he called me to see if I could help.

From 5000 miles away, I worked nonlocally with Edgar's holographic image, which I projected in front of me every two weeks, for six months. I found it very effective to imagine energetically wringing out the tumor in order to dry it out. I instructed Edgar to visualize drying out all of the vascular connections that this tumor had, effectively cutting off its survival capabilities. He did not undergo any other treatments, but simply continued with his healthy diet, exercise regimen and meditation. After one month, a CT scan showed that the size of the tumor was markedly reduced. Six months later, the growth had disappeared completely.

Edgar understands that we all possess our own healing abilities, making wellness our personal responsibility. This is the essence of self-empowerment. Working with a healer is always a participatory process, the healer a guide on a two-way street. Experience has previously shown Edgar that energy treatments work, so his beliefs and expectations were already in line with the treatment. As well, his body remembers how a successful outcome was achieved previously. Body memory or cell memory, as well as beliefs, influence outcome.

"We are simply blinded by the limitations of our current scientific paradigm," says the sixth man to walk on the moon. "The most parsimonious explanation for my recovery is Adam's energy healing ability. Eventually we'll have a more complete scientific explanation of abilities such as Adam's (and our own)," Mitchell believes. "What we know so far about the subatomic realm and quantum holography is only the tip of the iceberg."

What do successful people from all disciplines have in common? They all have high self-expectations and a strong belief in themselves. They are visionaries, whether their vision is to win an Olympic gold medal or create a corporation. The belief in what they are setting out to accomplish is clear and unwavering. I have noticed that when it comes to their health challenges, they approach them with the same commitment. Belief and trust in themselves is reflected in the discipline and effectiveness of their healing visualizations.

It is often straightforward to positively influence sports injuries. I know that professional athletes could benefit tremendously by working with energy, as their careers depend on a speedy recovery. In recent years, sports psychology has played a major role in the success of many athletes. Many have come to understand the importance of visualizing what they want to achieve: They know what a powerful tool visualization is.

The media can also play a powerful role in shaping our society, including our beliefs. In the media's coverage of my treatment of Ronnie Hawkins, it brought the discussion of a less than mainstream topic to the fore. Rompin' Ronnie Hawkins has been described as the performer who brought rock and roll to Canada from his home state of Arkansas back in the 1950s. During his more than fifty years as a performer, he has met just about everyone in the music business. Outside Canada, he is best known for the major stars that performed with him. The backup group for Bob Dylan, The Band, was originally Ronnie's backing band and was later famous in its own right. In 1969, John Lennon and Yoko Ono stayed at Ronnie's place during their peace crusade.

A few years ago, I read an article in the local newspaper about Ronnie Hawkins and his battle with inoperable pancreatic cancer. He had gone in for surgery to remove the tumor the month before, but the doctors were unable to operate because the tumor was wrapped around an artery. According to the newspaper article, chemotherapy was not an option for Ronnie, and his cancer had been pronounced terminal. When I looked at his photograph in the paper, I thought that I could help. I contacted his manager, who responded that Ronnie was eager to try anything. He had never heard of distant healing but figured he had nothing to lose.

He said, "Five of the best doctors in the world have told me that this is it. They said three to six months, tops—I'm gone." His friends organized a private party in Ronnie's honor in Toronto, Canada. Many celebrities attended, including well-known Canadian music producer David Foster, former U.S. president Bill Clinton, comedian Whoopi Goldberg, singer-composer Paul Anka, Ronnie's tycoon friend Don Tyson from Arkansas and Canadian industrialist Peter Pocklington. The evening was full of laughter and tears; Ronnie was very ill and was expected at most to live out only the rest of that year.

Two weeks later, in October, Ronnie was inducted into Canada's Walk of Fame. This ceremony is usually held in May, but he wasn't expected to live that long. Just a week before this, I had started distant treatments on Ronnie. Using a photograph, I energetically connected to him from 3000 miles away. Over the next six months, I did approximately sixty treatments with him. Ronnie was amazed to feel these treatments. He reported a fluttering feeling in his abdomen that persisted throughout the sessions.

Almost immediately, Ronnie's health began to improve. It was a surprise to everyone that he greeted in the new year. Even more wonderful was the news that his CT scan showed no evidence of any tumor remaining. An MRI a month and a half later confirmed that Ronnie was cancer-free. Now it is years later, and Ronnie continues to perform on stage and enjoy life.

Shortly after Ronnie was declared cancer-free, an article appeared in a popular American magazine. This piece produced an interesting yet unexpected effect. The magazine's target market is eighteen- to thirty-five-year-olds, younger than most people requesting treatments from me. Instead of health challenges, many of the readers were interested in how this information related to their own unusual experiences with energy. Some people who read the article had never heard the word "aura" before, yet they realized they had been seeing auras for years. Some saw colors; others had a feeling or just a sense of knowing. One woman reported that she always got information when she was physically close to others—for example, information about their moods and events that preceded their meeting. She was also able to help alleviate pain in others. When she confided in her mother, she was told to take a pill and lie down; her mom thought she must be ill. Others also reported that instead of receiving confirmation that their atypical experiences were real and worth exploring, their accounts were dismissed, which left them feeling confused. A number of readers reported being moved to tears as they recalled a meaningful personal experience that was disregarded or ignored.

It is always reassuring to people with unusual abilities to know that they are not alone. The magazine article gave many people permission to reveal their own experiences.

Children are keenly aware of reality beyond our five senses. It was wonderful to know that many young adults haven't forgotten what they once knew to be true. If these abilities are continually dismissed, their intensity often diminishes over time. Yet, with practice, one can revive these abilities. It is a matter of intention, learning to refocus and remembering what you have forgotten. Of course there is no age restriction on knowing that our abilities extend beyond our usual perception.

SPIRITUALITY

Spirituality is based on our intuitive knowing that there is more to our existence than what is dictated by our five senses of sight, hearing, taste, smell and touch. Merely inquiring as to what spirituality is suggests that you are spiritual. It is the act of contemplating our own existence. Since the beginning of time, humans have asked perplexing questions. Why are we here? What is our purpose? What is our role in this universe? Contemplating the meaning of life is in essence being spiritual. All organisms that are aware of their own existence are spiritual in some sense.

Our interconnectedness with everything in this universe plays a major role in defining our individual spirituality. How we view ourselves is not in isolation from everyone and everything else. The path each of us takes to understand our existence differs widely, but the search is nonetheless an integral part of our being. The spiritual search can be both personal and global. Our individual and collective quest to experience, express and explore the deeper meaning of knowledge and new ideas makes us spiritual. People vary greatly in their progress along a spiritual path. Some dedicate almost no time to understanding the universe; some devote their entire lives.

There is no limit to the number of questions that could arise as we ponder our role in the universe. I tend to take a scientific view on things, including life itself. What is the purpose of life? I personally do not like using the word "purpose" in this context because it implies that everything is predestined. I believe that life simply evolved in this vast amazing universe—from singularity to the incredibly complex world we experience today. All along there were unlimited probabilities, some of which manifested and some did not. We can't study the quantum world for long before coming face-to-face with mysteries of our seemingly nonphysical nature.

The scientific perspective on life is difficult for many people to accept. As conscious entities, our wish is not only to understand the universe—an exciting, never-ending quest—but to find meaning. The connectedness that quantum physicists describe has a meaningful aspect. This interconnection between each of our individual consciousnesses is something so complex that striving to understand it is a productive and fulfilling objective. There will always be something yet to be explored or beyond our understanding, and the human appetite to pursue answers cannot be ignored. Science is one of our best tools to use in this pursuit.

Many people feel that religion answers the question of how we came to be. There are many religions in the world today, and each follower believes that his or her religion is the true religion. Spirituality is definitely a part of religion, but one does not have to be religious to be spiritual. Religion is an organized group activity, while spirituality is an individual knowingness emanating from within. Belief in God or Allah or Jehovah then becomes a matter of individual faith and experience.

Other belief systems not recognized as organized religions also embrace a spiritual way of life. North American Native cultures have always had a great respect for the spiritual world. These beliefs provide them with their direction and timing for action and reflection. Their culture speaks of many guides, which are evident in their practices and customs. Totem poles are an artistic representation of important cultural information, such as clans, spirit guides and significant events, representing a set of beliefs at a particular time. These images include many of animals that act as messengers to guide them.

North American Native nations understand that individual contentment is based on the collective needs of all. This belief underlies everything they do in their daily activities and ensures harmony within their culture. Their philosophy of cooperation rather than competition was foreign to the Europeans who took over the Native land and tried to dominate their cultures. When the Europeans came to North America, they outlawed the spiritual beliefs of the Natives. Yet, what was seen by the Europeans as a primitive and regressive culture is actually the direction in which we all must move to achieve global sustainability.

Many wars throughout civilization have been based on misguided religious beliefs. The message that can unite all religions is: We are all one. Since we are all connected to the same field of information, ideally we would all have a unified understanding about consciousness and spirituality. Can you imagine the peace in the world if all religions started preaching from the same page? This is the unification that is required for our world to survive.

It is of the greatest importance to be open to learning and not get bogged down with dogmatism that divides us and stifles our progress. Your beliefs are ultimately a personal and private matter. Whether you define yourself as Christian, Jew, Hindu, Buddhist, Muslim, agnostic, atheist or what have you, the important thing is that we all embrace our differences and accept one another.

I see the difference between various religious philosophies as primarily a matter of semantics. The quantum physics term "energy field" is interchangeable with "the divine power of a deity." I generally avoid religious and cultural terms and prefer to speak from a scientific perspective. Scientific terminology is inclusive of everyone, rather than exclusive to only those of a particular cultural heritage or religious belief. Balancing of spiritual thoughts and ideas to form a collective consciousness for all of humankind should be everyone's goal. A unified approach would view "God" (or "Allah," or "Jehovah," and so on) as a different name for the same thing: the One Mind; the collective consciousness or energy source. The collective consciousness of all organisms in the universe has a tendency to influence events in various ways. Our overall goal should be to understand these interconnections of consciousness that we share with each other and everything else in the universe for the greater good of all.

Spirituality is based on our intuitive feeling of knowing that there are more subtleties to our existence than are picked up by the five senses. We must respect life by being aware. Sometimes life is to be heard, at other times it is to be seen and, almost always, it is to be felt. Our inner knowing will guide us. By becoming more aware, we move toward understanding ourselves. Through a better understanding of ourselves, we become more accepting of the harmony required for all of us to benefit from each other within a cooperative system.

Spirituality is ultimately a deep belief within yourself; it is the basis of your belief system and includes what you desire, expect and know will happen. Connecting to your own spirituality will allow you to move forward and achieve anything you can imagine. When you understand the origin of your thoughts, you are more in tune with yourself in every thought, word and action. Clarity of awareness is available to us to interpret every experience so that we can go forward with confidence. We can then embrace every new situation and challenge. This is the key to happiness.

Many of our spiritual beliefs lie in our subconscious minds. By uniting our subconscious beliefs and conscious intentions, we truly awaken our spirituality. We can then synchronize our thoughts, intentions and actions.

How does suffering—particularly, suffering from an illness—relate to spirituality? On an individual level, physical suffering can serve as a pivotal point in our lives: It is often a powerful wake-up call demanding our immediate attention. View this as a chance to take control of your health, reflect upon your life and notice where you are heading. In the long run, such suffering may force the development of self-responsibility and self-empowerment. Recognition of spiritual issues is part and parcel of this development.

In a more global view, when someone suffers, we all suffer, because we are all connected. Of course, those people closest to that person feel the most pain from their loved one's suffering.

As our global community shrinks, we increasingly find that people of every religion are becoming our neighbors, friends and relatives. Religion is a particular set of answers, within a historical and cultural context, to the spiritual questions people pose. We must learn to embrace the differences in interpretation since ultimately what is similar in each religion is the principle of love and acceptance. Our growing connections will help rid us of intolerance—an essential step in the survival of humankind. Our increasing global consciousness reflects the interconnectedness that we all share and is the basis of the ongoing paradigm shift in our thinking.

Sometimes a person might not get well because it is their time to move on—it is their time to die. You have said that you often intuitively pick up this information. Since beliefs play such a major role in our well-being, how do you handle that?
I believe that it is not something I should tell a person. I am not always right. Even if I were, it would not be appropriate to share any information that might influence a person's beliefs and their intention to get well.

How many treatments do people typically require? Does it depend on the person's belief system?
The number of treatments depends primarily on the illness, though the manipulation of energy in the body can be enhanced or slowed by the healee's specific beliefs. Many illnesses can be helped significantly with only a few treatments—joint pain, lower back pain, migraines and asthma among them. Even though some of these health challenges have been with a person for decades, they can sometimes be relieved in just a few treatments. Other illnesses, such as cancer, may require many treatments. This is why it is imperative that people understand what they can do for themselves. As in so many aspects of life, you can always count on yourself.

Have you ever worked with someone you couldn't help?
Most people I work with notice a difference, and if they stay with the treatments, they usually improve. About 90 percent of those I work with notice sensations during treatments.

Some people are curious to try energy healing but find it difficult to get their heads around it. Indeed, some may begin to follow the exercises in this book but be unable to keep with it. Energy healing is participatory and requires clear motivation and persistent practice on the part of the healee. Any conflicting beliefs that a person has may impede the journey to wellness. That is, the person may consciously want to get well but is unconsciously blocking the healing process.

Chapter 8

Reincarnation

*Reincarnation allows for the ultimate learning curve
in the progress of all things.*

—ADAM

*R*eincarnation is the mechanism for the transmission of information from one lifetime to the next. It is the process of repeated rebirth in a never-ending cycle of birth, life and death. I have some memories of past lives. Most are fragmented, but some are quite clear and some are traumatic.

Hundreds of years ago, I was a member of a Native American tribe. My home was surrounded by grassy hills, and a river flowed nearby. Life was peaceful. One day, a scout returned home with disturbing news. He had witnessed the decimation of a neighboring tribe, and the killers were headed toward our village. Immediately, a meeting was called. The elder medicine man told us that twelve men would stay behind to defend the village. Everyone else was to leave at once and get as far away as possible.

Within minutes, the women, children and many of the men left. My younger brother and I remained behind with ten other men. That was when the shaman said that he saw our main purpose in staying behind as giving the others a head start, thereby escaping the impending attack. He also revealed that all twelve men who stayed behind would be killed defending our village. Many years before this, when I was young, he had told me that my brother and I would die together.

That night as we gathered around the fire, no one spoke.

Each of us gazed silently into the flames, absorbed by our own thoughts. Just after sunrise, we were attacked by several men from another tribe. They were accompanied by white men. One of the white men pointed a stick at me. I charged at him with my mallet-like weapon. As I reached him, I realized that I was bleeding. I hadn't recognized his stick as a gun, since I had never seen a gun before: I had no way of knowing that I had been shot.

As I dropped to the ground holding my chest, my head turned to the side. I found myself gazing directly into the eyes of my brother, who lay only a few feet away. He was pinned to the ground by the attackers and being scalped alive. He saw me and our eyes locked. The look of terror in his eyes ripped through me. There was nothing I could do to help my little brother; I was dying too. So I smiled at him. That was all I could give him: a smile.

It is still an emotional experience for me to recall this life. Because of this, I understand the impact that memories can have on people. Some people have vivid memories of past life experiences, others remember fragments and many people have no recollection at all. Regardless of what we do or don't remember, our past lives have an impact on our emotional and thus physical health.

Reincarnation is a natural process, one of the everyday events in the universe. A scientific definition of reincarnation would draw on theories derived from our current body of knowledge of physics, especially of how energy behaves in our universe. One of the laws of physics is that energy can be neither created nor destroyed. Reincarnation, which involves a person's energy essence being passed on from one lifetime to another, is no exception to this rule: One's composite of energy (light) frequencies does not cease at the time of death but transfers to the next life.

Reincarnation is not all that mysterious in the context of the subtle energies and light emissions that I have been discussing. As

I described earlier, each of us has a unique frequency connection to the universal field of information; this is our signature link to everything at any time, and our eternal energy essence. This energy essence is referred to as the soul in many religions. It is all the information from all your previous lives—the unique way in which light has coordinated all of your cells throughout all of your incarnations. This is who you are. The cumulative light frequency emitted from a multi-cellular organism (such as a human being or animal) coordinates and unifies all of the cells within it into one harmonious organism. At the time of physical death, this unifying frequency of light goes through a transformation process as it becomes the essence of life in a new organism.

Reincarnation, as a means to preserve energy essence, is essential for human evolution, as well as for all other creatures great and small. It allows for the ultimate learning experience in the progression of all things.

Every living organism has a focal point of light emissions. This point is the center of information exchange and is where the light emitted within the body is at the greatest concentration. When I connect to someone's hologram, this focal point appears to me as a bright white light near the center of the brain. It is from here that we tune in to the field of information.

In life, the body is always in a dynamic state of disequilibria in terms of biophoton emissions and biochemical reactions. The constant state of rebalancing, or flux, is the state of disequilibria. In life, our energy is never totally balanced. Life is a constant balance and counterbalance process between emissions and reactions. At the point of death, the body reaches a state of equilibrium. A balance is finally achieved. The light frequency—the energy essence—dissipates, and then eventually manifests in the new organism, identical to what it was in the previous form.

One's state of mind and intentions at the moment of death have a great influence on what will occur as one passes from one physical life to the next. Your characteristics throughout your life—what you are like, the kinds of thought patterns that you typically have—will influence the pattern of your energy essence in your next life. The thoughts, both conscious and subconscious, that you have at the time of death play a large part in determining your next incarnate, or bodily, form. Those thoughts, of course, are usually in sync with your typical personality patterns.

Generally, if you had good thoughts and intentions throughout your life, these would be on your mind at the point of departure, or death. It's possible that someone who has lived an exemplary life is not connecting to positive intentions at the moment of death. Conversely, another person might have lived his or her life as an angry, self-centered person but managed at this transitional time to emanate positive thoughts and intentions. Although it is possible to change your focus toward the end of life, it is much easier to transfer a well-established path. It is a lot more work to instantly forge a new one.

Where your intention is focused at the exact moment of death determines the direction your new life will take. Your thoughts emit a particular energy frequency that links to and affects everything else. This influences the exchange of information at that time. If your thinking and intentions are vague and unfocused, your successive incarnate body will be selected as randomly as your thoughts are random. If you are thinking with clear, focused intention, you are more likely to influence what occurs. Your thoughts at the time of death are affected by the circumstances of your death. A violent, emotional or painful death would have a different influence than a peaceful parting in your sleep.

Our intentions are like a compass needle in the sense that they direct our energy through this transfer. Where the compass is pointing at the time of death guides us. We can influence this through our choices. Intention affects everything much more than we may be aware. It is important to understand how essential self-reflection and self-assessment are in maximizing our influence on our destinies. Your intention is the main guiding process in the transition from one life to the next. Of course, many factors line up at the time of death to pave the path of transition, the path to the next life: The outcome is a result of the sum of all of the smaller influences and experiences of your life journey too.

It is important, at the time of death, to reflect on what your intentions are and what you want to happen. It all comes down to intention. What messages are you sending out to the field? By aligning your conscious and subconscious thoughts, dealing with emotional and psychological baggage and thus lessening the impact of it on your daily life, and giving yourself daily affirmations, you can learn to focus your intention.

Your consciousness, present in every atom and cell, also exists externally of your physical self. Your own consciousness, rather than some external force, guides your new life and your new incarnation. The power to be your own guide lies totally within yourself.

Your combination of attitudes and degree of awareness puts you at a certain vibration level, and you will resonate with or be influenced more by the consciousness, or energy, of others at a similar vibration level. You are also affected by the collective consciousness, though not to a degree that redirects your own intention.

Many of us have been intrigued by accounts of near-death experiences. They almost always involve an intense, bright light and sometimes feelings of warmth more powerful than the sun. People report intense emotions such as overwhelming love, happiness, joy and contentment. Their entire lives replay before them in their mind's eye—every thought, word and deed. Feelings of peace and calm often linger with the person long after the experience.

These accounts by adults and children alike are consistent throughout history, transcending culture and religion. An out-of-body experience is felt as a spiritual conscious awareness such as we all will experience during the process of death and reincarnation. The difference, of course, is that in a near-death experience, death does not occur, so the person regains consciousness in the same physical self. The process of transformation is incomplete. In the process of reincarnation, on the other hand, there is a point of no return, when our connection to memories in the field is shifted from the conscious and subconscious level of self to the subconscious of the new self.

Based on the reports of people who have had a near-death experience, at the point of death, we experience an intense light. Some people report seeing this light, others feel it. This bright light imprints all data contained within us at our particular frequency or vibration—our signature. Next we go through what appears to be a tunnel as we experience an overwhelming sense of interconnectedness to everyone and everything else in the universe, and therefore the field. Accompanying this feeling of being a part of everything is our knowing that we are not separate consciousnesses. We are truly a collective consciousness.

One's new physical body is imprinted with the information that contains all of the data from all of one's past lives. As I discuss above, the connection between this information in the old body and the new incarnate is directed, through intentions and thoughts at the moment of death, by the person's unique frequency.

To appreciate the process of reincarnation, it is essential to understand the pivotal role energy and light frequencies play in human reproduction. The energy of the egg is different from the energy of the mother. The egg alone doesn't yet have the life force, which is the light that binds the cells together. At the moment of conception, when the energies of the egg and sperm merge, the newly created entity acquires the life (light) force. This signature frequency of light information starts to influence an embryo, coordinating the development of the new organism. Consciousness re-emerges in this new form.

In this way, our connection to all information in the field is complete, and our biophoton emissions light up with the light of life. Light emanates from every cell and an aura appears around the new body as the energy of all cells starts coordinating the cells' functions in synchronicity with the frequency. This energetic self is the essence of life. It is this that lives on, reconnecting to a new body during the process of reincarnation.

Death is an inevitable part of the reincarnation process. I haven't witnessed a person dying, but I witnessed the death of our cat and the energetic process of death must be the same, as cats and humans are both multi-cellular organisms. When our cat was euthanized at twenty-one years of age, I stared into her eyes the entire time she was dying. As she died, the harmonious flow of her aura became fragmented. All of the brilliant colors began to fade to grayish tones. Then a static-like pattern emerged as the speed of the aura's motion gradually slowed. After about half an hour, her aura was completely gray and almost stagnant. I kept my thoughts on what a wonderful friend she had been to me all of my life, knowing that this would influence her last thoughts and impressions in this life. Her new incarnate will receive guidance and direction from this in the same way that it does with humans.

The question of how long we remain between incarnations without a physical body has no real meaning when we are out-of-body. In that state, we are no longer restricted by space and time limitations. We are only energy as information, as we always have been. Our illusion of physical self provided us with rules that no longer apply. At death, our energy is in the form of waves, which do not operate as a function of time in the way energy does when it is particles of matter.

Once again, each of us has the ability to influence our incarnate selection as we manipulate our own energy through thoughts and intentions while we are alive. What we can accomplish in one life is a continuation of what we can accomplish in the next. We learn and we continue to learn.

If there is any reckoning that we must face, it is that which we arrive at through self-reflection of our thoughts, words, actions and intentions. Only we know our every thought and deed during our lifetime. Only we can visualize what impact our lives have had on anything and therefore everything else. We must stand before ourselves and review what we have done. This should not be thought of in a judgmental way, as it is an extension of our lifetime learning process. Any lessons that we need to address become clear to us upon self-reflection. This is the same self-reflection process that you have used to access your own self-talk and beliefs.

Our memories in this life cease at the point of death. A shift takes place, which transforms the connection of all memories in the field into the subconscious of the new body. The energy that is reincarnated is specific and, in that sense, our connection to the field remains identical. When this frequency connects to the new body, however, change inevitably starts to occur with every experience of the new environment. Once our conscious awareness returns to a new physical form, these various experiences start to shape our perception of events. Your subconscious self, the repository of your energy essence, is the accumulation of your many lifetimes. You are, in effect, the sum of many existences.

Two perspectives are joined with each reincarnation: the person in the previous life and the person in the new life. From the perspective of the person in the previous life, everything ends at the point of death. The energy information transfer from the old body to the new is beyond conscious awareness. However, the memories of the past life are continuous in the new life whether the "new" you is consciously aware of them or not. These memories resonate within every cell of your being, since your unique connection to the field of all information is ubiquitous—that is, everywhere at the same time. Reincarnation allows us to accumulate the wisdom and understanding to choose wisely through our developing spirits. This is spiritual evolution. Ultimately, a greater understanding of this process should lead to a deeper appreciation of all of humanity.

We can influence who, what, where and when our next life will be through focused intention. We can choose with whom we share the closest relationships, what we want and need to learn and what we can contribute toward the collective good. Your intentions have a much greater effect than you may be aware. Choose your wishes wisely.

How and when does the holographic information from a former body imprint on the new incarnate? How and when does this information get transferred?

I'm not exactly sure. It might be at the point of conception because that is when the biophoton emissions start coordinating the development of cells. Those cells are who you are—what is unique to you. The way in which light emissions are organizing your cells is what constitutes your mind—your consciousness. As soon as light begins coordinating the formation of cells, consciousness is present. What comes with that consciousness is all information from all previous lives.

What form do we take after dying and leaving the body behind?
We become a different form of energy—or what I call a wave function. That is what you are—a wave function, whether you are in a physical body or not. Without a physical body, you will be absorbed into the field and will continue to have energy properties. You may not consciously be aware of where you are or what's happening, but your intentions will still influence things.

Can an animal reincarnate as another type of animal—as a human, for example?
Yes. For example, in the case of my cat, the vast majority of her memories are of people. Her intentions throughout her life and at the time of her death are going to be focused on people because she was around people all of her life. If her intentions were constantly on people, the chance of her coming back as a human is high. The intentions of both humans and animals at the time of death are a main factor in what form the incarnation will take.

Chapter 9

Karma

Our reality is influenced, but not determined, by karma.

—ADAM

I am often asked at my workshops about karma—the nature and influence of the energy that is transferred from one incarnation to the next—and its relationship to illness. Health and healing is part of who we are and who we have been. For instance, I have had a health issue revisit me from the past.

Several years ago, I was one of the healers invited to the First Nations International Healing and Medicines Gathering held at the Nekaneet First Nation in Saskatchewan. The setting is the beautiful grasslands where Cree people have lived for centuries. It was an honor to take part in the traditional Native ceremonies and to work with shamans from around the globe.

During the entire week of the Gathering, there was always a long lineup of people outside one particular shaman's teepee of the ten that made up the healing circle. When I arrived at my teepee each morning, people were already lined up outside that teepee. When I left in the evening, a lengthy line remained. I wasn't able to catch even a glimpse of the shaman, as he never left his teepee, choosing to eat and sleep there too.

After the closing ceremonies, I was packing my belongings when a man approached me. He introduced himself as the assistant to that shaman. The aide said that the shaman would like to meet me now if it was convenient. My mom also wanted to meet the shaman, so we went together to his teepee.

The shaman and I recognized each other immediately and we spoke, in telepathic images, of knowing each other in a past life. He and I had been close in a previous life. We were in the same tribe, I being the older of the two of us. He remembered us both being on horseback and my being shot in my right shoulder with an arrow. Telepathically through images, he asked how my shoulder was. I rolled up my sleeve and showed him a scar on my right shoulder.

The past life shoulder trauma seems to have followed me into this lifetime, because when I was thirteen years old in my current life, I injured my right shoulder in a bus accident and had to have surgery on it. There would have been a number of ways for me to break my fall as the bus driver slammed on the brakes, but it was my shoulder that took the brunt of the impact. This doesn't necessarily mean that the shoulder injury in my current life was a certainty. It was not inevitable or unpreventable. Karma does not directly cause things to happen. Rather, the tendency or likelihood of an event is present as a karmic influence: Karma influences events to occur in a particular manner or sequence. My shoulder injury wasn't directly caused by the karmic influence, but that influence did play a role in my breaking my fall with my shoulder. My reaction may have been in my subconscious when I reacted to the event.

After a brief conversation, the shaman and I parted, as there was still a lineup of people outside his teepee waiting to see him. I am sure our paths will cross again.

Karma is commonly thought of as the baggage that we carry with us from one life to the next. However, once again, a law of physics provides us with a more accurate perspective on karma: For every action, there is an equal and opposite reaction. This suggests that energy seeks equilibrium. Some people take this law and apply moral considerations to it, calling it karma. For example, a common belief is that if you have evil intentions in one life, your karma will be to make restitution in the next, thereby balancing out good and evil or achieving equilibrium.

It seems to me that some people underestimate the role of karma in events and others overestimate it, by claiming that unfortunate events are due to karma. Karma plays a subtle role in our everyday lives. It is not operating to punish you for actions in a past life. I understand karma to be less rigid than a system of restitution, and not predestined. It is just energy—and, remember, there is no good or bad energy; energy is just energy—that works and moves in various ways according to natural laws. And karma is not limited to humans but applies to all living organisms.

Offspring can be influenced by their parents' karma—but in an environmental sense rather than a genetic sense. In the womb, the baby is growing and developing, surrounded by the mother's energy. The mother's energy is like a conductor of electricity. The fetus attracts the mother's energy but has its own energy patterns. Yet, it generally moves energy in a similar fashion to that of the mother and so experiences a similar flow.

As I discussed earlier, every organism emits a unique frequency of light that connects to the field of information. This connection can increase the likelihood of certain events occurring. These frequencies of light emitted from your body can influence events in subtle ways, which cumulatively can influence larger events that may seem unrelated.

For instance, if you are angry all the time, you will outwardly demonstrate this emotion, and your frequency will closely correlate with that of anger. The events that occur around you will thrive in an environment of anger. Certain events will be more probable, such as conflict with another person, leading to a chain of events that makes you think that you have bad karma. What is actually happening is that your angry attitude is attracting more anger. What you refer to as your karma is the result of your habitual thoughts and intentions.

As one's essence reincarnates, some similar traits or inclinations from a previous life tend to carry over to the next; that, too, is karma. Those inclinations, in turn, will affect the events that may happen in your new life. So a person's energy essence, you might say, while not identical to that in a previous life, has some similarity. There are always differences; things are constantly changing. Each life is a new beginning. Remember that when you reincarnate, your new body is in another time and often a different place, which means new experiences. You will have a different genetic makeup and be raised in a different environment. These influences can mitigate karma. Environment plays a more influential role in our lives than does genetics. Certain environments allow specific energies to thrive and others to be less important. If you are raised in an environment that encourages growth, then growth characterizes your thoughts and intentions and you will progress accordingly. Conversely, if you have to cope in a fear-based environment, that negative conditioning will become a particular challenge to overcome. This is why karma can only be an influence, and not a certainty. Nothing is predetermined.

We choose our own paths; free will guides our journeys. Our subconscious memories from previous lives and the similar frequency from one life to another do have an impact. But we can look at these tendencies as challenges to overcome. We create our own destiny: Karma is only an influence on events. Within our new selves, we can intend and create new possibilities to positively influence any existing karmic patterns. There is always the choice—and hence the potential—to wipe the slate clean. We can consciously choose how we are going to react to any karmic influences, subconscious programming and the environment in which we find ourselves.

There is no karmic law that you must relive all of the bad and ugly events of past lives, even if you vividly remember some events and experiences in this life. But past life memories can be traumatic. This is because the most vivid memories often occur at transition, or the moment of death, as we have the clearest recollection of our most emotionally charged events. Those moments where intense emotions intertwine with memory give us recall of the experience. Memories from past lives are usually subconscious feelings triggered by events in the present life.

Every one of us gets impressions or feelings about past, present or future events. People react to such sensations differently. Many people rely heavily on their gut instincts. Others try hard to dismiss these signals that their subconscious is sending them.

I am often able to pick up images from a person's past lives. Generally, the images are brief and random. Sometimes they make a lot of sense to the person when I relate them, and other times not. The images won't resonate with the person unless he or she has experienced a meaningful event connecting this subconscious information from a past life to events in the current life.

To access past life information, I connect to the person the same way as I would if doing a treatment. I then access the center of the brain, where there is the highest concentration of light and therefore the highest concentration of information. It is here that I receive information about past lives.

One woman I met wanted to know what I could see of her past lives. When I did a reading on her, I telepathically received two brief images. In the first image, she was descending a staircase, lit by a torch, to a dungeon; the next image was of prison bars. These images made perfect sense to her when I told her of them. Many years earlier, she was touring in Europe. As she approached a castle, she became nauseated and fearful. She refused to go inside and skipped the tour. At the time, she could not explain this reaction, but she felt strongly that she could not enter the castle—and she followed her feelings. My past life reading therefore immediately resonated with her. If we can understand what triggers our fears and negative emotions, we can control our reactions to them. It is possible to reestablish all of the positive learning experiences while repatterning the negative ones. Again, there is no karmic law that you must relive all of the bad and ugly events, so only keep what you need for self-enlightenment.

Living life with a positive outlook and expecting positive outcomes is important for achieving your goal. Your intentions must be clearly focused on what you want and expect to happen. If good health is your objective, be clear in your intention. Positively influence any karmic patterns with your intentions. By doing the exercises in this book, you will align your conscious and subconscious thoughts, effectively adjust emotional reactions to be more favorable and be able to focus on what you want through affirmations. Emphasize what you want to achieve in order for the best possibilities to manifest themselves.

Our seeking a purpose for the existence of karma is a very human activity, one growing out of the desire for meaning in life. The transfer of energy from one life to the next is a natural evolution. Since energy cannot be destroyed, it transmutes into another life.

From an evolutionary perspective, karma is one of many variables that influence the energetic aspect of the self as it continues from one lifetime to the next. Another variable is how quickly you reincarnate to another life—the physical transition is not necessarily instantaneous. Another influence on our energetic self is the thoughts and intentions that are in your mind when you die, as discussed in the previous chapter, on reincarnation. Of course, you are influenced by the body you are going into and the who, what and where circumstances of your new incarnate. For example, the challenges of a prince are different than those of a pauper. Everything changes somewhat: your personality, the environment that influences you, your appearance. The process is dynamic. You are always evolving, from one incarnation to the next, just as you evolve and make changes within each lifetime, which is itself the sum of all of your incarnations.

What is relatively stable is the manner in which light coordinates your cells—the frequency of that light remains somewhat the same. As I discuss in the previous chapter, this is the essence or soul of a person. So, from lifetime to lifetime, certain patterns will be similar. But if the incarnate does not encounter a challenge from a previous life because of entirely different circumstances in the new life, karma may not be much of an influence.

Often a variety of small effects—small changes—cause a series of events to occur, which can result in interesting coincidences between different lifetimes. One of my mom's past lives illustrates this point. In that past life, she was a nun in a clinic, dedicated to helping and healing people. She had been born into a poverty-stricken family and had many siblings. When she became an adult, she had the choice of getting married into equally abject poverty and repeating the cycle, or becoming a nun. She chose the latter because it offered more possibilities. Her empathy for others led her to start a clinic dedicated to healing. I intuitively knew that my mother would recognize the way she referred to the work she did in her clinic in her past life—as healing "hearts, minds and souls." When I told her about this during a past life reading, she shivered; the recollection of this past life resonated with her. She now finds herself helping others in this lifetime as well, by helping me with my healing workshops.

We are in control of pointing our own compasses—another way of describing free will. At first it might seem that karma and free will are contradictory concepts. But this is not so: Your free will has determined your karmic influences. Your choices have all been of your own free will. We are constantly making choices—every minute of every day. Our environment influences the choice we make, but we are always the driving force; the chosen route is not externally imposed upon us. When we change our minds about something, karmic influences are changed accordingly. Nothing is written in stone, so to speak. As I've said before, energy is a neutral force that behaves according to how we direct it. One obvious characteristic of the universe and evolution is constant change. We exist in a dynamic system.

I have been asked whether karma affects thoughts as well as actions. There is no distinction between an action and a thought in terms of karma. A thought has a particular energy, which initiates its link to everything. An action also links to and has an effect on the energetic flow, thereby setting a certain chain of events into motion. The only difference between the two is that an action alters the awareness and reactions of others. In a domino-like effect, others see the action and their collective attention amplifies the energetic effect of that action.

Many people believe that the root cause of an illness can be traced to an incident from a past life. In my view, there is no illness that karma or a past life event is solely responsible for. Nobody deserves to be ill. Some people take some comfort in the concept of karma as a reason for their illness. They say that it is a lesson that must be learned from a past life. This is not a productive outlook for anyone embarking on a healing journey through self-empowerment. A healthier perspective is to put all past events aside and travel forward on the path of healing. Simply consider the lesson as having been learned and that it is now time to get better. Take responsibility for your way forward in thought, word and action. Start making changes from within.

In no circumstances should you play the role of the victim. Life is as dynamic as you are. Make the changes that will be beneficial to you on your health and healing journey. Be flexible. Make sure that you are ready, willing and able to accept change. We must focus on re-creating what we want to achieve. Always see the glass as being half full rather than half empty. Imprint this attitude into your being until it is ingrained within everything you think, say and do. Give credit where credit is due when good things are achieved, especially if it is your own accomplishment. Sometimes it may seem impossible to reach your goals, but two steps forward and one step back is still progress in the direction you want.

Life is for learning. Regain your footing. Blaming an illness on past lives and karma is not productive. In our current life, we *can* directly influence events and carry on. Failure occurs only by not trying in the first place. Establish your goal and make it happen.

You mention that the role of karma on events is sometimes overemphasized. Why is this a concern?
Each time you reincarnate, you start with a new environment and a new body. Your intentions may change with the new incarnate, thus influencing your energy. You can always change your present intentions and influence your present health. I'm concerned that if people feel that their illness involves a lesson to be learned, they might tend to accept it as fate rather than changing it. Life is a dynamic experience; it is not predetermined. It's important not to use karma as an excuse to be sick, as this will undermine your intention and determination to get well.

How have your past lives been revealed to you—through dreams, waking memories, visions?

Some have come to me in dreams, some in visions and some occur when I go to certain places—I just know I've been there before and I recognize specific locations and recall events. Often these past life memories are as clear to me as my childhood memories from this life.

Chapter 10

The Spirit World

After physical death, the essence of life exists without physical form until it unites with a new incarnate.

—ADAM

At my workshops I meet many people who feel strongly connected to spirits and the spirit world. This issue weighs heavily on their minds, as our society is reluctant to address such issues as valid ones. Yet anything that concerns us spiritually influences our physical and psychological health and wellness. In this way, the spirit world is inseparable from our health and healing. How we view life after death most certainly influences our lives. Culture plays a dominant role in our views about the spirit world, as does religion and our own experiences throughout our lifetimes.

Many people are sensitive to our energetic connections. At my workshops, I am often asked whether I see spirits—what some people refer to as ghosts. In response, I sometimes relate this story about one encounter I had with a spirit.

I was on a canoe trip with my parents along a river that snaked through the mountains. While heading up the river, I became aware of a spirit trying to get my attention. To me, spirits look like an aura without a physical body. As I had encountered them many times before, I was curious, but not afraid. This spirit followed us along the shoreline, in the thick bushes. As we paddled, it sent me a message. Several minutes later, I asked my parents that we pull over, and so we stopped on a stretch of beach. I felt compelled go into the bush and connect with this spirit.

When I emerged from the bush, my dad said I looked like I had seen a ghost. I told him that the spirit was of an old Native elder. The information this spirit shared with me was about the massacre of his friends and family, including him. When I connected to this spirit, I received vivid images of the massacre. I could see Natives being scalped and murdered with axes and knives. For me, it was an intense experience to relive, in a sense, his experience. I could telepathically see this event from his perspective as his story in images repeatedly replayed. It was like watching a movie in which the elder's last intention as one of the murder victims was the storyline. His intent was to tell someone what happened and not let the murderers get away with the crime.

The spirit told me to "go where the eyes look." At first I didn't know what this meant. Then I intuitively knew to look up over my right shoulder at the mountain behind me. I found myself staring up at a steep, heavily forested mountain. The mouths of two caves near the top looked like large eyes in the mountainside. The spirit had instructed me to "go where the eyes look," so I allowed my gaze to follow the line of sight of the "eyes" in the mountainside. From where my parents and I stood, they appeared to be looking at a spot on another densely forested mountain. The hike to that mountain looked like an extremely difficult one. Since I believed the spirit's story about the massacre, I felt it was not necessary to go to the spot itself.

This fragmented piece of information appeared to me in images that repeated like a movie running in a loop. It was this elder's emotionally charged intent to have someone verify what was done to him and his family. Since time is of no relevance in the spirit world, he would have no inkling of the time that had passed. Of course, from our perspective, the lapse of time has made punishment, retribution or justice for the massacre by legal means unfeasible. I believe that what connected his energy to mine was not only my ability to tune in to such fragments but a resonance that exists with my Native ancestry. But there are many other factors to this connection, including the intense emotion that the elder felt during this event at his life's end.

When discussing the spirit world, it is important to remember that all of the information in the universe is within the field. This means that nonphysical fragments—those fragments that were once part of the energy systems of living organisms (that is, previous entities) but are no longer part of any organism—can be accessed. The host organism has died and reincarnated, but some residual information was not attached in the process. A fragment of data was left behind, so to speak. Although this fragment will eventually dissipate and be absorbed into the field, it stays together as a unified fragment for an undetermined length of time. I do receive information as it gets bounced off such fragments.

Sometimes what remains after death is a very large fragment, which can appear in the general shape of a human. This is what most people mean when they speak of spirits or ghosts. These fragments of information may seem to have some awareness as they go about their activities; they may carry a sufficient amount of information from when they were in material form that makes them appear to function like a person still. For instance, they may be engaged in activities such as walking or talking. However, most of the time they appear to me as just a repetitive loop of data on a seemingly endless replay, which represents the fragment of information left behind. This energy fragment is usually of a very emotional event that occurred in the last life. One way to think of spirits is as being similar to an audio recording of someone's voice. Even though the person might be long dead, the taped voice remains and can be replayed over and over.

People who interpret fragments as actual personalities of deceased individuals—or angels—may be overstating the role of fragments. I think that rather than these spirit fragments helping or protecting us, they exist merely as information remaining from their former life.

Nevertheless, even a fragment of information can have some influence on us, since any intention of any sort affects everything else. A fragment may have a connection to a person; for instance, Native spirits have an affinity to connect with me, likely because of my Native heritage. Because of that attachment, the spirit will naturally tend to exert an influence, just to keep that connection. There are many ways a person could have a connection to one of these fragments. Your simple thought or intention could be similar to the thought or intention of that spirit at that time. This creates a momentary connection, sometimes enough for the spirit to turn its attention to you. That is an automatic, natural process. So, fragments have an influence as part of a chain of events, but not a direct influence. Many fragments have no influence at all.

If you feel that your life is disrupted by a ghost, what you may actually be aware of is a fragment of information that does not have consciousness. No matter how we perceive spirits, we have to recognize that we are all connected to this spirit information. In most cases, we pass spirits off as nothing and ignore them. Once a person becomes more aware of these connections, he or she will be more influenced by them.

Not everything or everyone who dies leaves information behind in this form. A fragment has a frequency—it is a vibrational entity just like everything else. When you die, your intentions at the time of death will determine whether any of your memory gets "stuck" in this frequency, in the sense that a piece of your memory remains in nonphysical form in this reality. That is, your intention may be to leave this reality, but your frequency might be a little off. As a result, there will be pieces of your information that are misdirected in the process and left behind. A fragment is left to influence our physical world in this reality for a time.

After death, a person is in spirit form—that is, in waves rather than particles. From the perspective of our physical selves in our day-to-day lives, time is very important. For example, it takes time to get from point A to point B. From the perspective of the spirit, which exists as a wave, the time it takes to make a connection or have an influence has no real meaning; time is irrelevant. The instant that you die you are in spirit form, or waves. If your intention—conscious or subconscious—at the time of your death worked, it has manifested.

Some people refer to spirits as beings from another dimension but, in my opinion, "dimension" is not the right word to use. These fragments occur within our reality of space-time. It is misleading to divide our universe into dimensions. We do this for our own convenience, as many concepts involving energy, time and space are very difficult to define. There are, however, an infinite number of multiple subsets of information that may be overlapping.

A fragment of information, or spirit entity, can be seen by people who are tuned to its visual frequency. Large spirit fragments are found in many places. I have seen them in graveyards, shopping malls, tennis courts and in the wilderness. To me, they look like auras, except with no energetic flow and without the physical host. In other words, I see an aura without a body. This is more likely to be the case if the fragment is from someone who died traumatically, as the imprint is emotional.

How do fragments differ from each other?
Some are more complex pieces of information than others. Some will have the vague appearance of a body and even appear to be engaged in an activity, such as walking.

What are spirits?
Spirits are simply pieces of information. They are not conscious entities deliberately trying to frighten us. Some people have told me that they have encountered spirits that are able to make noise or move objects. It could be that an information fragment is complex enough to manipulate matter in some way. I haven't seen this, but theoretically it is possible.

Can we influence these fragments with our intentions?
Yes, theoretically we could influence fragments with our intentions, allowing them to be absorbed into the field more quickly, if that's what we want. Our intentions are always much more powerful than we may be aware of. It's just a matter of time until these fragments disintegrate and are reabsorbed into the field.

PART 3

Healing Visualizations

An overwhelming need for healing exists in our world. No one or two, or even several hundred, healers can meet the demand. One of my main goals is to remind people of their innate healing abilities and to teach them how to heal themselves. I urge you to ponder the ideas I've presented about the origin of the universe, our resulting oneness and our enormous energy-healing potential. We all have this built-in healing ability because of our connection to universal energy. We simply need to learn how to develop it and discipline ourselves to use it.

Energy healing is not magic. It is a real shift in a person's actual energy system, resulting in bodily changes occurring in real time. Healing is a process of change. The visualizations presented in this part of the book can be used for small aches and pains as well as for serious health challenges. The steps for each healing visualization are not hard. The concepts are simple. The visualizations are simple. The challenge is self-discipline. The challenge is setting aside time and actually doing the visualizations over a period of days, weeks and months. Then you will see the results.

The following words emphasize the main steps of self-healing:

The DreamHealer is within us.
DreamHealer, awaken!
Connect to yourself with healing intention.
Plant your vision of your future.
Grow it in your dream state.
Wake up to your new reality.

WHY DO VISUALIZATIONS?

Many people ask me, why do visualizations, specifically? I respond by telling them to take responsibility for their health by taking action. Think healthy, be healthy.

All of our attitudes and daily activities have a real physiological effect on our bodies. Our brains imprint an impression from visualizations we do, so they are processed as real events, even though they are created in our imaginations. This imprint sets off more electrical charges in the neurons of the brain. These signals flash between the synapses, which connect the neurons to one another. By repeating the visualizations regularly, the connections between neurons become stronger, more permanent and more accurate in making the visualizations realistic and our physical reaction to them real. Brain cells form a network. We can create a permanent pathway of change in our brains, which will create the beginning of a permanent memory adjustment in our bodies.

When I observe someone doing visualizations properly, I can see the flow of energy that they are directing within themselves. The impact on their physical self is indeed powerful. This is why I highly recommend visualizations: because I have seen their positive effects. One's own ability to influence oneself is an amazingly effective ability, and it can easily be harnessed with a few simple tools.

Think of yourself as a director creating a movie of your future—which then becomes your conscious reality. This is what

Healing Visualizations

you are doing by actively being in charge of your thoughts, words and deeds. Visualizations grant us this unlimited creative license.

Top athletes use visualization techniques because they realize that physical agility and skill is only a fraction of the game. In every sport, it is the psychological aspect that separates good athletes from great ones. The entire game plan is unfolding very precisely in the mind's eyes of top athletes of every sport. Optimal performance is just as much a psychological challenge as a physical one.

Each and every year, world records are broken. The record for the fastest runner in the world in the 1950s is now often broken by university track team members. What was once deemed an impossibly fast running speed is still admired but is no longer viewed as exceptional. Once records are broken, athletes know that increased performance is possible, and they believe they can do it. This is more of a psychological breakthrough than a physical one.

See yourself as you want to be. If you are an athlete, imagine with as much detail as you can what it feels like to wear that Olympic gold medal. See it, feel it, hear it, believe it. Make it real. Your body will respond to this as if it were the real event. Now you actually have a memory imprint that you have achieved this, and therefore you can do it again: You already know how to do it.

The same technique applies to healing visualizations. Imagine yourself doing all the things that you will be able to do once you achieve your goal of wellness. Make sure that your visualization is as detailed as possible as you imagine the physical challenges that you want to overcome. Do what you love to do once again. Envision this as if it is already your new reality.

It is vital that, as you do the visualizations, you sense them as being dynamic and fluid. Use all of your senses to imagine vividly the events happening to you, until your brain interprets these images as real experiences. Your brain will compute the information as if the thought is an event that is actually occurring. You will know that your visualizations are working when you start to feel changes in your health. Make your visualizations realistic with clear positive intention for optimal results. You are re-creating yourself in your new experience of wellness. Create your new healthy reality now. Remember that energy is being processed as new information within your body.

Your return to wellness is an ongoing learning process. The objective is not eternal life in our present form. Rather, the objective is to empower yourself to create an optimally functioning immune system, a balanced emotional state and a reawakening of your spiritual awareness.

Practice the exercises and visualizations in this book for a comprehensive lifestyle change. Incorporate visualizations into your daily routine and you will realize the advantages that they bring. Soon, doing them will be as natural as breathing. Enjoy your newfound sense of inner peace as you relax and grow in the mastery of this skill.

STRATEGIES TO ENHANCE HEALING VISUALIZATIONS

Preparing yourself psychologically in order to get the maximum benefit from visualizations is essential. In many respects, doing visualizations is like painting a house. The first half is all preparation work. Filling all the small nail holes and cracks must be done first. This is followed by sanding and taping. It seems like forever before one gets to see the actual color of the new paint on the walls. We have all experienced what happens if we skip these meticulous preparation steps: The end result is not satisfactory because the improvement is flawed and doesn't last.

Likewise, to achieve long-lasting benefits from energy healing, we must realize that the groundwork *before* this journey is just as essential and time-consuming as the journey itself.

We can use our dreams most effectively by doing visualizations at bedtime. This is how we set them in our minds for the duration of our sleep. Our most imaginative state of mind is during our dream state. This is also our least judgmental phase, so visualizations will more easily become real to us and be processed as actual events at this time. Actively embed into your dream state a visualization that is most helpful to you and your well-being. You can accomplish this by thinking about a particular visualization as you drift off to sleep, so that it is rooted in your subconscious thoughts.

Breathing Exercise

Breathing effectively during your visualizations is important for providing oxygen, and hence energy, to all of your cells. You can easily do this by paying attention to your breathing in and out. Breathe in vital life energy and the mental picture will become more realistic.

Here is an easy two-step breathing exercise:

1. Inhale energy as deeply as possible, filling your lungs and abdominal cavity with air. Imagine when doing this that you are providing your body, mind and soul with everything you need to achieve your goal of wellness.
2. Strongly exhale the air from your lungs and abdominal cavity, releasing with it what you do not need or want in your body. In this way, rid your body of any emotional blockages and problems.

SPEED MEDITATION

To reach a calm, meditative state, most people prefer to be in quiet surroundings, with their body in a physically relaxed position. This is not always easy. We live such busy, stressful lives that there are often random thoughts in our heads or noises in our environment that prevent total quiet. The good news is that meditation can still be achieved, since this consciousness-expanding state originates in the mind. Environmental challenges such as noise and being physically uncomfortable will distract you only if you let them.

The means of entering the relaxed frame of mind that is meditation may vary, but what is important is that you are able to reach that level of calm consciousness vital for reflection. Once achieved, the quiet, altered state of mind operates in the same manner, no matter how it was reached.

Here is a meditation technique I use when my environment lacks physical comfort, calm and quiet. I call it speed meditation. The extreme sense of motion experienced during speed meditation causes confusion in our thought patterns, which disrupts our state of consciousness. This disruption in logic activates the subconscious mind, where calmness can be found.

1. Close your eyes and visualize in your mind's eye a merry-go-round. Visualize it as it sits motionless, capturing as much detail as you can. See the multi-colored roof and the stilled positions of the dancing animals.
2. Start up the motion. Watch the animals move up and down as the carousel spins around.
3. Increase the speed. Watch the animals go by faster and faster, concentrating on seeing as much detail as possible.

    Some people may find this dizzying until they get used to it. If you feel a little off balance, visualize the carousel rotating in the opposite direction. This will rebalance you. Then try increasing the speed again.
4. Take the speed to its limit. The carousel is moving as fast as you think it can go. No matter how fast it is spinning, keep accelerating the speed. This makes you visualize faster than

the speed of your thoughts. You will feel a rush and will find yourself thinking of nothing. From this point onward, it is as if the carousel spins beyond conscious awareness.

This heightened state of awareness through the visualization of speed at the breaking point leads to a peaceful and relaxed feeling. The mind-body resets itself into a frame of consciousness in which a meditative state can quickly and easily follow.

MAXIMIZING FOCUSED INTENTION

Now that your beliefs, intentions and expectations are aligned toward your healing, the next step is to know that you are ready, willing and able to implement self-healing. Information is constantly being exchanged between your quantum hologram and your physical self. Visualizations are tools you can use to be in control of this information exchange process. You know where to direct your immune system for optimum performance. Visualizations enable you to reset yourself to your own maximum capacity for accomplishing this.

Visualizations, when done with clear intention and detailed focus, incorporate all five senses into a dynamic and realistic feeling of experiencing the event. What you envision in your mind's eye with the vividness of a true experience triggers your subconscious mind into action. This maximizes your focused intentions in order to optimally guide your immune system in correcting the problem.

Chronic problems are often no longer recognized by your body as difficulties because it has become accustomed to them. They are often overlooked or ignored so that your body can concentrate on the new incoming information. Visualizations can reawaken your body to the awareness that there is a problem so that your immune system can respond. Your unwavering intention to change an unhealthy status quo will activate a shift in the subconscious mind.

Expand on your visualizations to include all of your senses. People have different dominant senses, so some may find it more realistic to hear their visualizations. Others may find that they can feel the visualizations more accurately and realistically than they can see them. Some people find that if they narrate aloud what is happening, it makes a more lasting impression, so they speak it. Self-talk can help boost self-confidence in this process of self-creation. These approaches, whether dramatic or reserved, are all equally valid and effective as long as they are meaningful to you. Trust yourself.

If you find that your mind wanders when you are visualizing, stop and relax. Refresh your screen, so to speak. This process involves reprogramming your mind and body. Be patient with yourself. Concentrate on the feeling and it will return. Refocus.

EXERCISE FOR PROJECTING A HOLOGRAPHIC IMAGE

A hologram, as noted earlier, is a three-dimensional projection containing all of the information (past, present and future) of a person, place or thing (see Illustrations 18 and 19). A person's optimal state of health is contained within it. It is not necessary to master this exercise in order to do visualizations, as you can imagine doing any visualization directly on your body. Using this holographic image is optional for self-healing, but it is useful. With practice, as you become more skilled, you may even find it most effective to visualize directing energy onto both your body and your projected image simultaneously. It is necessary to at least be familiar with projecting an image before assisting others with their healing.

The first few times you practice this exercise, you will find

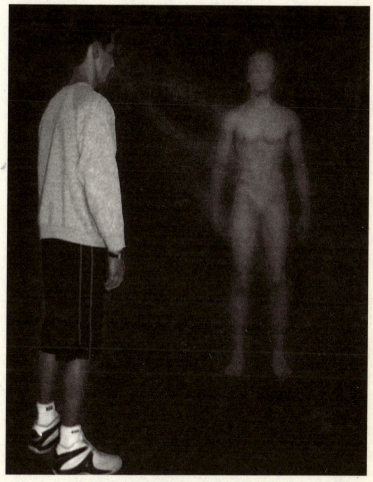

Illustration 18: Projecting a holographic image.

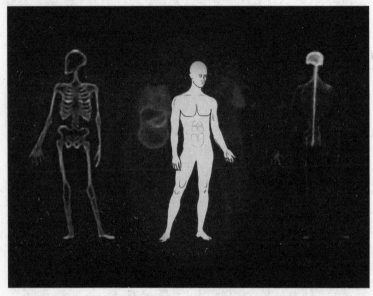

Illustration 19: Various holographic views. Access these subsets of information for healing.

it easier to visualize a simple two-dimensional image rather than the actual three-dimensional image. With practice, your intuition and intention will connect you to more information, until you are linking to the hologram itself.

1. Stand in front of a full-length mirror and take a careful look at your reflection. Try to remember every detail of your image—all your physical characteristics.
2. Close your eyes and burn this image of yourself into your mind's eye.
3. With eyes closed, project this two-dimensional image of yourself about two feet in front of you, as a base for your visualizations. This image of your body can be any size, though two feet in height is typical.
4. Through your visualizations, direct energy flow onto this image for optimal health.

You can also direct healing visualizations to others as follows:

1. Look at a photograph of the person's face.
2. Concentrate on the person's physical characteristics as you close your eyes and burn the image into your memory.
3. With eyes closed, project a hologram in front of you.
4. Direct the energy flow through visualizations with your focused intention to achieve optimal health.
5. Dispose of the person's energy blockages by throwing them into a vacuum, the garbage or a black hole. Energy blockages need a host organism in order to thrive; without one, they dissipate quickly.

SPECIFIC VISUALIZATIONS

It is important to remember that the following visualizations are guidelines only; they are meant for you to tailor to your individual needs. It would be impossible to cover here visualizations for every ailment. This is where your imagination is of the utmost importance; set your imagination free to reach what you desire. Adjust the visualizations in whatever ways will most efficiently and effectively heal the ailment. Experiment with them, and modify them to suit you. Be creative. Think of them as clothes that you can change into and out of to adapt to any occasion. If white light is too hot for you, try a cooler color such as blue or purple. Perhaps your mythical dragon (discussed below) breathes out red flames. Play with images and experiment. This also keeps visualizations alive, dynamic and exciting.

Do the research necessary to find out what your problem looks like anatomically. Also find out what the optimally healthy functioning of this area looks like—this is what you are striving for. Build your personal visualization from this information. In this sense, it is important to make your visualizations as realistic as possible to you, so the images you use should be as realistic as possible.

It doesn't matter if you are standing, sitting or lying down when you do the visualizations, as long as you are comfortable. The main thing is to relax and focus your intentions on what you expect to achieve. The primary factors in all healing strategies, including the visualizations, are your attitudes and intentions. Be confident as you set out to master your new skills.

Light-Hearted Visualization
For any condition, but especially for self-love and acceptance, and mending a broken heart (see Illustration 20)
An effective general visualization, which can be modified for all conditions, is the ball of bright white light. This exercise makes maximum use of the heart's ability to synchronize universal energy available to the body, mind and spirit.

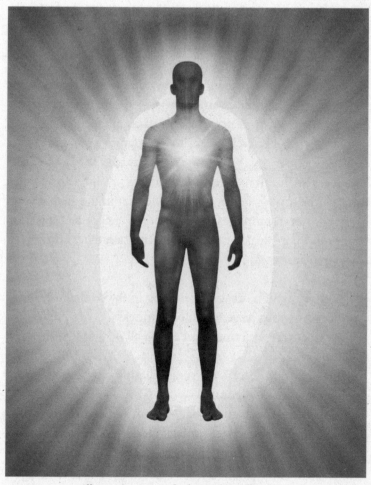

Illustration 20: *Light-hearted visualization:*
Collect light in your heart area, then radiate it to every cell as you become as bright as the sun.

Many people have written to me about having a broken heart. I have recommended that they do the light-hearted visualization, and they report wonderful results. In fact, it is effective for all matters of the heart, especially when we need to increase love and acceptance of ourselves.

Increase your love for yourself and the result will be increased self-confidence in your ability to transform yourself. To know you can do it is an essential step on your journey to success. As you experience greater self-acceptance and deeper knowing, you effectively begin to reprogram your mind and body.

This visualization pulls universal energy into your body through the top of your head and collects it in the area of your heart. Your heart amplifies the intensity of energy, and it is near your body's core, which makes its distribution to all other areas of the body easy.

1. With inhalation, imagine bringing in the sunlight through the top of your head and into your heart.
2. Breathe in several times, collecting all of that light in your heart area.
3. Imagine your heart is the sun, radiating out beams of pure light energy. Be the sun.
4. With exhalation, radiate that warmth and love to every part of yourself. See and feel yourself literally shine from within. This opens your heart to universal energy, to your own energy and to the energy of everyone and everything else.
5. Feel the strength as you become unified with everything. Experience the energy of peace and harmony.

See your heart radiating as brightly as the sun.
Feel yourself glow with energy.
Hear your heart pumping.

Smell and taste the heat.
Make it real.

Light Bulb Visualization
For illnesses that affect or have spread to the entire body, such as infection, cancer and AIDS (see Illustration 21)

As I obtain more experience and practice, I am able to incorporate more specific visualizations into my healing. In workshops I have held, there have been many requests for visualizations to deal with illnesses that affect, or have spread to, the entire body, such as AIDS and cancer. An effective visualization for healing such an illness is one that recruits every cell in the body to recognize the problem. The light bulb visualization does this.

1. With inhalation, bring in universal energy through the top of your head. (See the Bring in Universal Energy exercise in Chapter 4.)
2. Imagine every cell as a magnet, attracting energy into each cell.
3. Let light energy radiate out to every cell. Imagine filling every cell with light until every cell becomes so bright that each looks like an individual light bulb, radiating its own light.
4. Imagine shaking your entire body like one of those vibrating belts that promise to jiggle away excess fat. With every shake, the individual cells begin to reach a similar frequency, until they are all resonating at the same coherent vibration. If you look in a mirror, your aura will be almost too bright to see your reflection.
5. Visualize your entire body as a guitar resonating with a single harmonious chord strummed in perfect tune. When your entire body resonates in harmony, you no longer see every cell as an individual light but the entire body as one

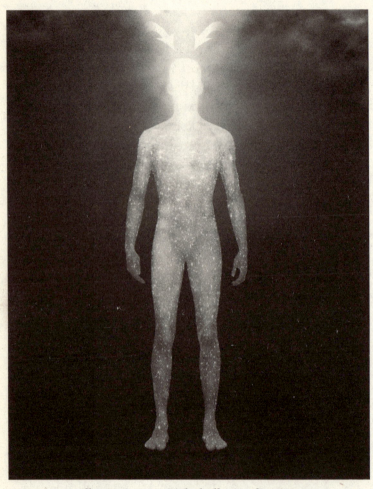

Illustration 21: *Light bulb visualization:*
Cells beginning to resonate at a coherent frequency;
soon your entire body will vibrate with a harmonious light.

continuous body of light. Every cell in your body is now working together toward the common goal of fixing the problem.

See your entire being light up.
Feel your harmonic flow of energy.
Hear your single resonating frequency.
Smell and taste the vapors.
Make it real.

Once all the cells are resonating at the same frequency, there is cooperation between cells, enabling you to more effectively communicate with your cells. Any visualization is more intense and effective when cell communication coherence is achieved. You may also find it effective to talk to your body as you guide yourself through the visualizations. Saying the steps aloud may help, especially when you first start doing them.

If you have cancer, imagine every cell in your body recognizing the problem and attacking it. Do not limit this visualization solely to immune system cells. Every cell must be included, even skin cells. Every cell has the ability to give at least some resistance to any illness. Getting every cell in your body working together creates a powerful force to eliminate the problem and simultaneously boost your immune system.

When a person with cancer undergoes chemotherapy and that treatment doesn't work, he or she is often dealt a double whammy. The cancer remains active, yet the chemotherapy has compromised the person's immune system. It is not uncommon to have a very low white blood cell count after several sessions of chemotherapy. The person's primary health challenge now becomes restoring a functioning immune system and, second, eliminating the cancer. No matter what your condition or what therapy you are pursuing, it is important to focus on rebuilding your immune system, since it is your primary source of health and well-being.

Even if you do not know exactly what your health problem is or do not have a clear idea as to how your body could heal, it is still useful to practice the light bulb visualization. Just imagine speaking to your cells as if you were speaking to a person. Tell the cells to find the problem and eliminate it. However, ideally, the visualization should be anatomically accurate. I therefore highly recommend that you research the illness and understand exactly what your problem looks like, and exactly what the area should look like when the problem is gone. Be sure to maximize your healing potential by improving your immune defenses too.

This light bulb visualization is also effective for emotionally based illnesses. Any problem you have, even if it is emotion based, has a physical effect on your body because of the various biochemicals that are released. When speaking to the cells involved in an emotional problem, imagine every cell in your body forgetting past emotions that are still causing you harm. Every cell essentially has its own memory, and you are simply telling each cell to release painful emotional memories.

Light Injections Visualization
For any condition that affects one target area, such as a specific organ; also for arthritis and pain (see Illustration 22)
Use this visualization for any localized health challenge, such as a specific organ. It can also be used for arthritis, pain issues and sports injuries. Many acute and chronic pains occur in specific areas, so they can be addressed individually. If you have several areas you want to work on, use this visualization on one area at a time.

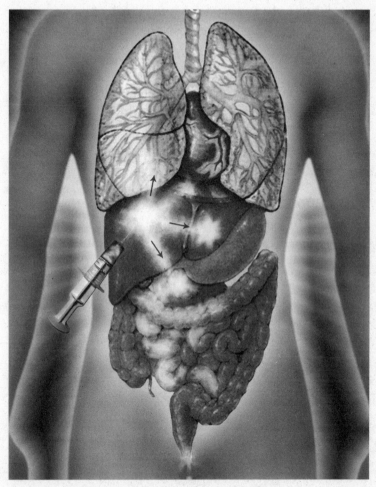

Illustration 22: *Light injections visualization:*
Inject light directly into the problem area, allowing the healing light to radiate to surrounding tissue.

1. Visualize filling a syringe with pure, white light.
2. Imagine injecting this pure white light into your problem area. As light fills the area, light glows and radiates from within.
3. As the surrounding tissues soak up the light, you will shine in wellness.

See your problem dissolving into the pure light.
Feel your calm energy ripple.
Hear your light radiating.
Smell and taste the energy.
Make it real.

Bright White Light Visualization
For connecting to your inner self (see Illustration 23)

When I connect directly to the bright white light that is at the center of the brain, I experience an incredible sense of connectedness. I see an image of the body in perfect health. Everyone has a problem of some sort—an old injury or an injury forming. The image inside the bright white light has no signs of any illness or injury of any kind. As I mentioned earlier, this is the area many people refer to as the soul.

The soul is the glue that unifies the energy systems of each cell into a coherent frequency that is consistent with the whole person. It is what keeps each cell working in unison with all others. Even though every cell interacts with its environment and has a consciousness, the soul represents our singular consciousness, observer of all of our experiences. It is what each of us refers to as "I"; it is the self, the observer.

Many conclusions could be drawn as to what this white light is; all interpretations would arise from our personal biased meanings. I perceive this white light as containing an image of perfect health—as the original perfect blueprint. It is this image of perfect health that we all strive to experience. I believe that

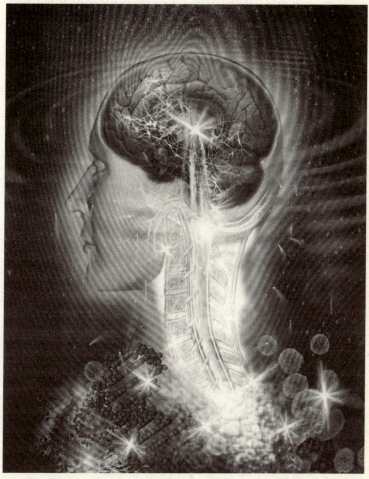

Illustration 23: *Bright white light visualization:*
Light the center of your brain with your internal light source and let it grow light energy roots that connect to every cell in your body.

the image of perfect health is in you. Your optimal image is what is looking out of your eyes at this very moment.

Many specific visualizations can be done utilizing this bright white light. People have found working with it to be especially effective for emotional illnesses.

1. With inhalation, bring energy from the universe in through the top of your head. (See the Bring in Universal Energy exercise in Chapter 4.) Collect and focus it at the center of your brain.
2. Light the center of your brain with your internal light source and watch it glow.
3. With exhalation, visualize light energy roots growing out of the bright white light.
4. Grow the roots and expand their network until every cell in your body is connected to these roots.
5. See pulses of light going from the center of your brain to every cell along these pathways as your body messages synchronize. With each pulse of light, you can see your problems or illness shattering like glass and falling away from your body forever.

See your light pulsing.
Feel your perfect self.
Hear your problems shattering.
Smell and taste the purity of energy.
Make it real.

The light from the center of your brain has effectively flushed out the old program about your health challenge and reverted to the original default image of your perfect self.

Bubble Wrap Visualization
For a localized problem, such as a tumor or fibroid, anywhere in the body (see Illustration 24)

Most of us have popped bubble wrap at one time or another; this visualization makes use of that experience. This visualization is useful when one wants to rid the body of something foreign that is in one location, such as a tumor or fibroid.

1. Imagine the problem area as layers of bubble wrap.
2. Move your focused intention to that location.
3. With inhalation, breathe fresh air and healing light energy into all the pockets of the bubble wrap, filling them nearly to the breaking point.
4. With exhalation, pop as many bubbles as you can. Imagine tightening your muscles in that area to make it happen.
5. Repeat the steps until every bubble has burst.
6. Exhale with force in order to expel all of the unwanted material from your body. Fill yourself with boundless healing energy.

See your bubbles pop.
Feel the rush of air as they burst.
Hear each mini-explosion.
Smell and taste pristine air.
Make it real.

Mythical Dragon Breathing Visualization
For eliminating stress (see Illustration 25)
This exercise can be very useful for the elimination of stress held tightly within your body. Focus on the area of your body where you are holding all of your worries.

1. With inhalation, imagine that you are breathing in white, hot flames.
2. Focus on moving these flames with your awareness to your place of stress.

Illustration 24: *Bubble wrap visualization:*
Breathe healing light energy into each cell-pocket; with exhalation, burst as many bubbles as you can, popping away your problem.

3. With exhalation, breathe out the flames and the ashes of your burned out stress.
4. With each successive breath, move your awareness lower in your body, until the flames shoot from the ground up. Each breath in fans the coals. Each breath out eliminates body tightness or stress.

See flames engulf your stress.
Feel ashes exit your body.
Hear your breath release it.
Smell and taste the smoke.
Make it real.

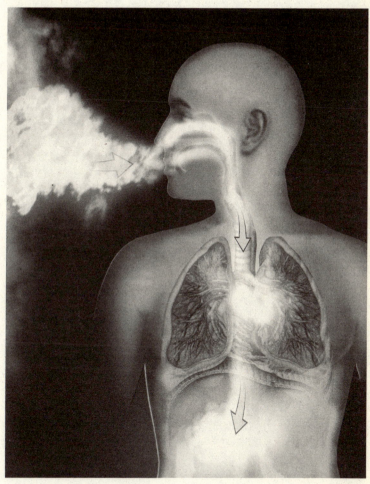

Illustration 25: *Mythical dragon breathing visualization:*
With inhalation, imagine that you are breathing in white, hot flames;
focus on moving these flames to your place of stress.

Reflection

*E*very thought and intention we emit is energy. When you throw a stone in the ocean, the ripples affect every atom in the ocean. When we think good intentions or thoughts toward someone, we affect everyone around us and beyond. Imagine what kind of a world this would be if we all had good thoughts and intentions. Such a world is possible if we all teach one another about the influence we have on ourselves and others. When the world comes to this understanding, there will be no wars and no killings, only harmony. Like the cells in our bodies, we all will be working together.

I see this as a realistic objective because I continue to receive countless emails from people who understand this interconnectedness we all share. Meanwhile, there remains the challenge of knocking down the many walls of fear that remain throughout the world. There are many people who have a strong awareness of our connection with one another but have had to suppress their abilities because of fear of ridicule. Yet, everywhere I see evidence that this wall of fear is eroding.

Self-empowerment spreads as we learn how we can influence our reality. Self-empowerment is contagious as each person passes on to others the knowledge of what we all are capable of achieving. There is a wave of understanding and acceptance of our interconnectedness and healing ability that is building. The momentum of this wave is increasing exponentially. Each of us can speed the process of change with our own unique gifts. Let us all hold this vision of a world that is healed.

Stay tuned!